CHAPTER

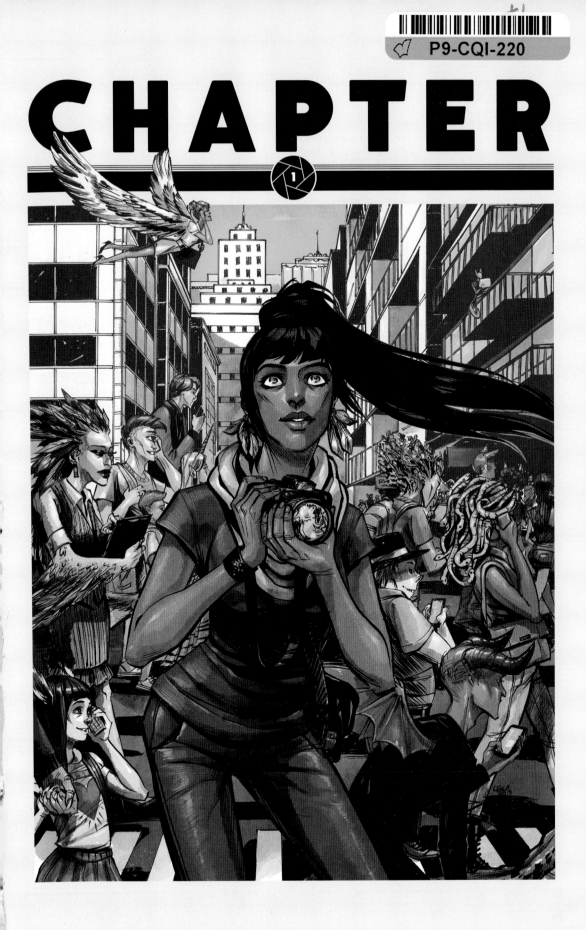

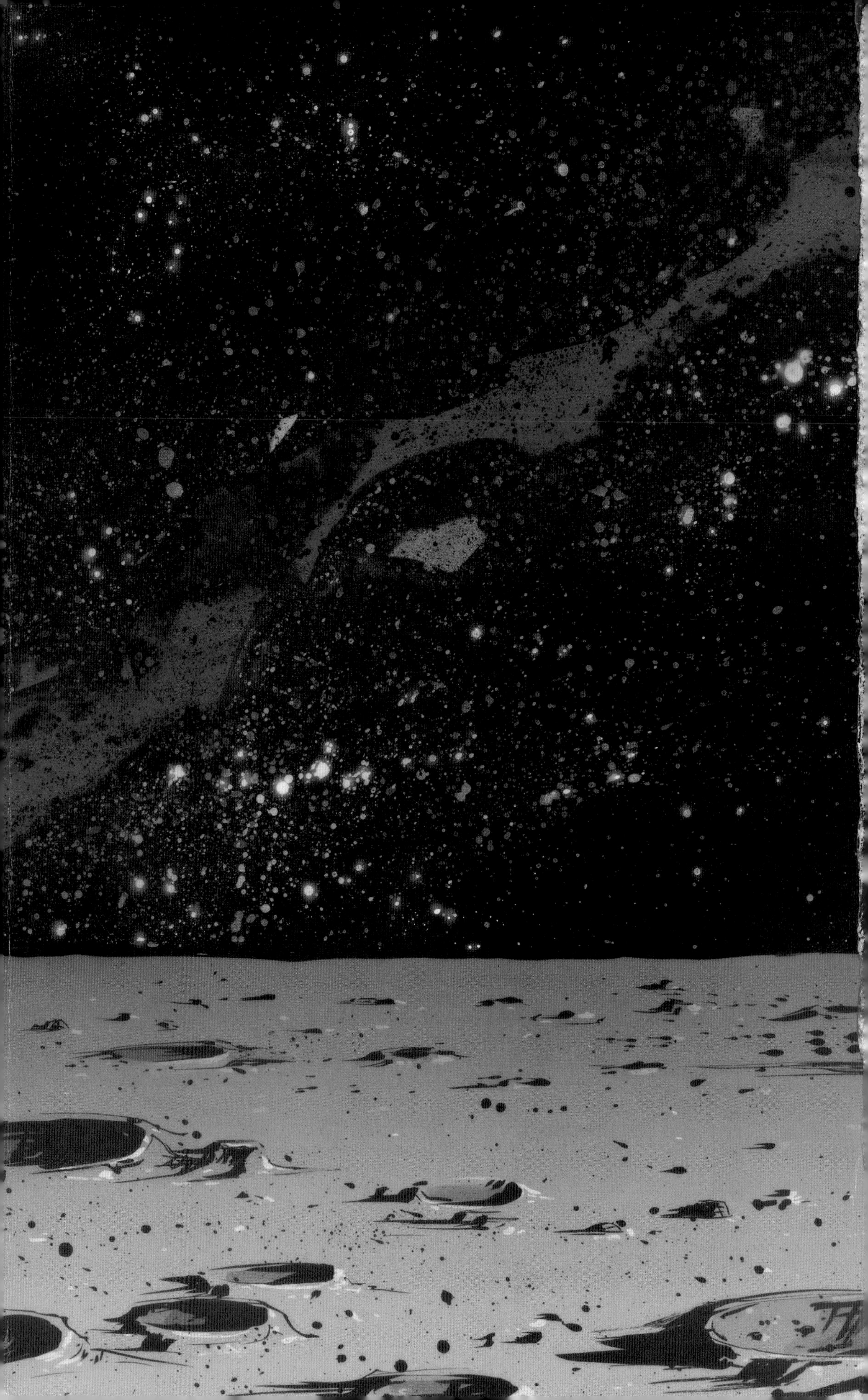

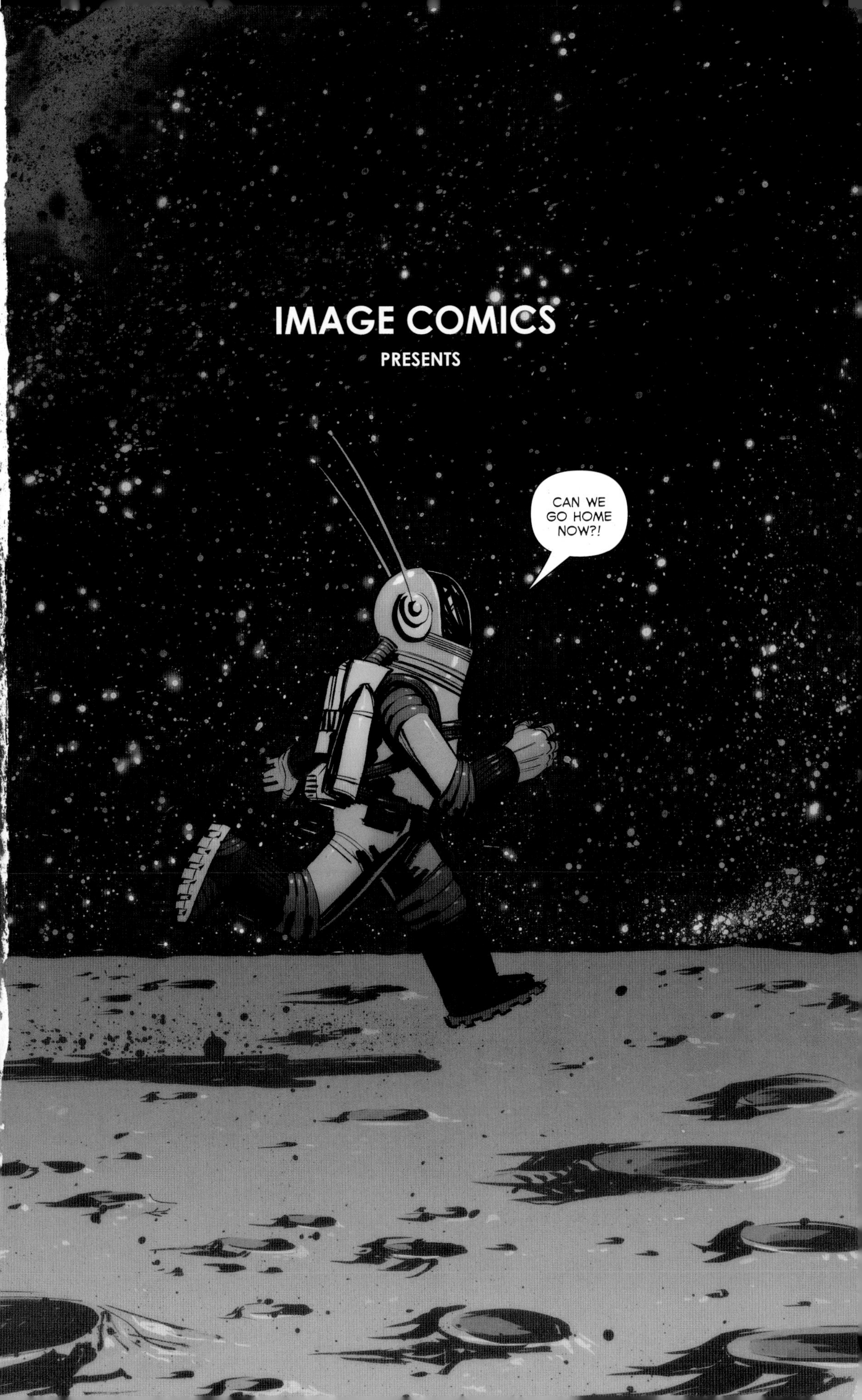
IMAGE COMICS
PRESENTS
CAN WE GO HOME NOW?!

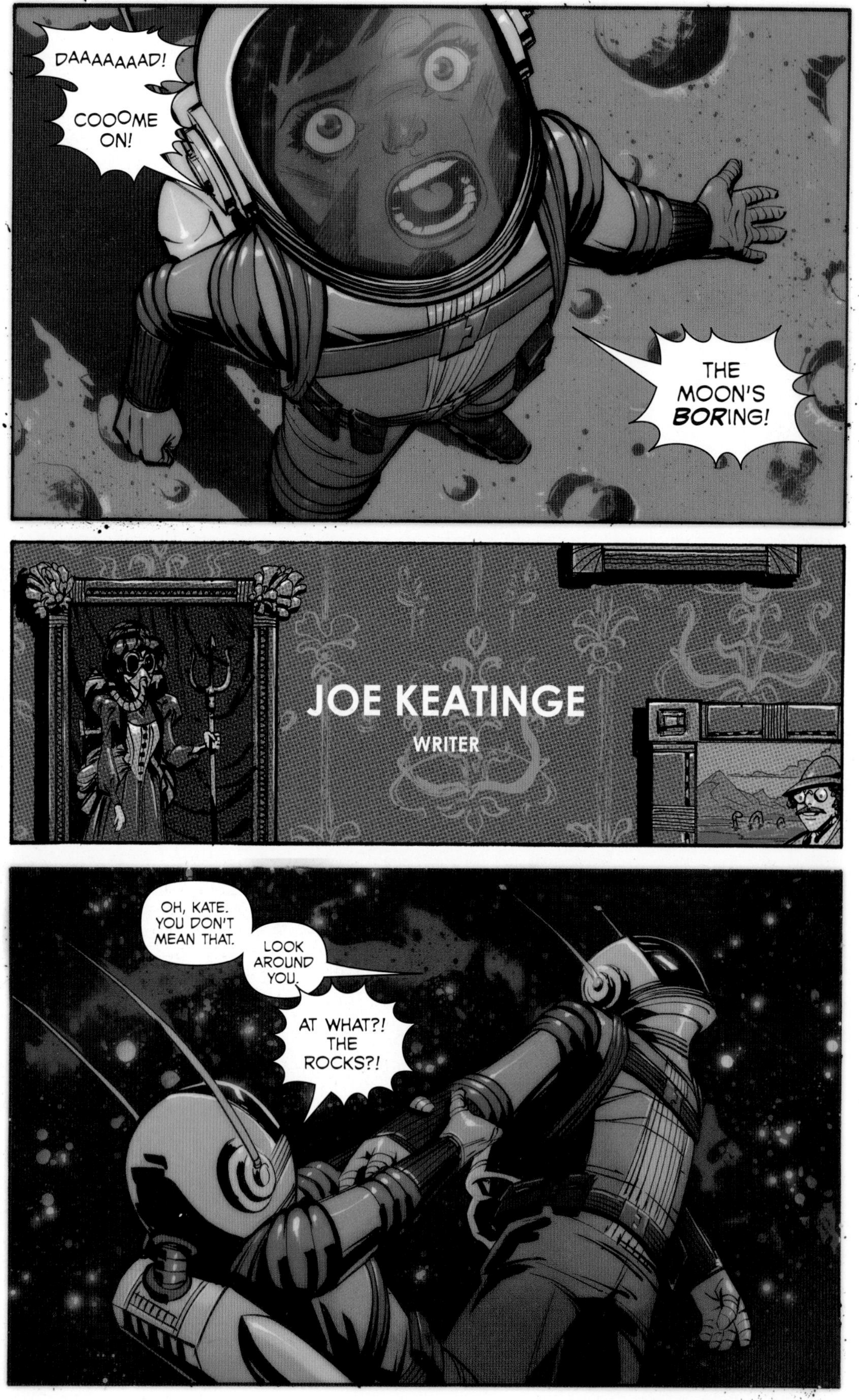
DAAAAAAAD!
COOOME ON!
THE MOON'S BORING!
JOE KEATINGE
WRITER
OH, KATE. YOU DON'T MEAN THAT.
LOOK AROUND YOU.
AT WHAT?! THE ROCKS?!

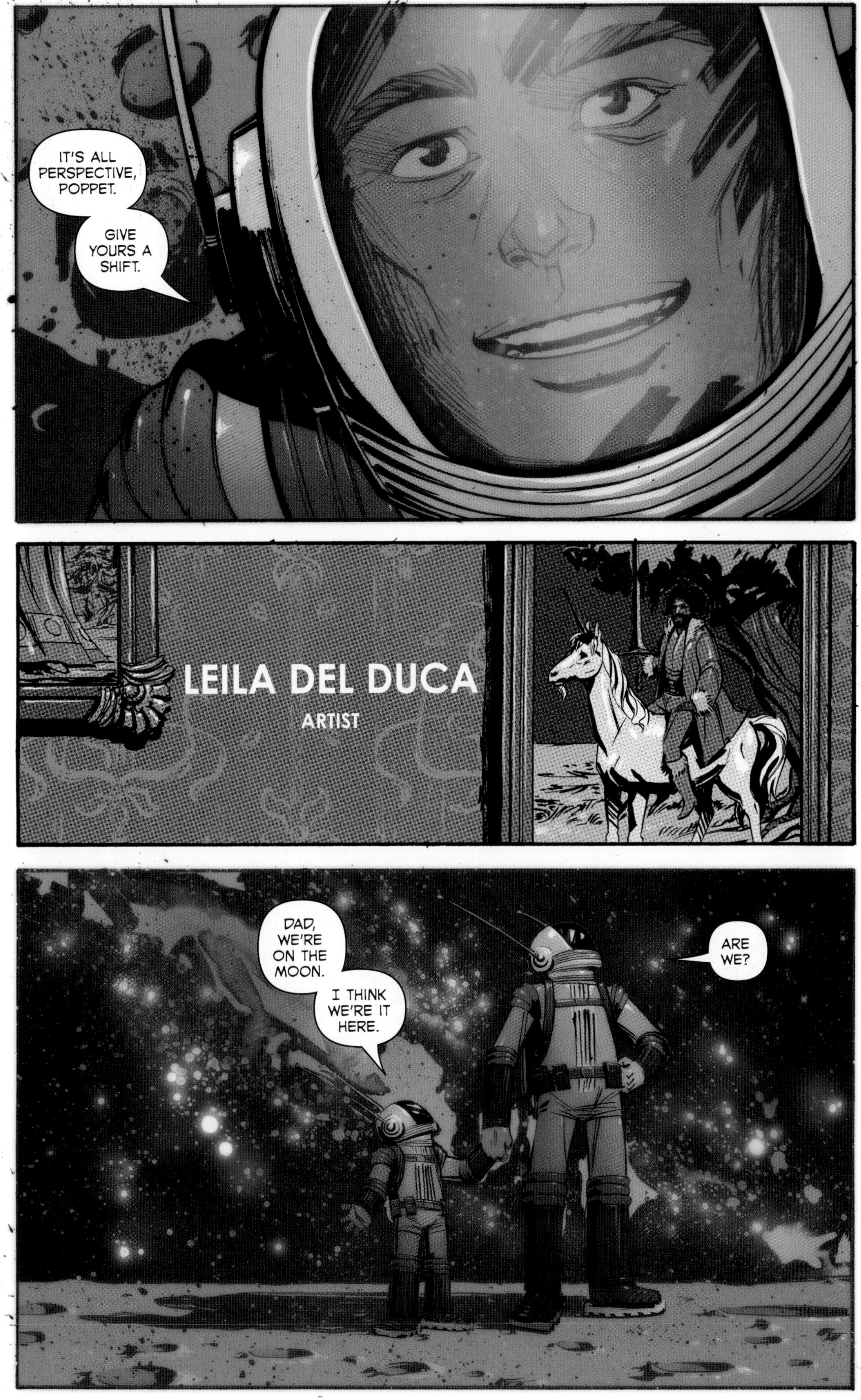
IT'S ALL PERSPECTIVE, POPPET.
GIVE YOURS A SHIFT.
LEILA DEL DUCA
ARTIST
DAD, WE'RE ON THE MOON.
I THINK WE'RE IT HERE.
ARE WE?

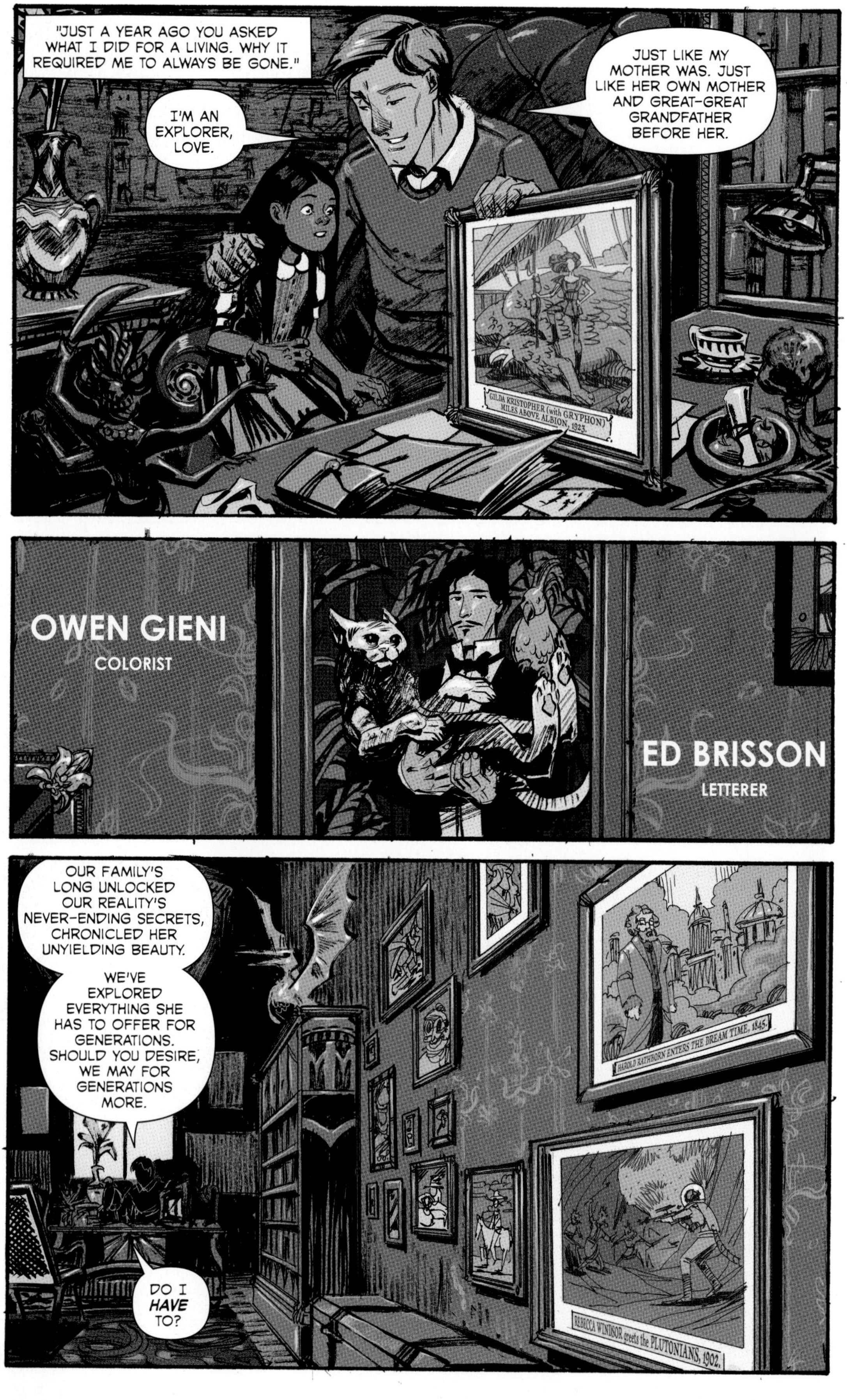
"JUST A YEAR AGO YOU ASKED WHAT I DID FOR A LIVING. WHY IT REQUIRED ME TO ALWAYS BE GONE."
I'M AN EXPLORER, LOVE.
JUST LIKE MY MOTHER WAS. JUST LIKE HER OWN MOTHER AND GREAT-GREAT GRANDFATHER BEFORE HER.
GILDA KRISTOPHER (with GRYPHON) MILES ABOVE ALBION, 1923.
OWEN GIENI
COLORIST
ED BRISSON
LETTERER
OUR FAMILY'S LONG UNLOCKED OUR REALITY'S NEVER-ENDING SECRETS, CHRONICLED HER UNYIELDING BEAUTY.
WE'VE EXPLORED EVERYTHING SHE HAS TO OFFER FOR GENERATIONS. SHOULD YOU DESIRE, WE MAY FOR GENERATIONS MORE.
HAROLD RATHBORN ENTERS THE DREAM TIME, 1845.
DO I *HAVE* TO?
REBECCA WINDSOR greets the PLUTONIANS, 1902.

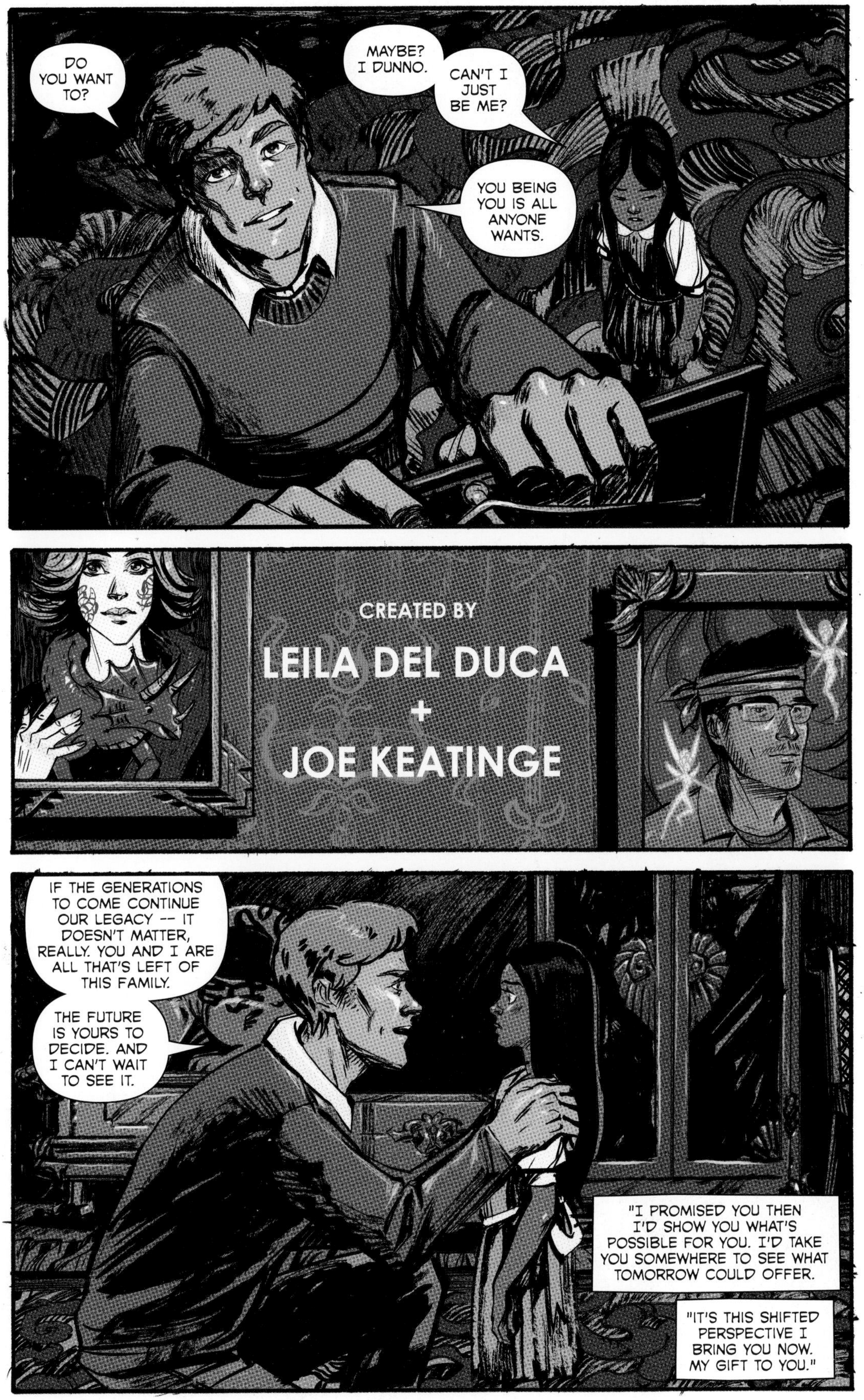
DO YOU WANT TO?
MAYBE? I DUNNO.
CAN'T I JUST BE ME?
YOU BEING YOU IS ALL ANYONE WANTS.
CREATED BY
LEILA DEL DUCA
+
JOE KEATINGE
IF THE GENERATIONS TO COME CONTINUE OUR LEGACY -- IT DOESN'T MATTER, REALLY. YOU AND I ARE ALL THAT'S LEFT OF THIS FAMILY.
THE FUTURE IS YOURS TO DECIDE. AND I CAN'T WAIT TO SEE IT.
"I PROMISED YOU THEN I'D SHOW YOU WHAT'S POSSIBLE FOR YOU. I'D TAKE YOU SOMEWHERE TO SEE WHAT TOMORROW COULD OFFER.
"IT'S THIS SHIFTED PERSPECTIVE I BRING YOU NOW. MY GIFT TO YOU."

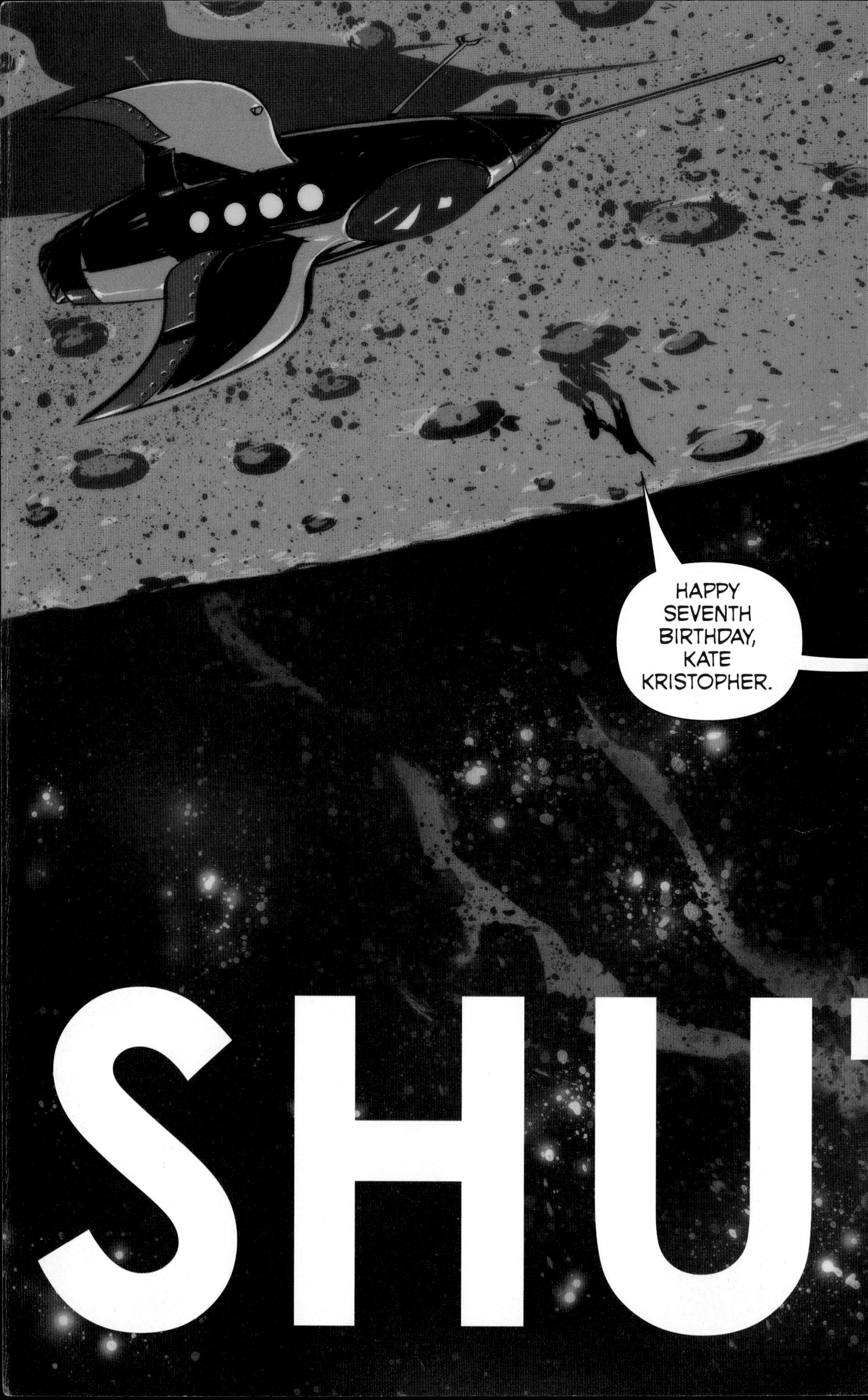
HAPPY SEVENTH BIRTHDAY, KATE KRISTOPHER.
SHU

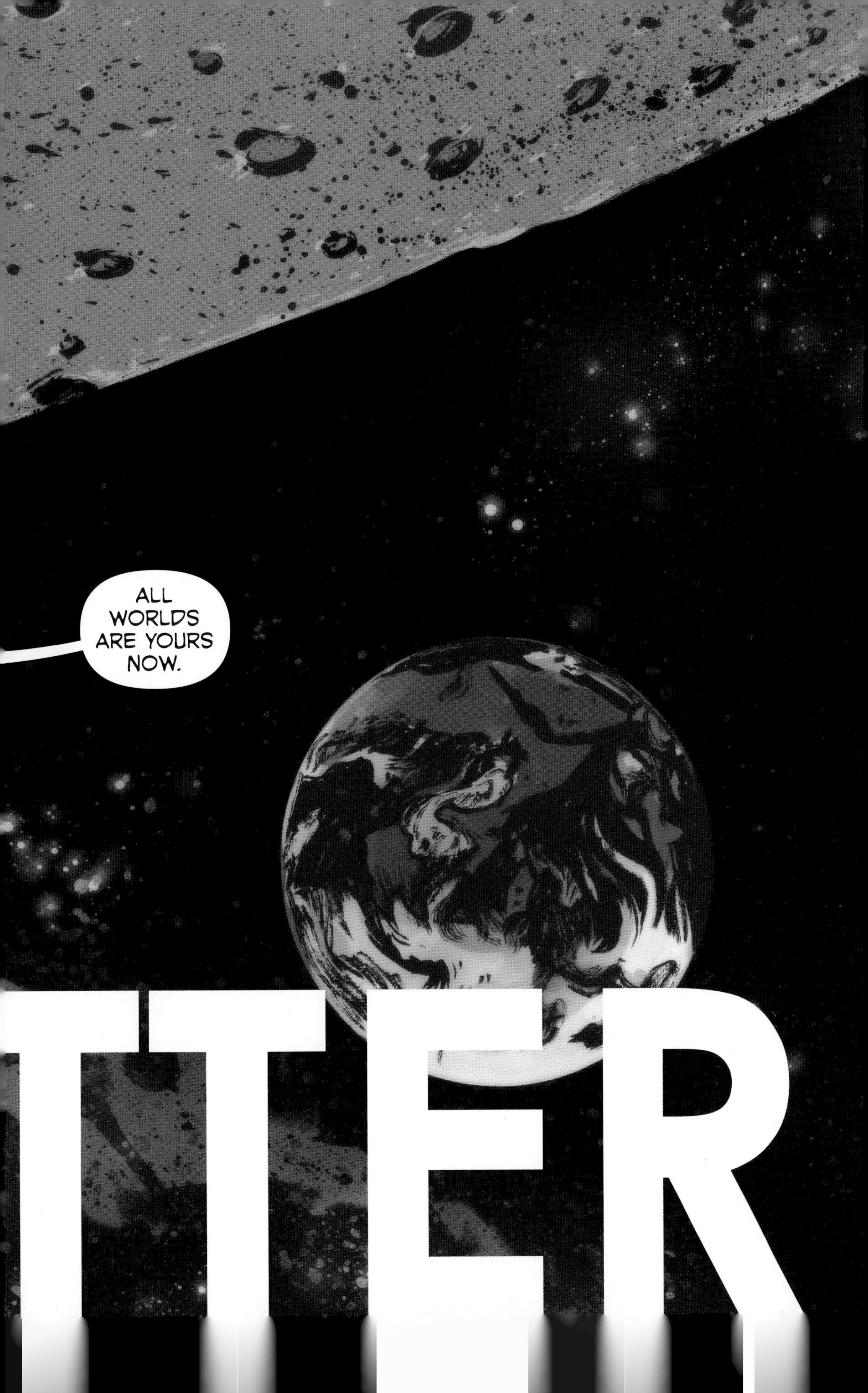
ALL WORLDS ARE YOURS NOW.
TER

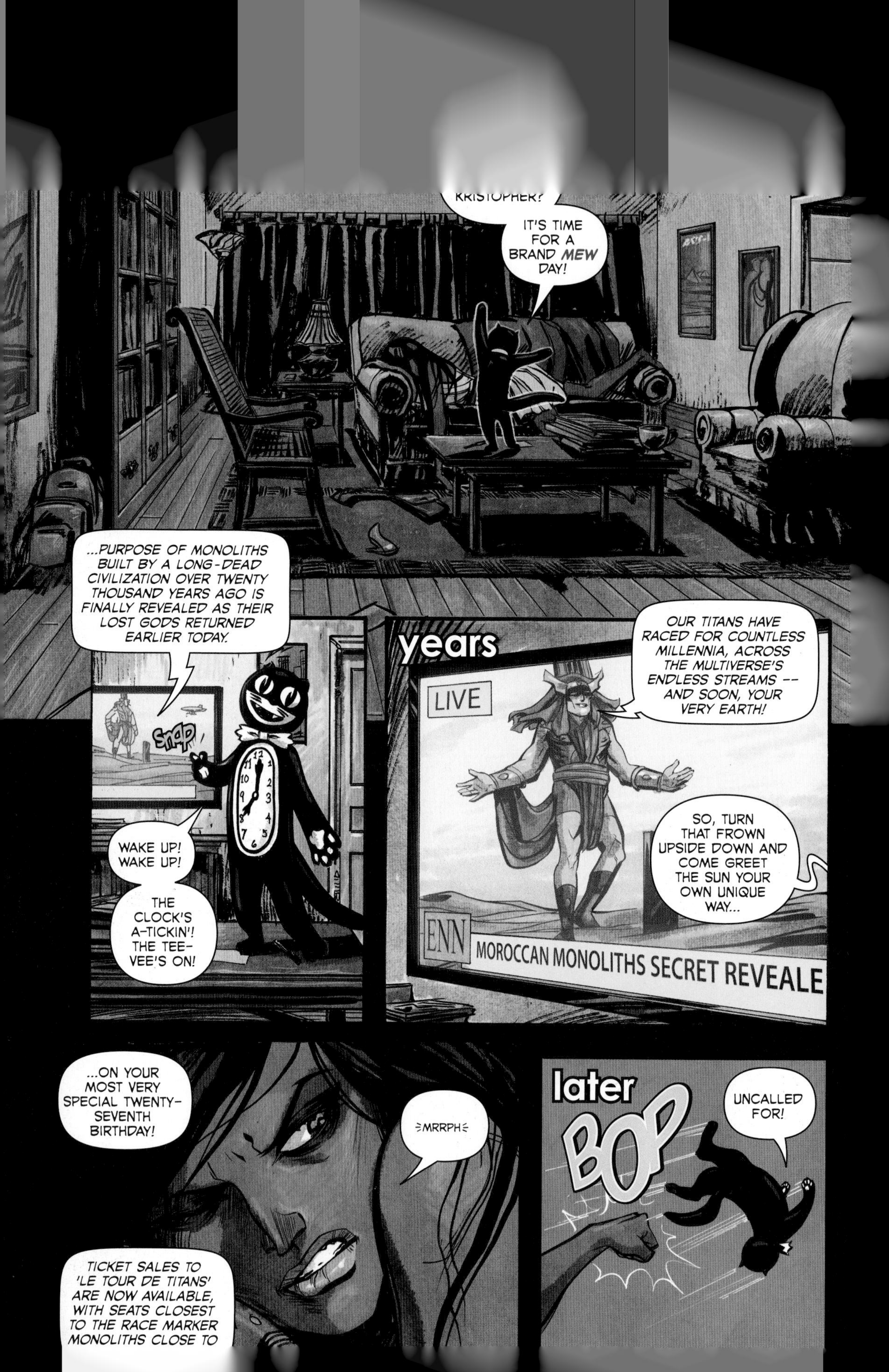
KRISTOPHER?
IT'S TIME FOR A BRAND *MEW* DAY!
...PURPOSE OF MONOLITHS BUILT BY A LONG-DEAD CIVILIZATION OVER TWENTY THOUSAND YEARS AGO IS FINALLY REVEALED AS THEIR LOST GODS RETURNED EARLIER TODAY.
SNAP
WAKE UP! WAKE UP!
THE CLOCK'S A-TICKIN'! THE TEE-VEE'S ON!
years
LIVE
OUR TITANS HAVE RACED FOR COUNTLESS MILLENNIA, ACROSS THE MULTIVERSE'S ENDLESS STREAMS -- AND SOON, YOUR VERY EARTH!
SO, TURN THAT FROWN UPSIDE DOWN AND COME GREET THE SUN YOUR OWN UNIQUE WAY...
ENN
MOROCCAN MONOLITHS SECRET REVEALE
...ON YOUR MOST VERY SPECIAL TWENTY-SEVENTH BIRTHDAY!
MRRPH
TICKET SALES TO 'LE TOUR DE TITANS' ARE NOW AVAILABLE, WITH SEATS CLOSEST TO THE RACE MARKER MONOLITHS CLOSE TO
later
BOP
UNCALLED FOR!

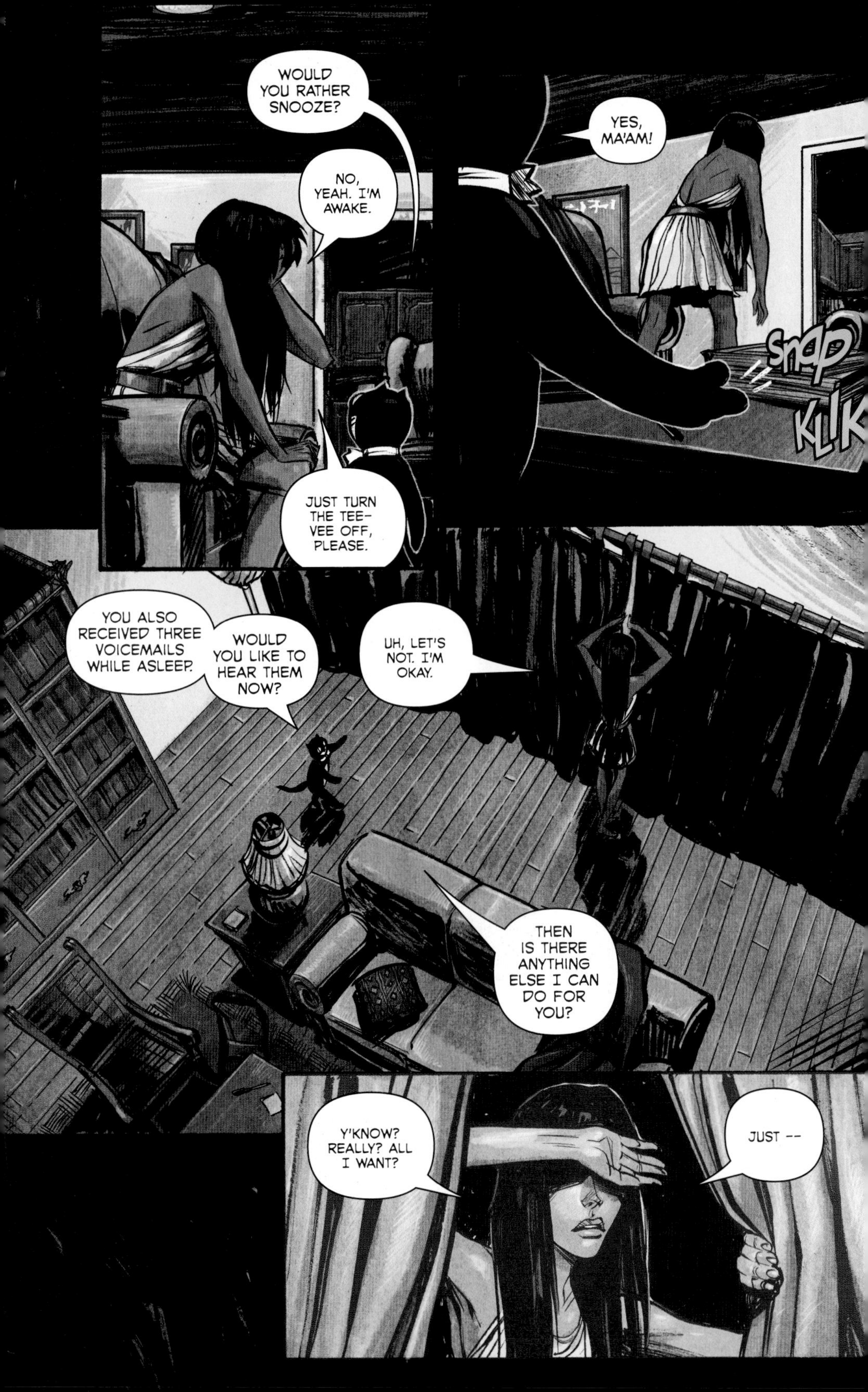
WOULD YOU RATHER SNOOZE?
NO, YEAH. I'M AWAKE.
JUST TURN THE TEE-VEE OFF, PLEASE.
YES, MA'AM!
SNAP
KLIK
YOU ALSO RECEIVED THREE VOICEMAILS WHILE ASLEEP.
WOULD YOU LIKE TO HEAR THEM NOW?
UH, LET'S NOT. I'M OKAY.
THEN IS THERE ANYTHING ELSE I CAN DO FOR YOU?
Y'KNOW? REALLY? ALL I WANT?
JUST --

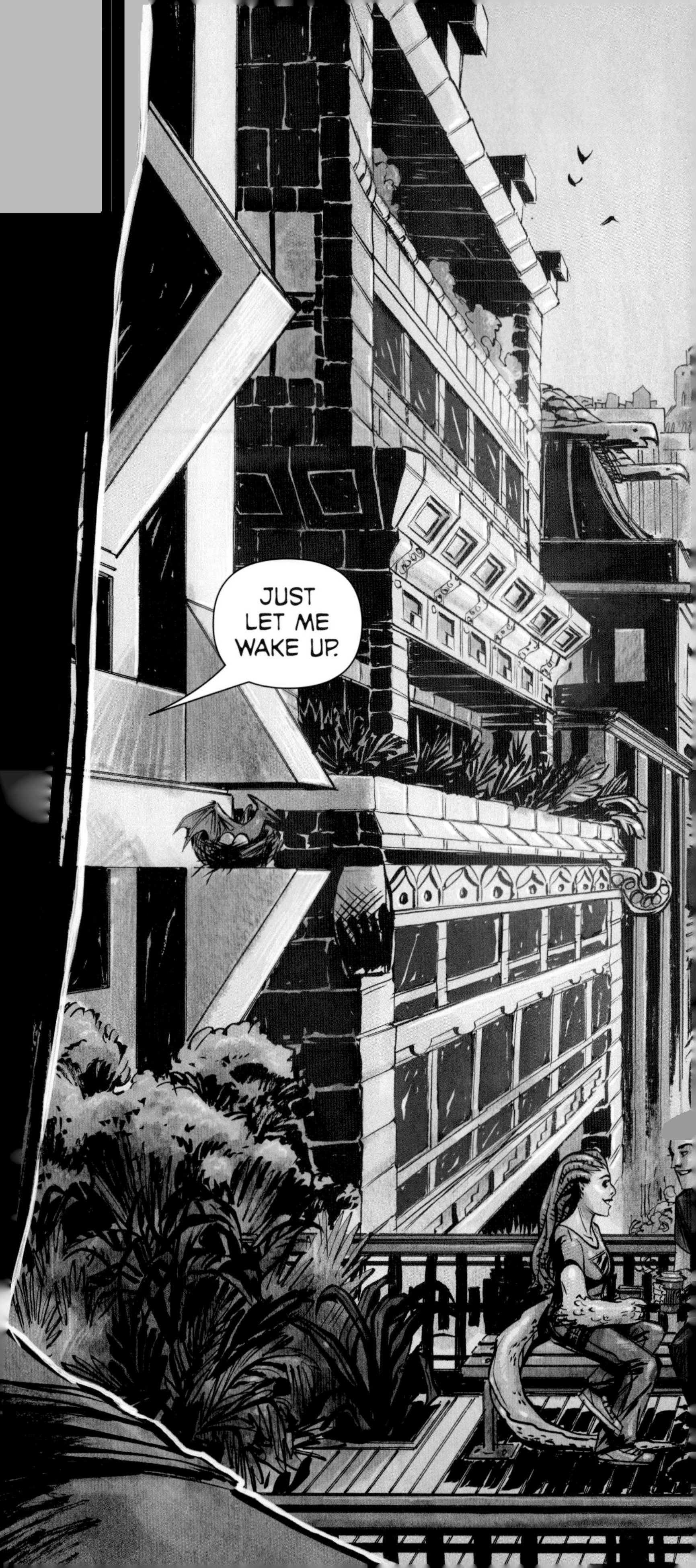
JUST LET ME WAKE UP.

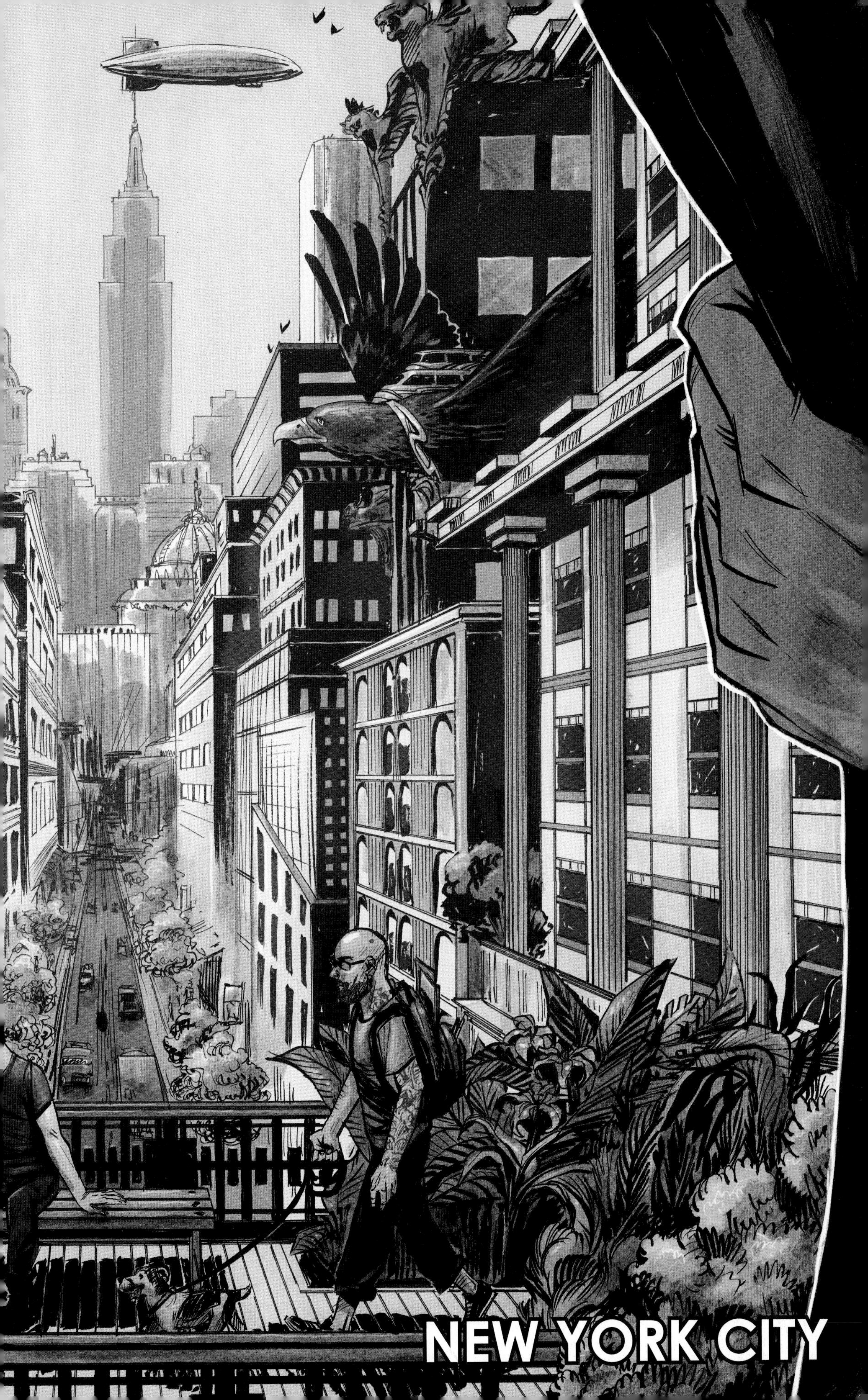
NEW YORK CITY

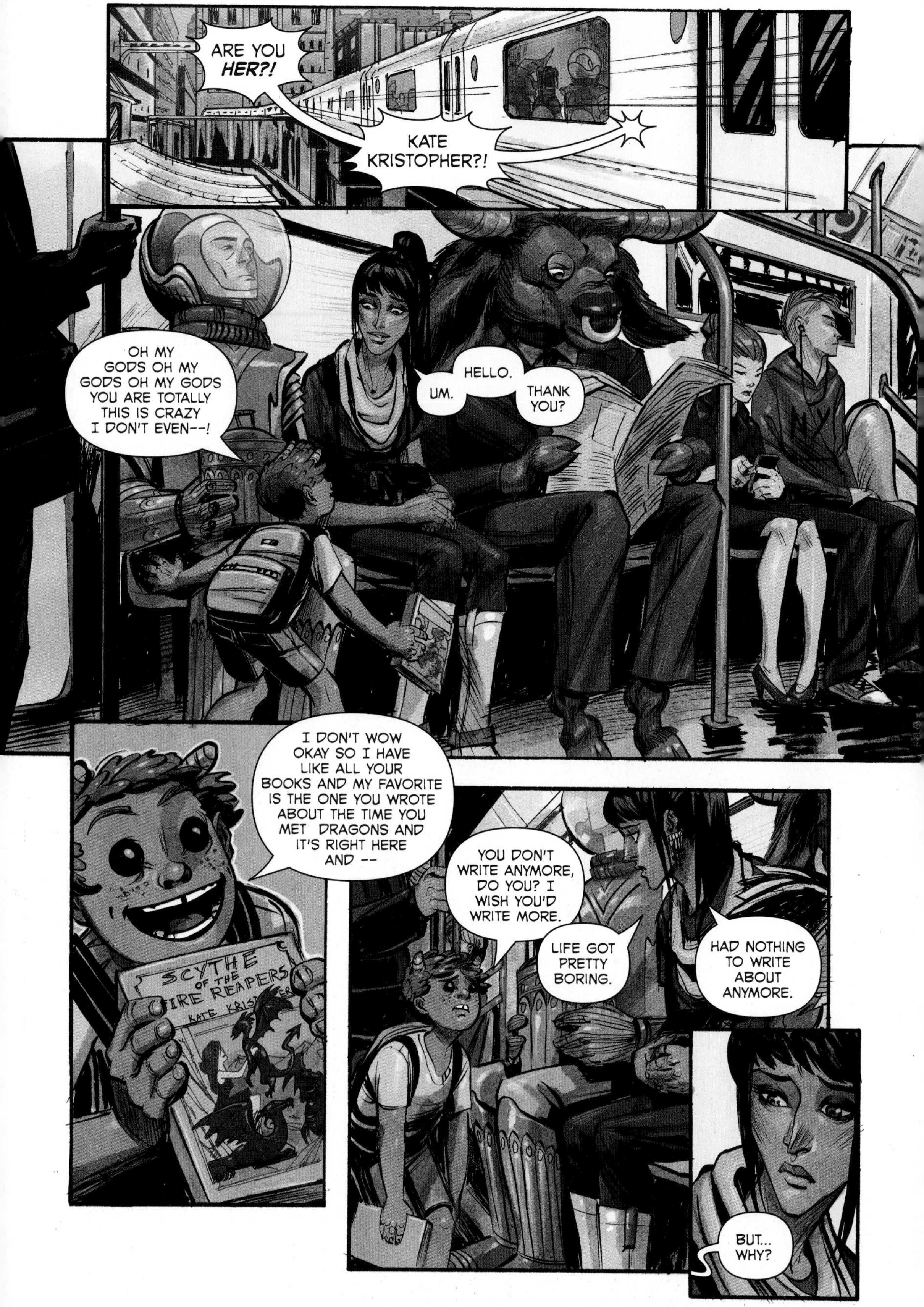
ARE YOU *HER?!*
KATE KRISTOPHER?!
OH MY GODS OH MY GODS OH MY GODS YOU ARE TOTALLY THIS IS CRAZY I DON'T EVEN--!
UM.
HELLO.
THANK YOU?
I DON'T WOW OKAY SO I HAVE LIKE ALL YOUR BOOKS AND MY FAVORITE IS THE ONE YOU WROTE ABOUT THE TIME YOU MET DRAGONS AND IT'S RIGHT HERE AND --
SCYTHE OF THE FIRE REAPERS
YOU DON'T WRITE ANYMORE, DO YOU? I WISH YOU'D WRITE MORE.
LIFE GOT PRETTY BORING.
HAD NOTHING TO WRITE ABOUT ANYMORE.
BUT... WHY?

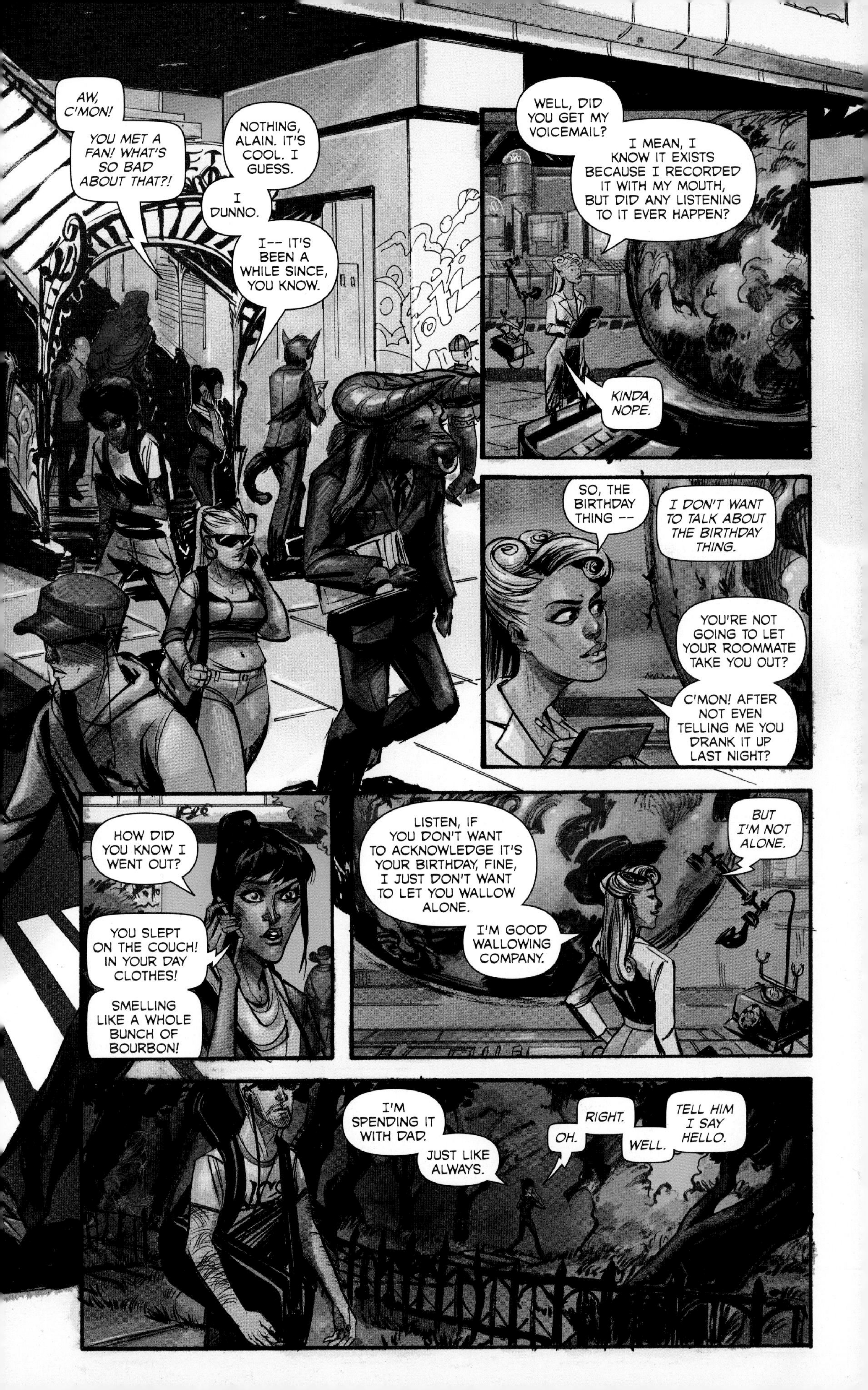
AW, C'MON!
YOU MET A FAN! WHAT'S SO BAD ABOUT THAT?!
NOTHING, ALAIN. IT'S COOL. I GUESS.
I DUNNO.
I-- IT'S BEEN A WHILE SINCE, YOU KNOW.
WELL, DID YOU GET MY VOICEMAIL?
I MEAN, I KNOW IT EXISTS BECAUSE I RECORDED IT WITH MY MOUTH, BUT DID ANY LISTENING TO IT EVER HAPPEN?
KINDA, NOPE.
SO, THE BIRTHDAY THING --
I DON'T WANT TO TALK ABOUT THE BIRTHDAY THING.
YOU'RE NOT GOING TO LET YOUR ROOMMATE TAKE YOU OUT?
C'MON! AFTER NOT EVEN TELLING ME YOU DRANK IT UP LAST NIGHT?
HOW DID YOU KNOW I WENT OUT?
YOU SLEPT ON THE COUCH! IN YOUR DAY CLOTHES!
SMELLING LIKE A WHOLE BUNCH OF BOURBON!
LISTEN, IF YOU DON'T WANT TO ACKNOWLEDGE IT'S YOUR BIRTHDAY, FINE, I JUST DON'T WANT TO LET YOU WALLOW ALONE.
I'M GOOD WALLOWING COMPANY.
BUT I'M NOT ALONE.
I'M SPENDING IT WITH DAD.
JUST LIKE ALWAYS.
OH.
RIGHT.
WELL.
TELL HIM I SAY HELLO.

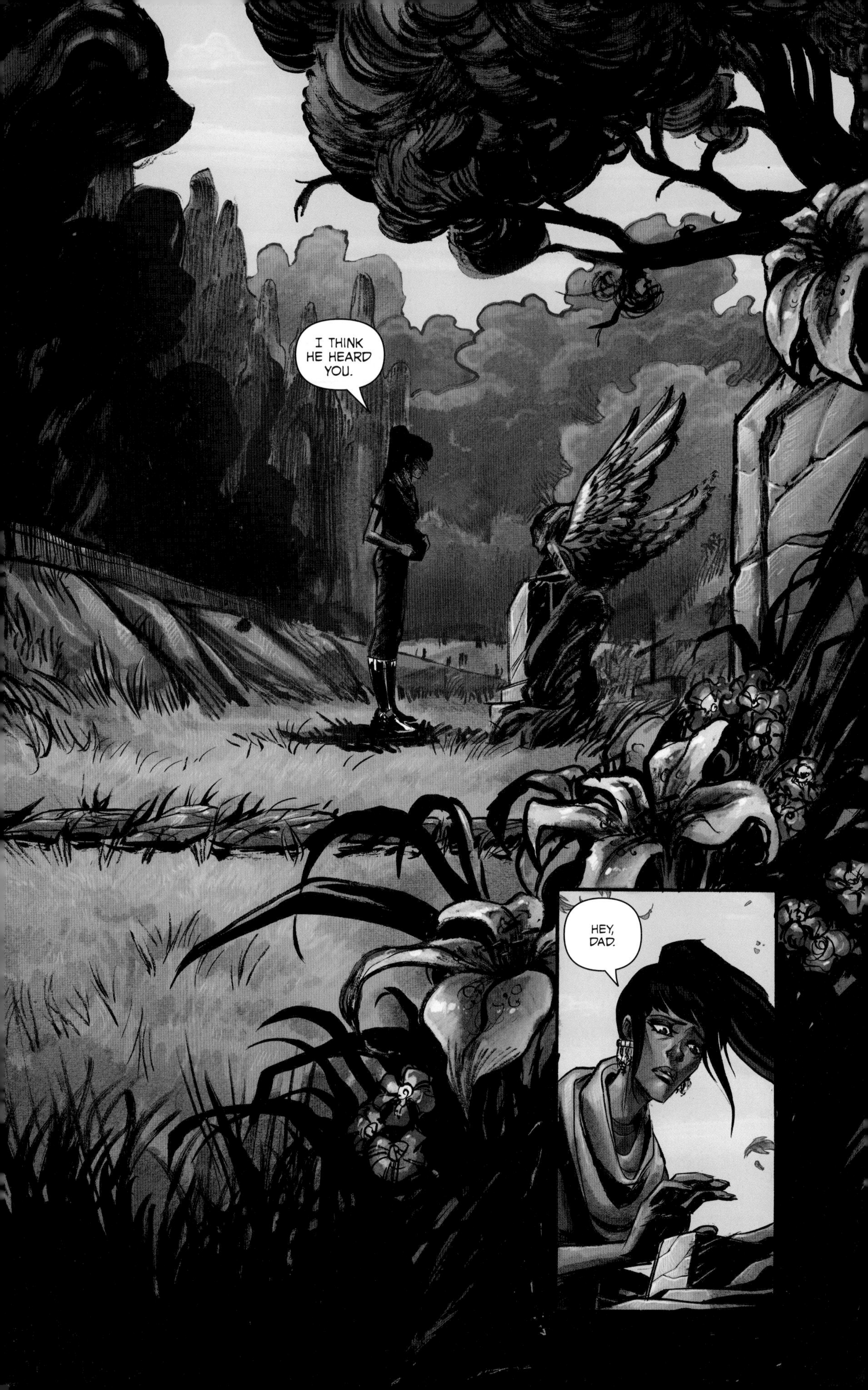
I THINK HE HEARD YOU.
HEY, DAD.

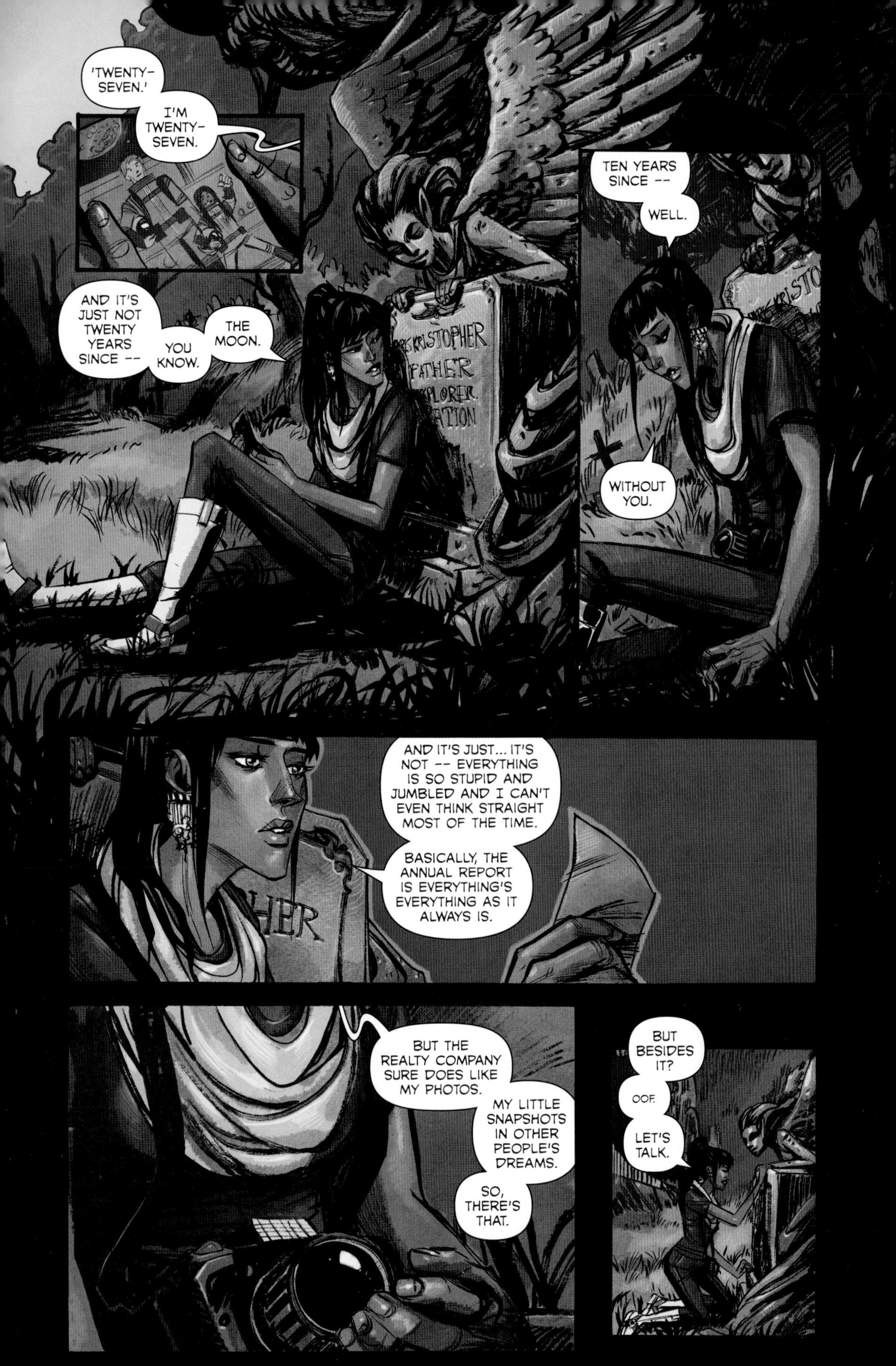
'TWENTY-SEVEN.'
I'M TWENTY-SEVEN.
TEN YEARS SINCE --
WELL.
AND IT'S JUST NOT TWENTY YEARS SINCE --
YOU KNOW.
THE MOON.
WITHOUT YOU.
AND IT'S JUST... IT'S NOT -- EVERYTHING IS SO STUPID AND JUMBLED AND I CAN'T EVEN THINK STRAIGHT MOST OF THE TIME.
BASICALLY, THE ANNUAL REPORT IS EVERYTHING'S EVERYTHING AS IT ALWAYS IS.
BUT THE REALTY COMPANY SURE DOES LIKE MY PHOTOS.
MY LITTLE SNAPSHOTS IN OTHER PEOPLE'S DREAMS.
SO, THERE'S THAT.
BUT BESIDES IT?
OOF.
LET'S TALK.

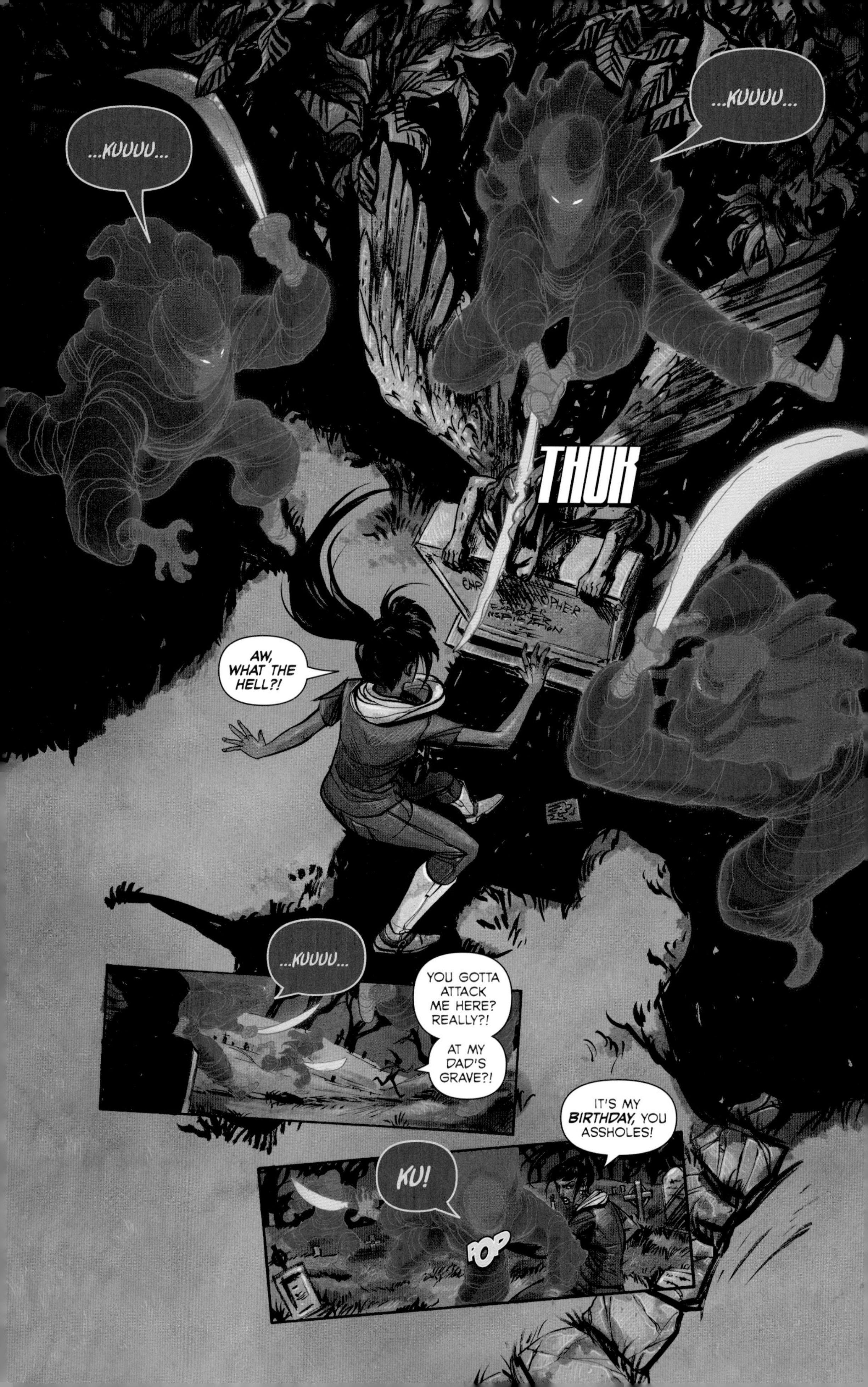
...KUUUU...
...KUUUU...
THUK
AW, WHAT THE HELL?!
...KUUUU...
YOU GOTTA ATTACK ME HERE? REALLY?!
AT MY DAD'S GRAVE?!
IT'S MY BIRTHDAY, YOU ASSHOLES!
KU!
POP

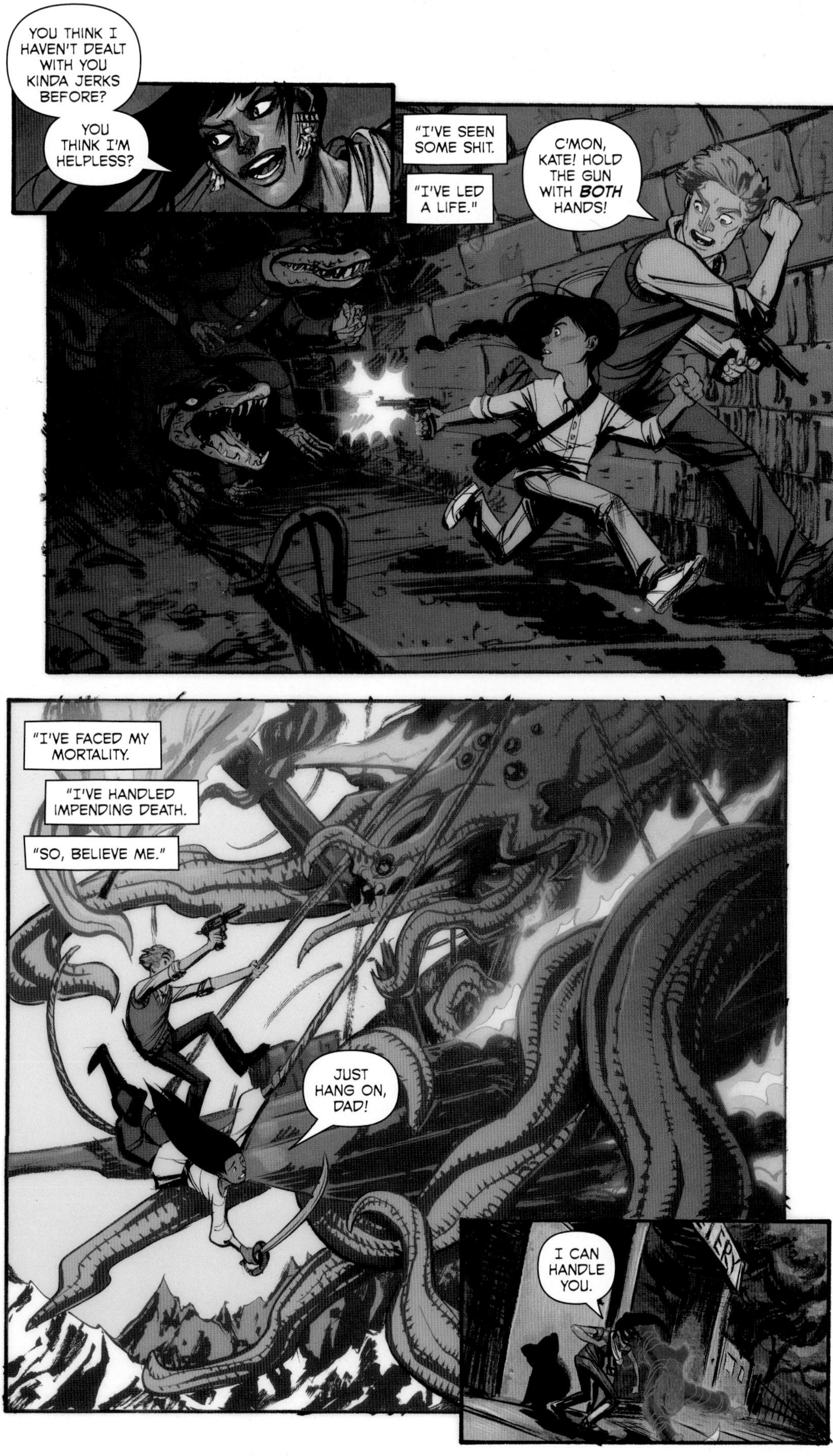

YOU THINK I HAVEN'T DEALT WITH YOU KINDA JERKS BEFORE?
YOU THINK I'M HELPLESS?
"I'VE SEEN SOME SHIT.
"I'VE LED A LIFE."
C'MON, KATE! HOLD THE GUN WITH BOTH HANDS!
"I'VE FACED MY MORTALITY.
"I'VE HANDLED IMPENDING DEATH.
"SO, BELIEVE ME."
JUST HANG ON, DAD!
I CAN HANDLE YOU.

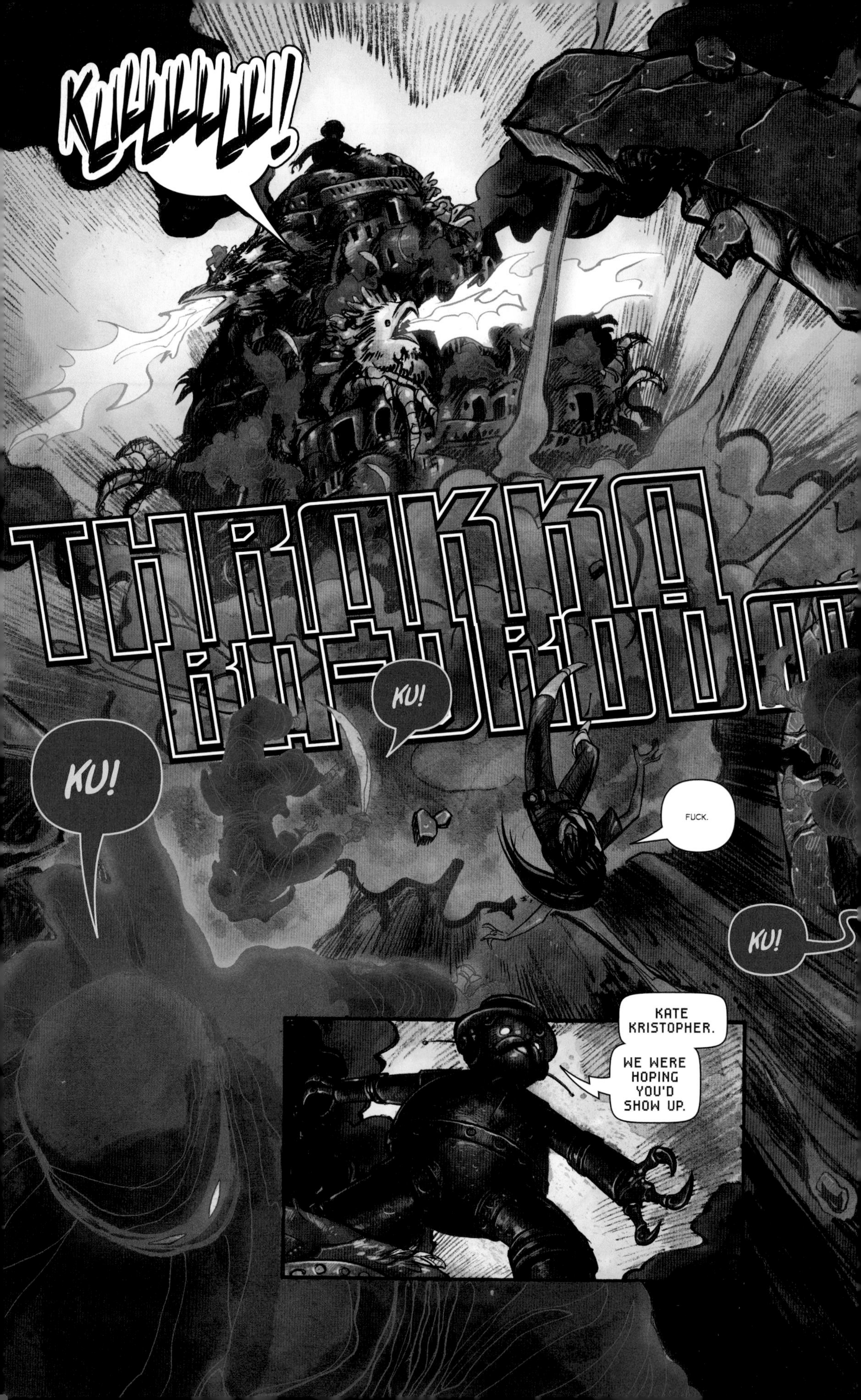
THRAKKA
KU!
KU!
FUCK.
KU!
KATE KRISTOPHER.
WE WERE HOPING YOU'D SHOW UP.

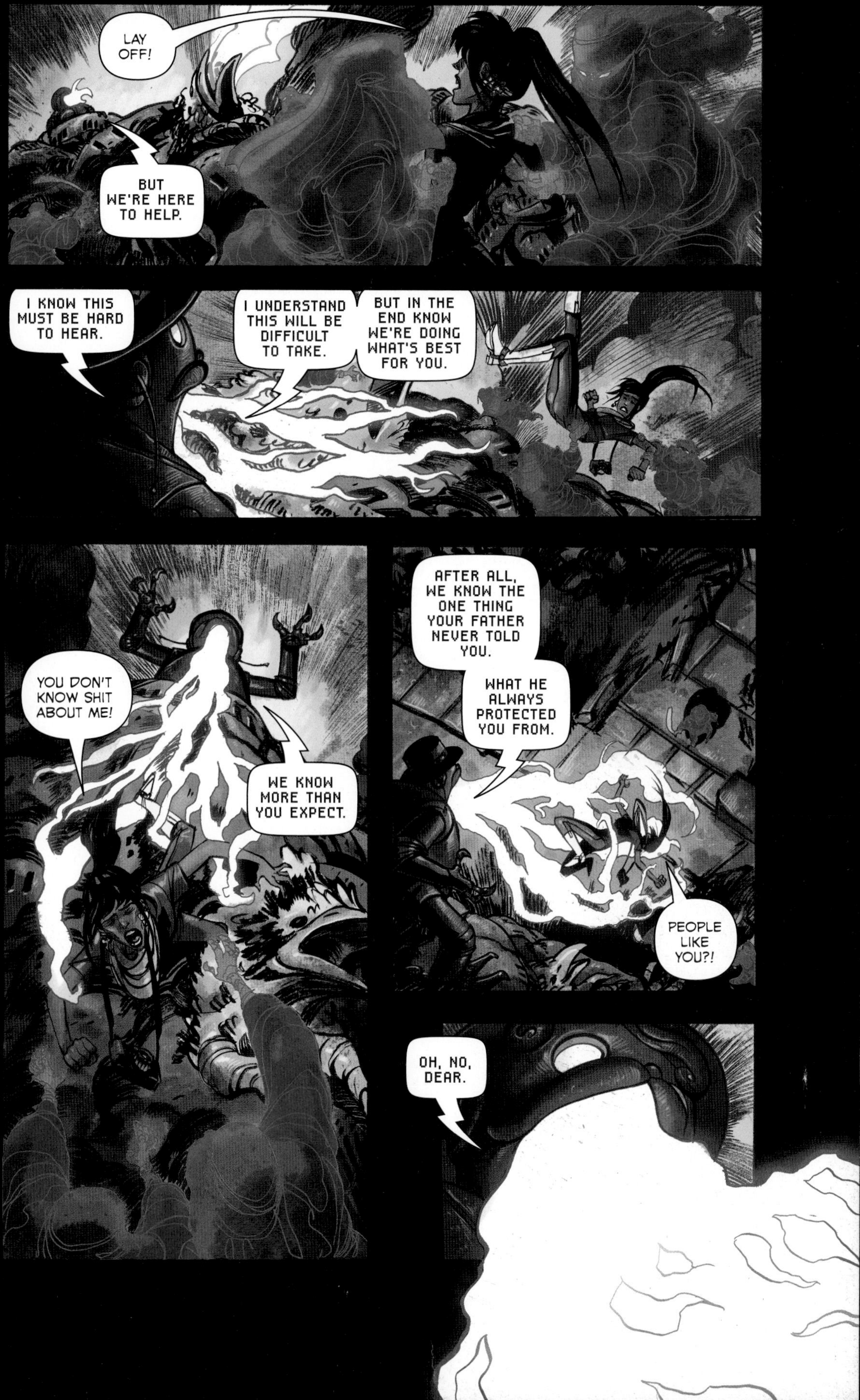
LAY OFF!
BUT WE'RE HERE TO HELP.
I KNOW THIS MUST BE HARD TO HEAR.
I UNDERSTAND THIS WILL BE DIFFICULT TO TAKE.
BUT IN THE END KNOW WE'RE DOING WHAT'S BEST FOR YOU.
YOU DON'T KNOW SHIT ABOUT ME!
WE KNOW MORE THAN YOU EXPECT.
AFTER ALL, WE KNOW THE ONE THING YOUR FATHER NEVER TOLD YOU.
WHAT HE ALWAYS PROTECTED YOU FROM.
PEOPLE LIKE YOU?!
OH, NO, DEAR.

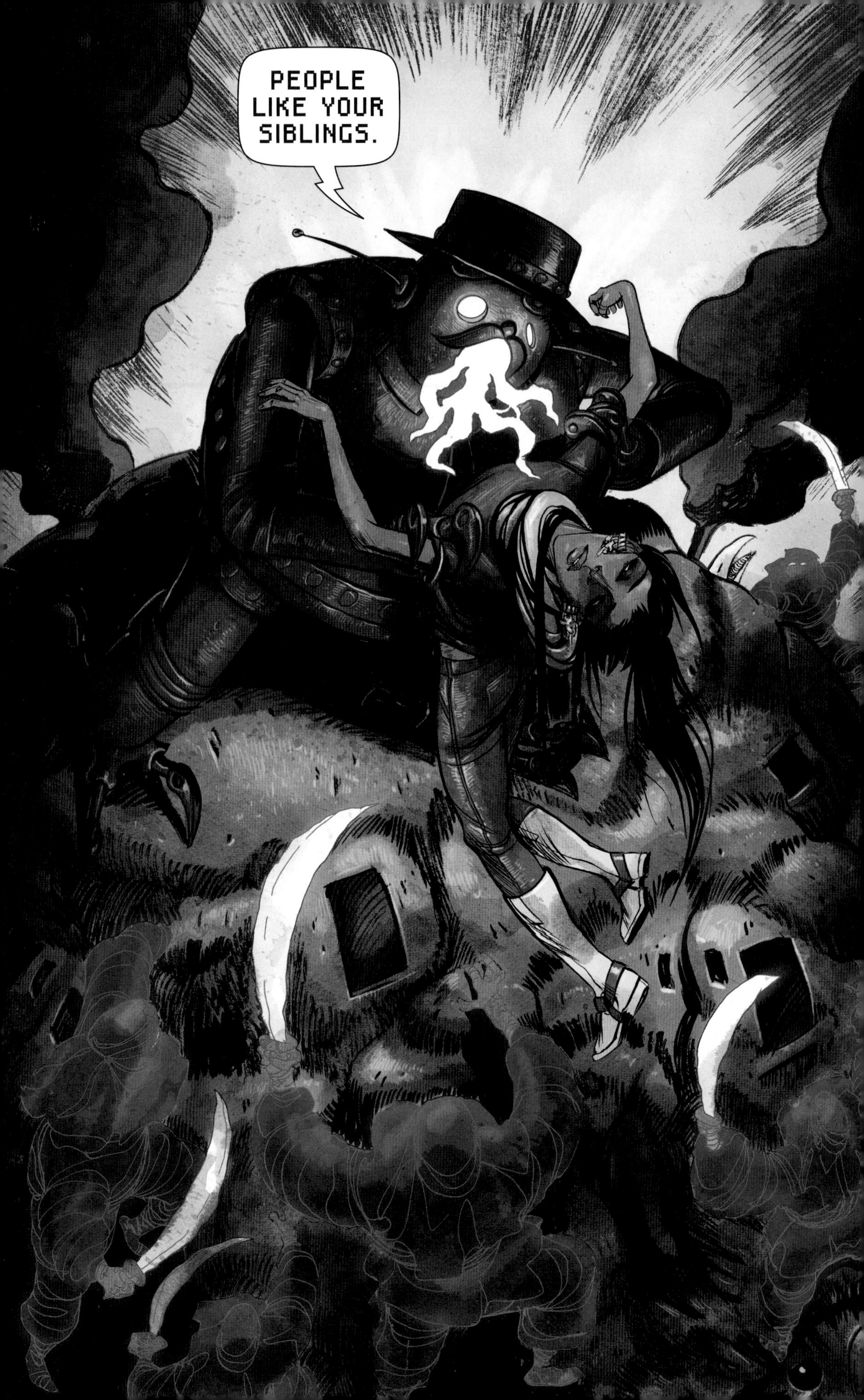
PEOPLE LIKE YOUR SIBLINGS.

CHAPTER

2

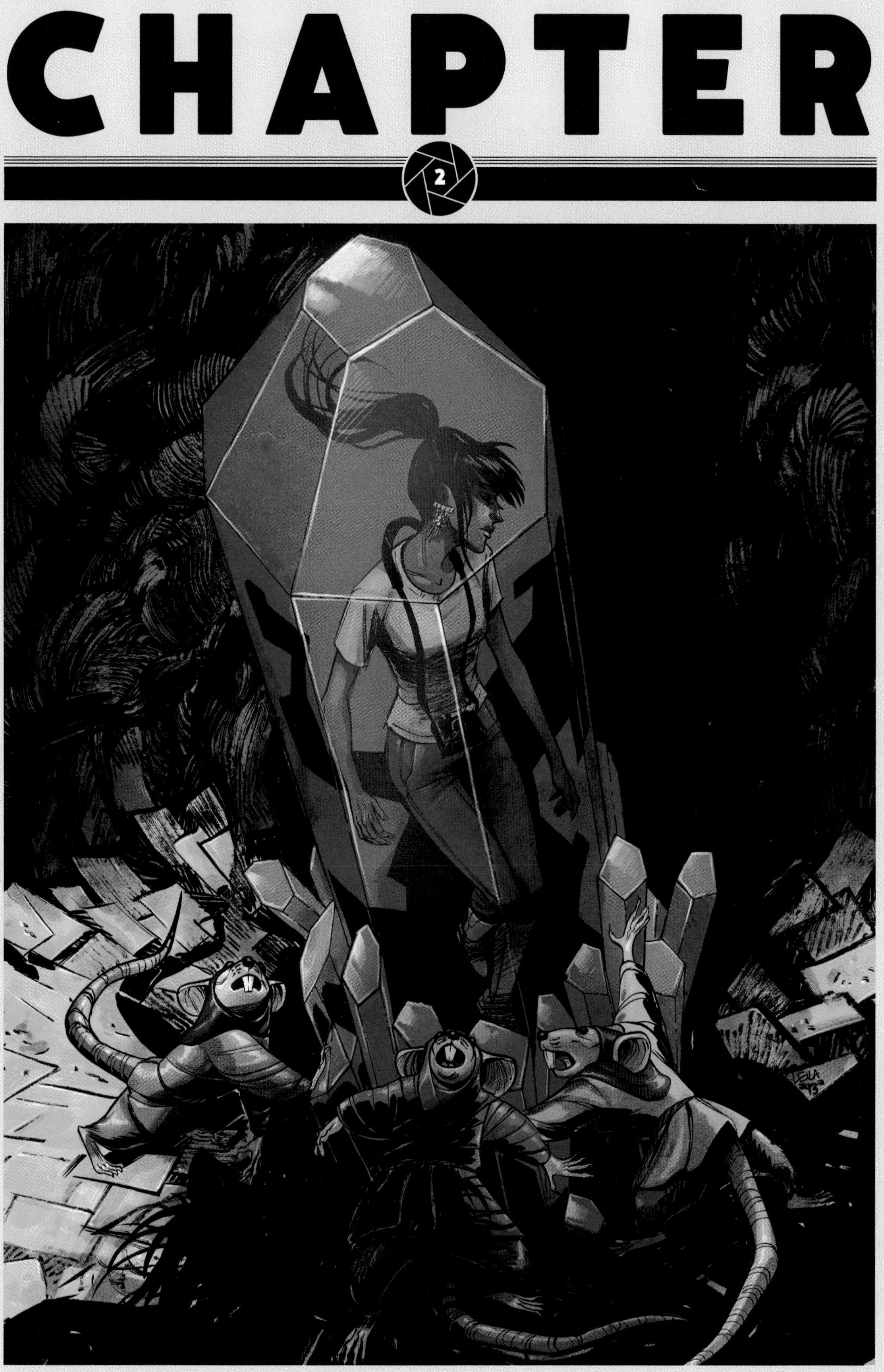

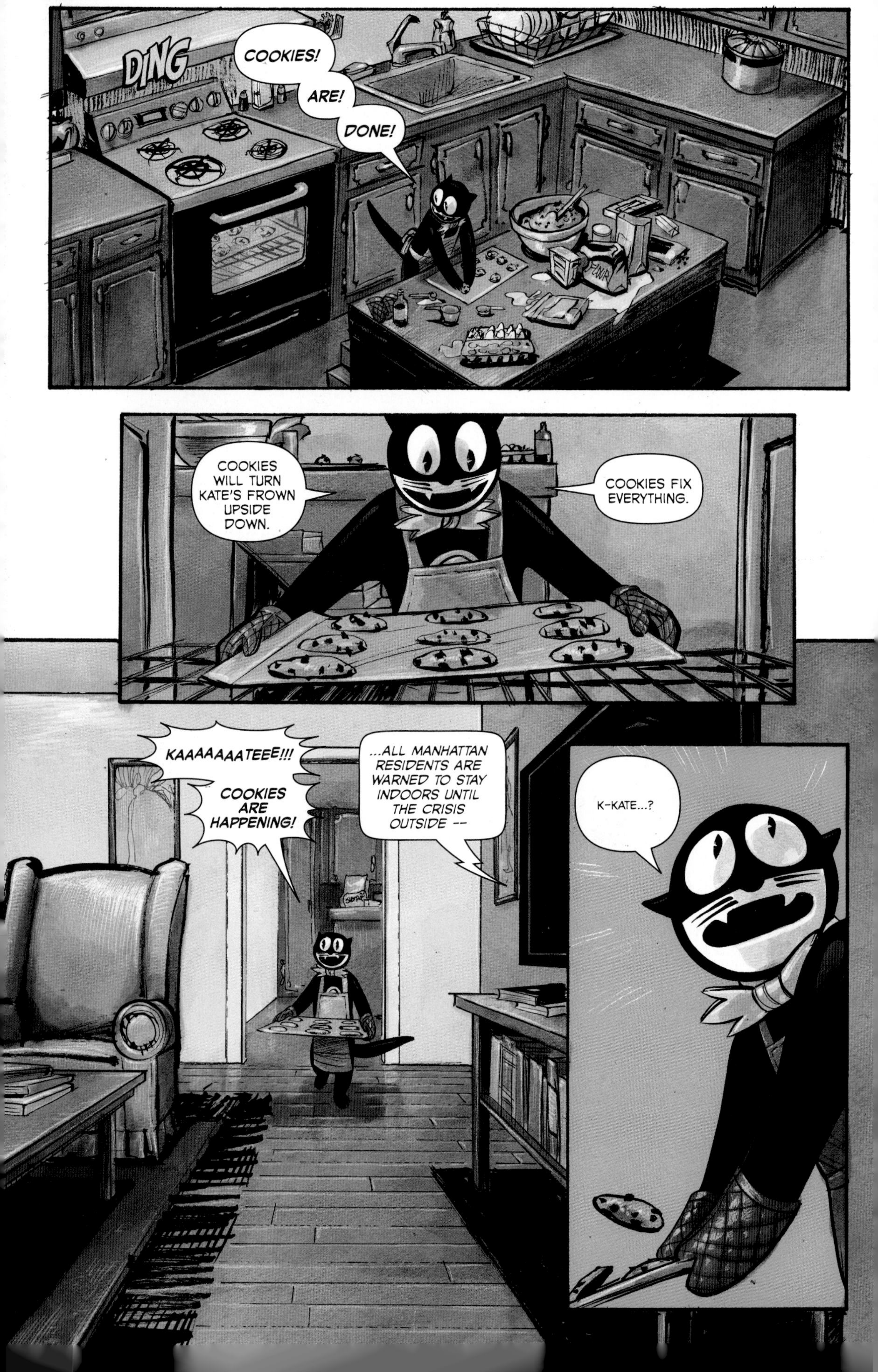
DING
COOKIES!
ARE!
DONE!
COOKIES WILL TURN KATE'S FROWN UPSIDE DOWN.
COOKIES FIX EVERYTHING.
KAAAAAAAATEEE!!!
COOKIES ARE HAPPENING!
...ALL MANHATTAN RESIDENTS ARE WARNED TO STAY INDOORS UNTIL THE CRISIS OUTSIDE --
K-KATE...?

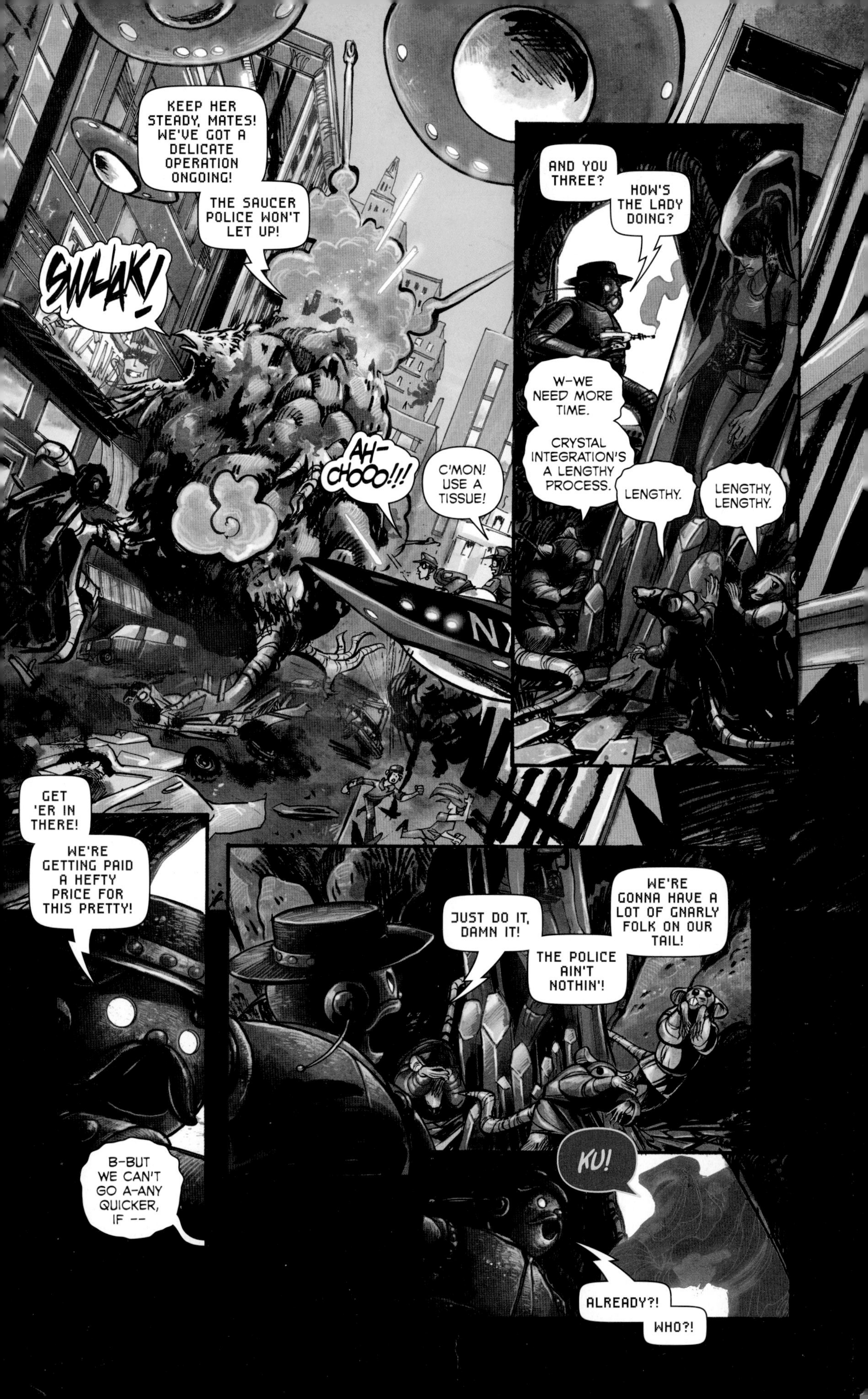

KEEP HER STEADY, MATES! WE'VE GOT A DELICATE OPERATION ONGOING!
THE SAUCER POLICE WON'T LET UP!
SWAK!
AH-CHOOO!!!
C'MON! USE A TISSUE!
AND YOU THREE?
HOW'S THE LADY DOING?
W-WE NEED MORE TIME.
CRYSTAL INTEGRATION'S A LENGTHY PROCESS.
LENGTHY.
LENGTHY, LENGTHY.
GET 'ER IN THERE!
WE'RE GETTING PAID A HEFTY PRICE FOR THIS PRETTY!
B-BUT WE CAN'T GO A-ANY QUICKER, IF --
JUST DO IT, DAMN IT!
WE'RE GONNA HAVE A LOT OF GNARLY FOLK ON OUR TAIL!
THE POLICE AIN'T NOTHIN'!
KU!
ALREADY?!
WHO?!

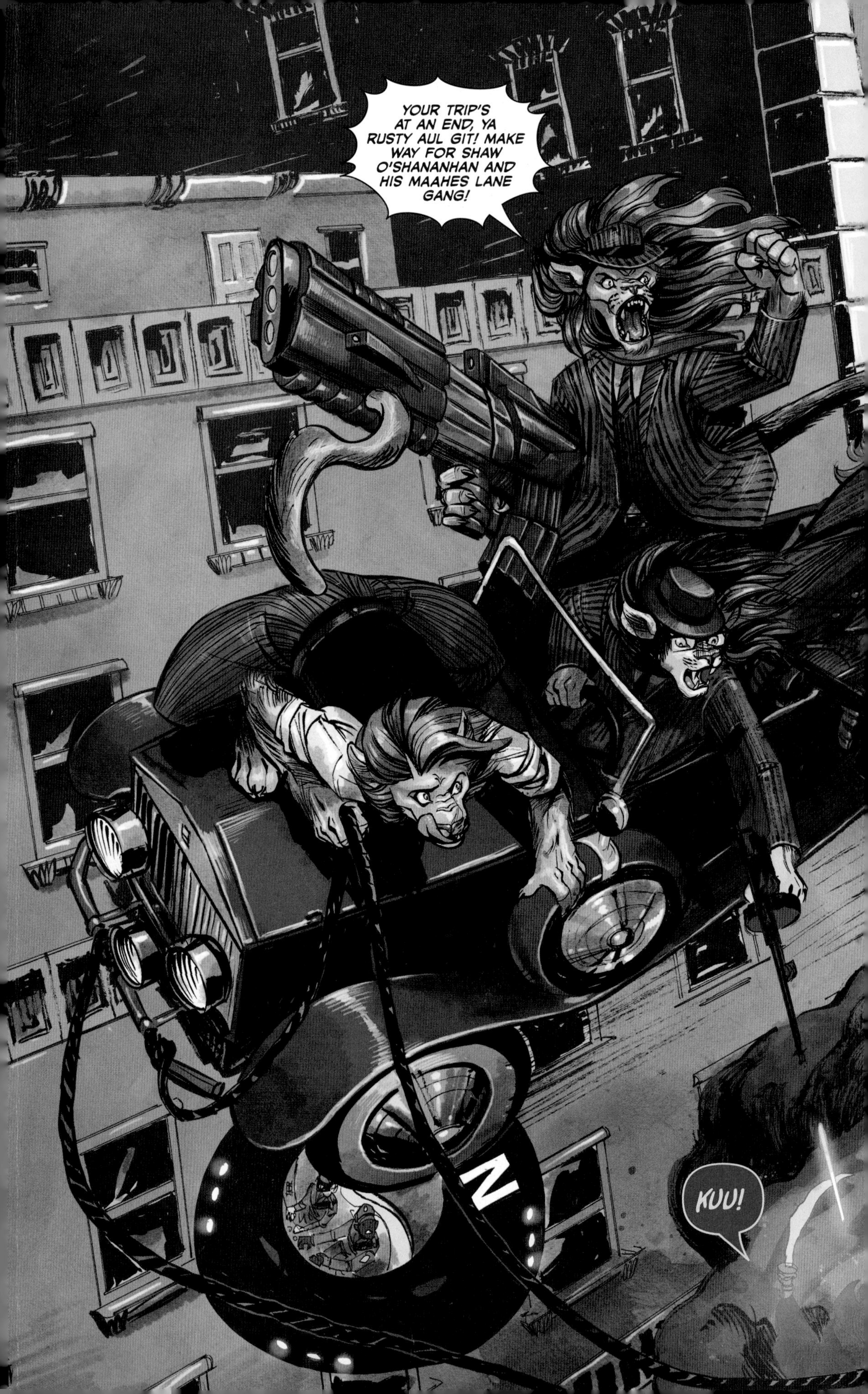
YOUR TRIP'S AT AN END, YA RUSTY AUL GIT! MAKE WAY FOR SHAW O'SHANANHAN AND HIS MAAHES LANE GANG!
KUU!

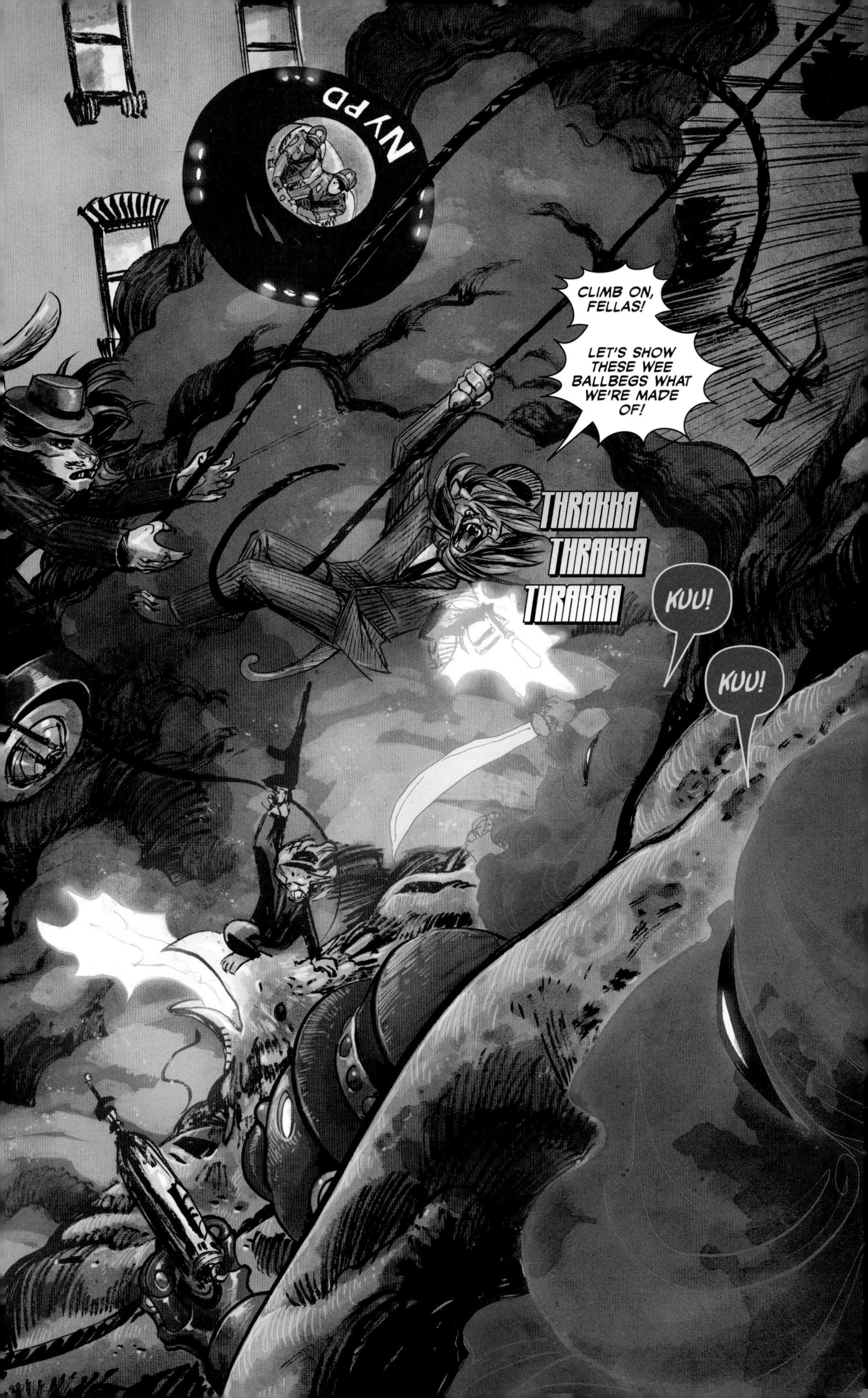
NYPD
CLIMB ON, FELLAS!
LET'S SHOW THESE WEE BALLBEGS WHAT WE'RE MADE OF!
THRAKKA THRAKKA THRAKKA
KUU!
KUU!

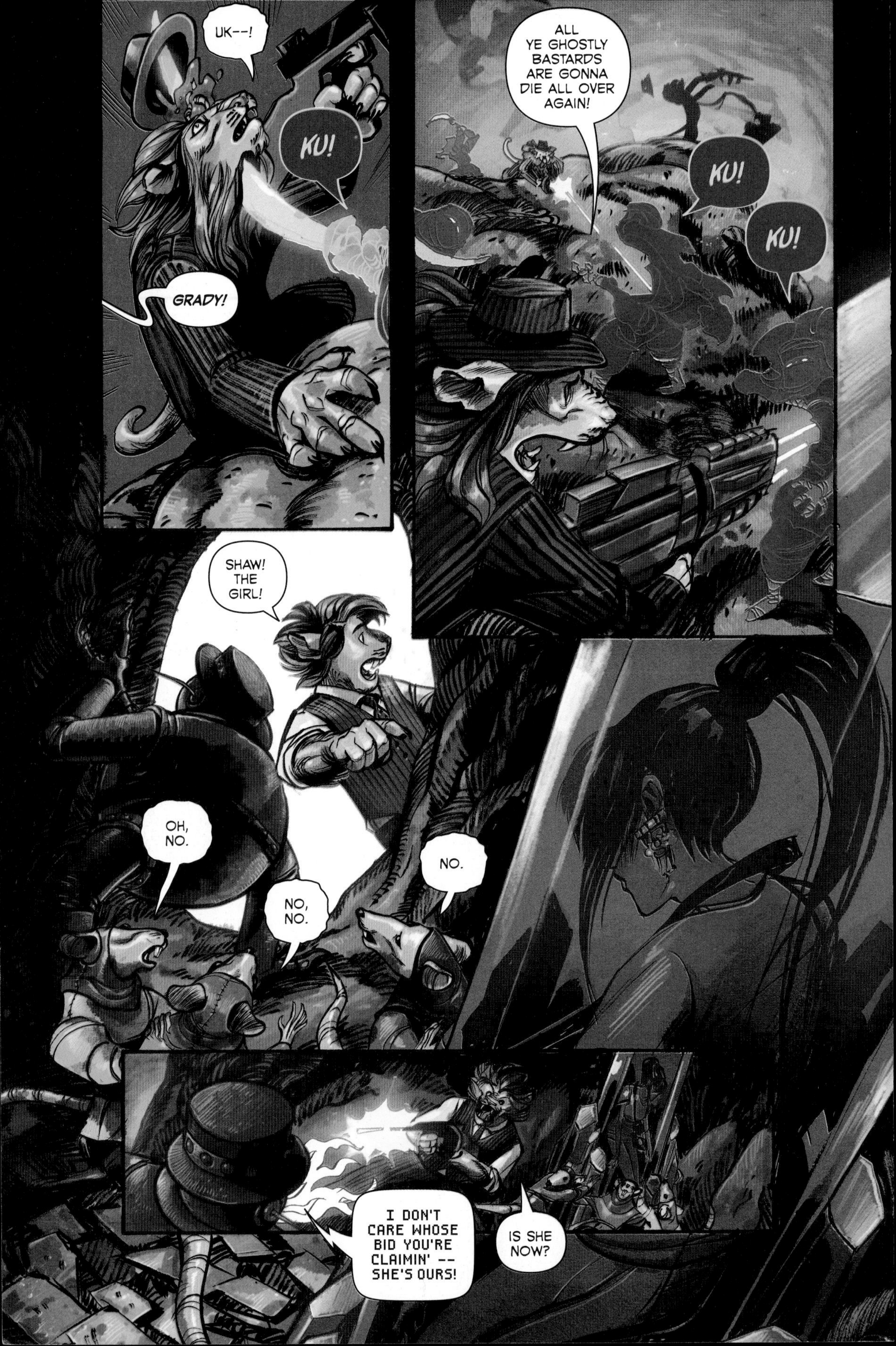
UK--!
KU!
GRADY!
ALL YE GHOSTLY BASTARDS ARE GONNA DIE ALL OVER AGAIN!
KU!
KU!
SHAW! THE GIRL!
OH, NO.
NO, NO.
NO.
I DON'T CARE WHOSE BID YOU'RE CLAIMIN' -- SHE'S OURS!
IS SHE NOW?

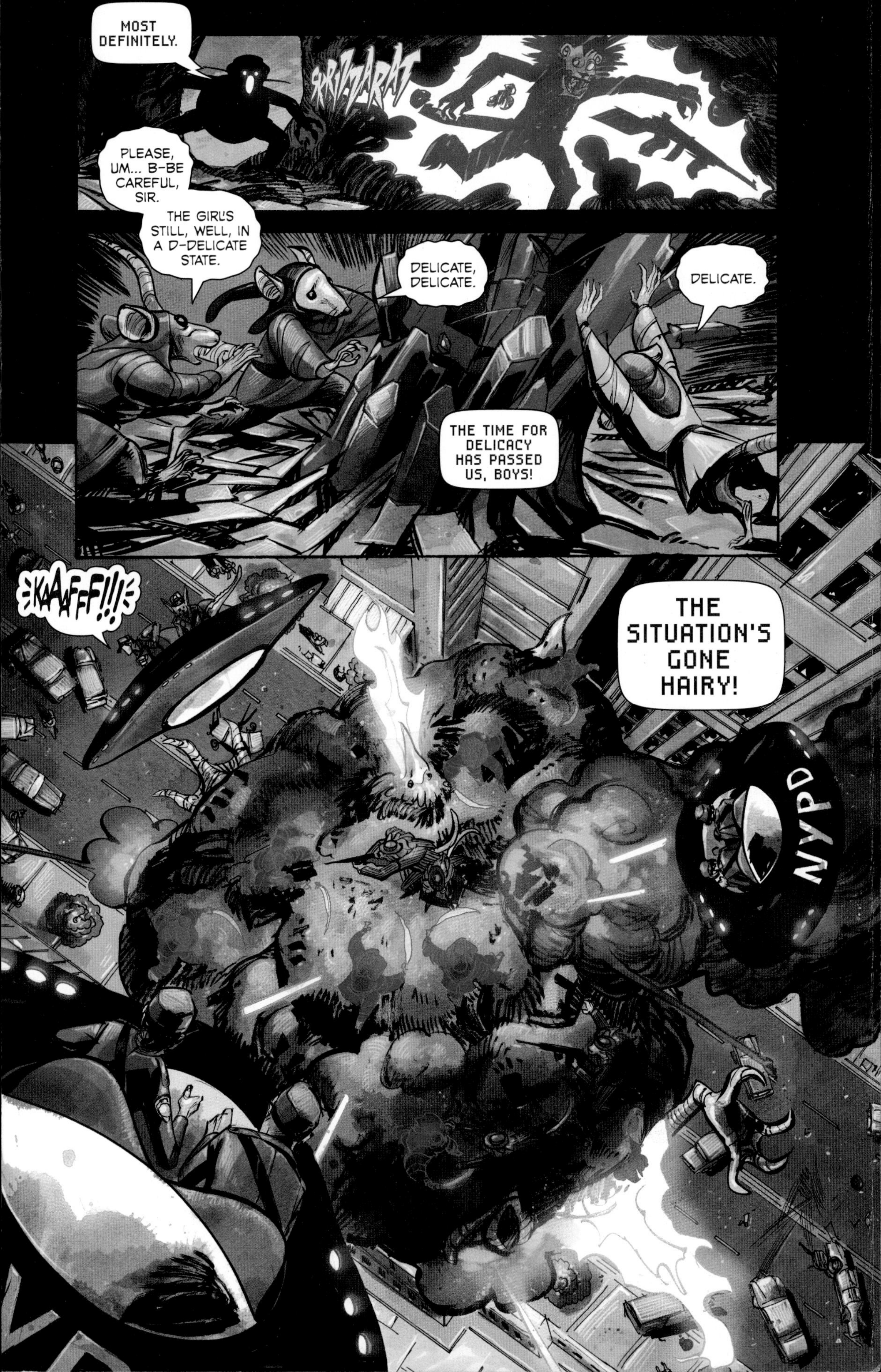
MOST DEFINITELY.
SPRIZZARAT
PLEASE, UM... B-BE CAREFUL, SIR.
THE GIRL'S STILL, WELL, IN A D-DELICATE STATE.
DELICATE, DELICATE.
DELICATE.
THE TIME FOR DELICACY HAS PASSED US, BOYS!
KAAAFFF!!!
THE SITUATION'S GONE HAIRY!
NYPD

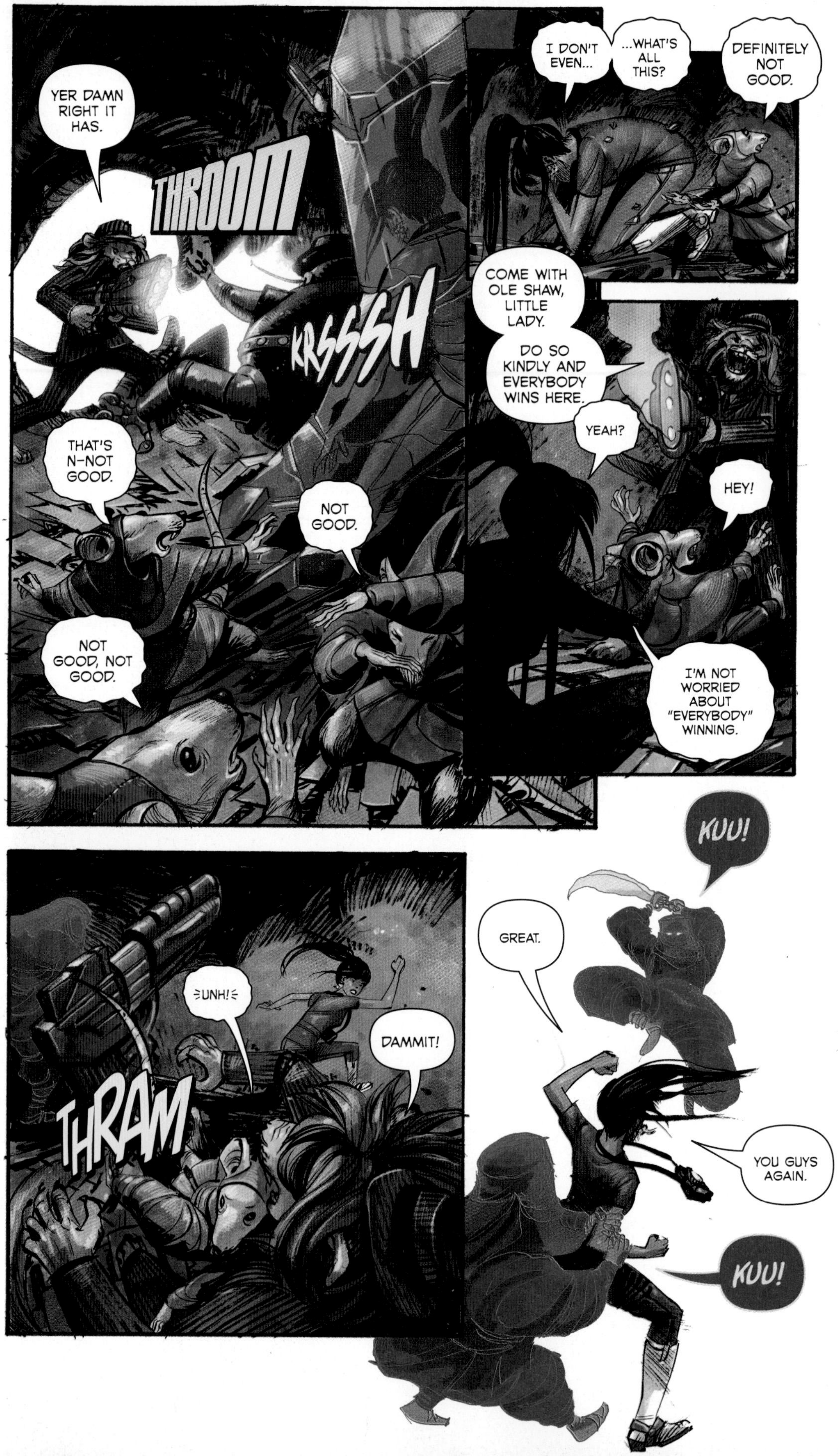
YER DAMN RIGHT IT HAS.
THROOM
KRSSSH
THAT'S N-NOT GOOD.
NOT GOOD.
NOT GOOD, NOT GOOD.
I DON'T EVEN...
...WHAT'S ALL THIS?
DEFINITELY NOT GOOD.
COME WITH OLE SHAW, LITTLE LADY.
DO SO KINDLY AND EVERYBODY WINS HERE.
YEAH?
HEY!
I'M NOT WORRIED ABOUT "EVERYBODY" WINNING.
UNH!
DAMMIT!
THRAM
KUU!
GREAT.
YOU GUYS AGAIN.
KUU!

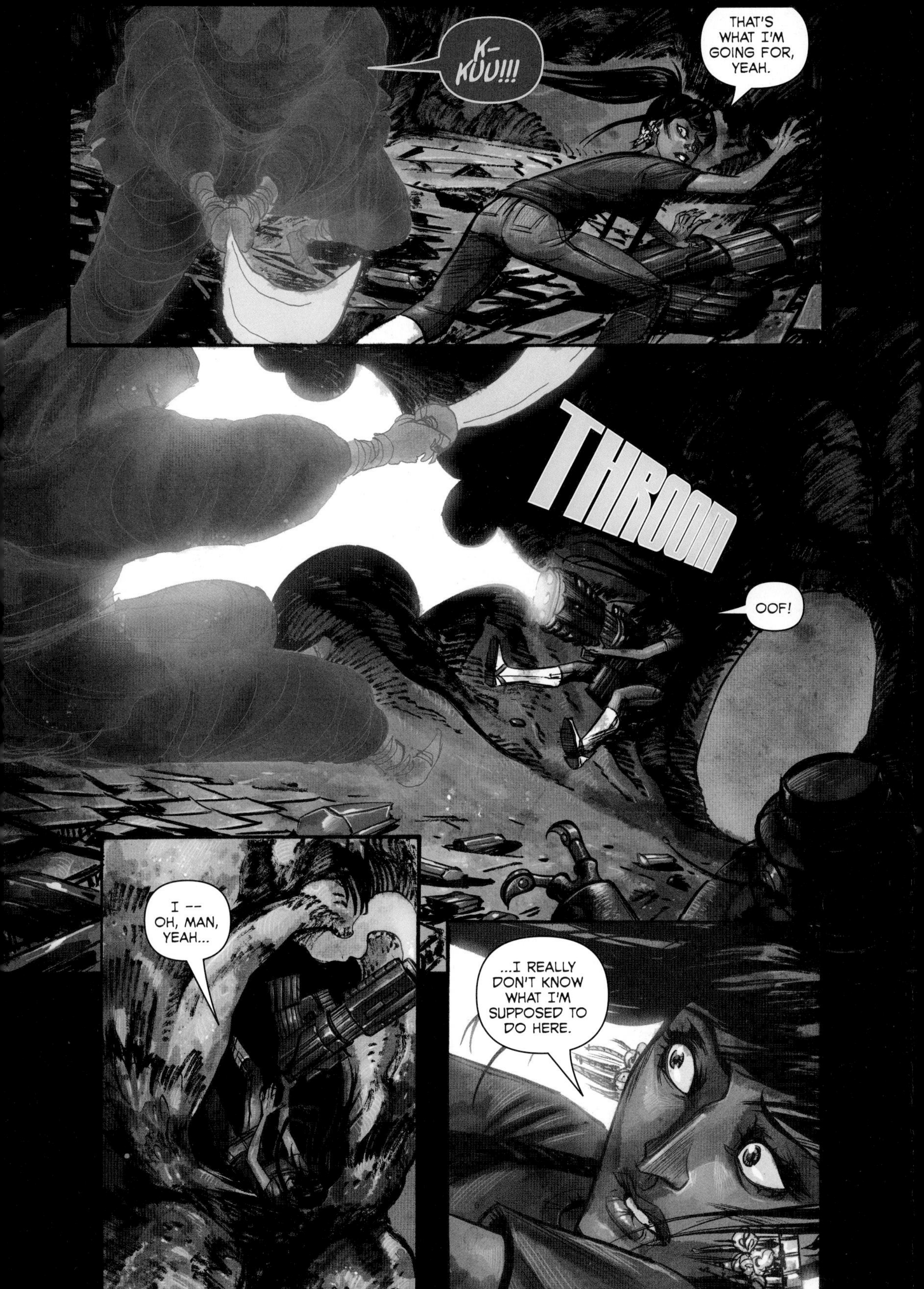
K-KUU!!!
THAT'S WHAT I'M GOING FOR, YEAH.
THROOM
OOF!
I -- OH, MAN, YEAH...
...I REALLY DON'T KNOW WHAT I'M SUPPOSED TO DO HERE.

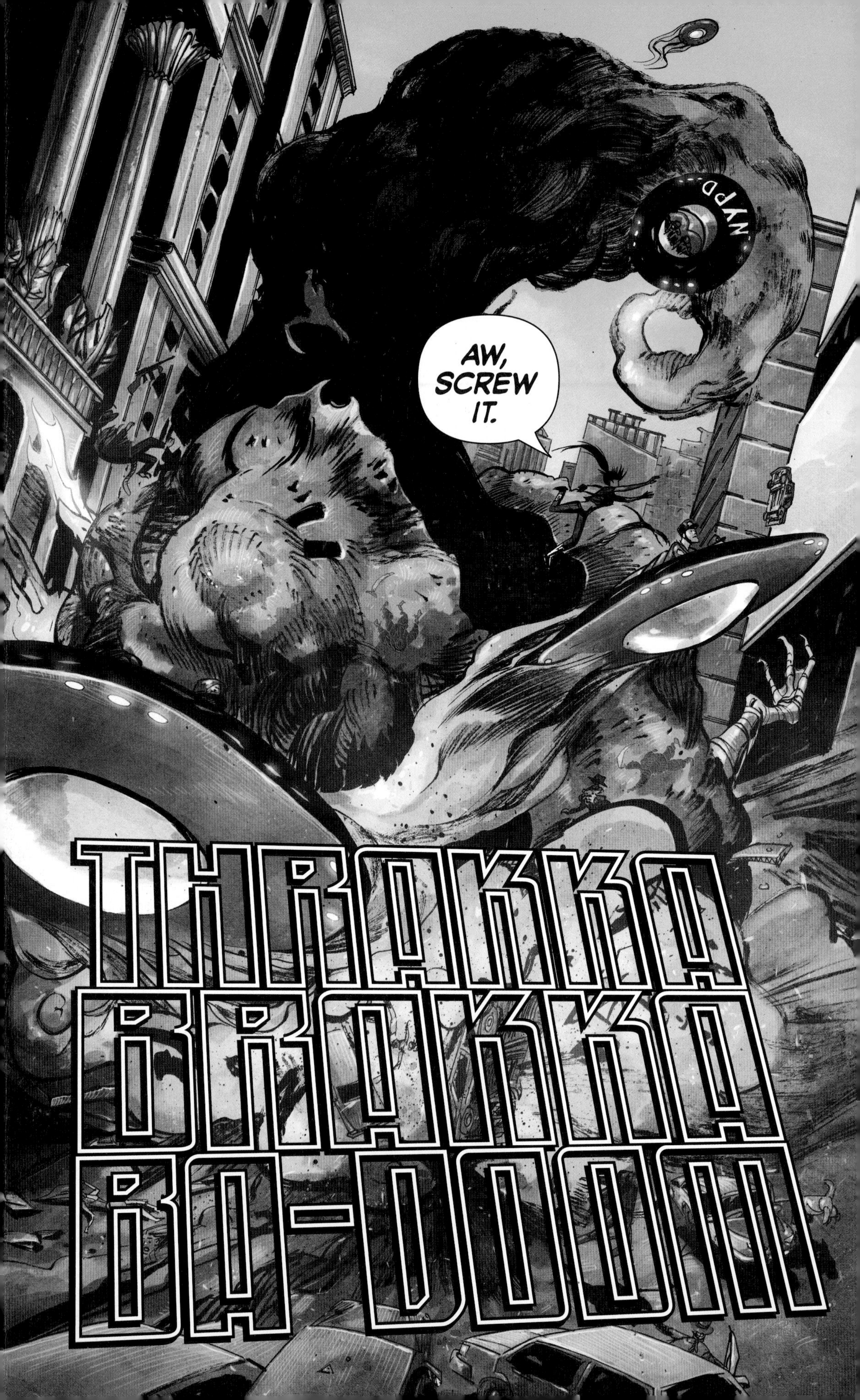
AW, SCREW IT.
THRAKKA BRAKKA BA-DOOM

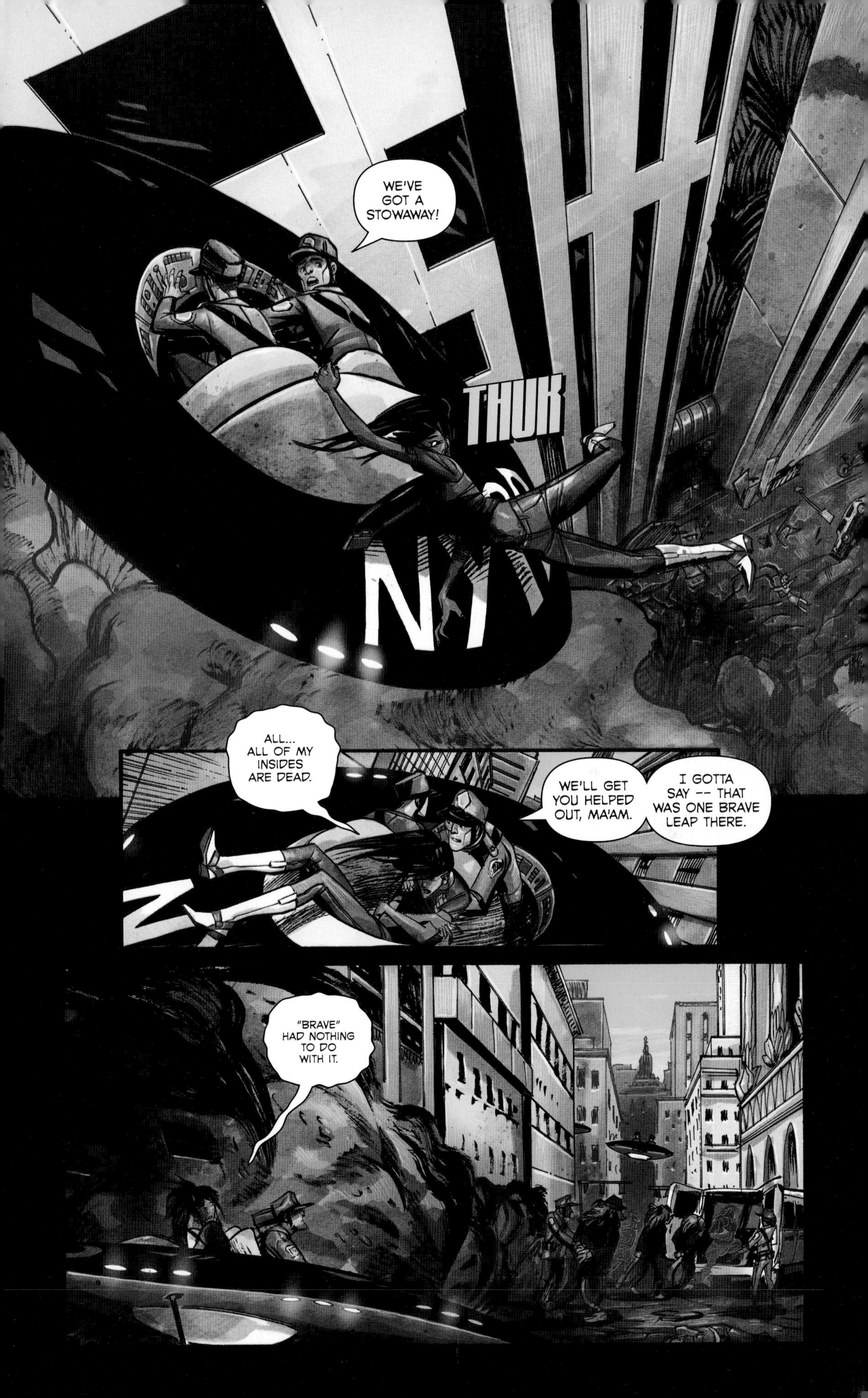
WE'VE GOT A STOWAWAY!
THUK
ALL... ALL OF MY INSIDES ARE DEAD.
WE'LL GET YOU HELPED OUT, MA'AM.
I GOTTA SAY -- THAT WAS ONE BRAVE LEAP THERE.
"BRAVE" HAD NOTHING TO DO WITH IT.

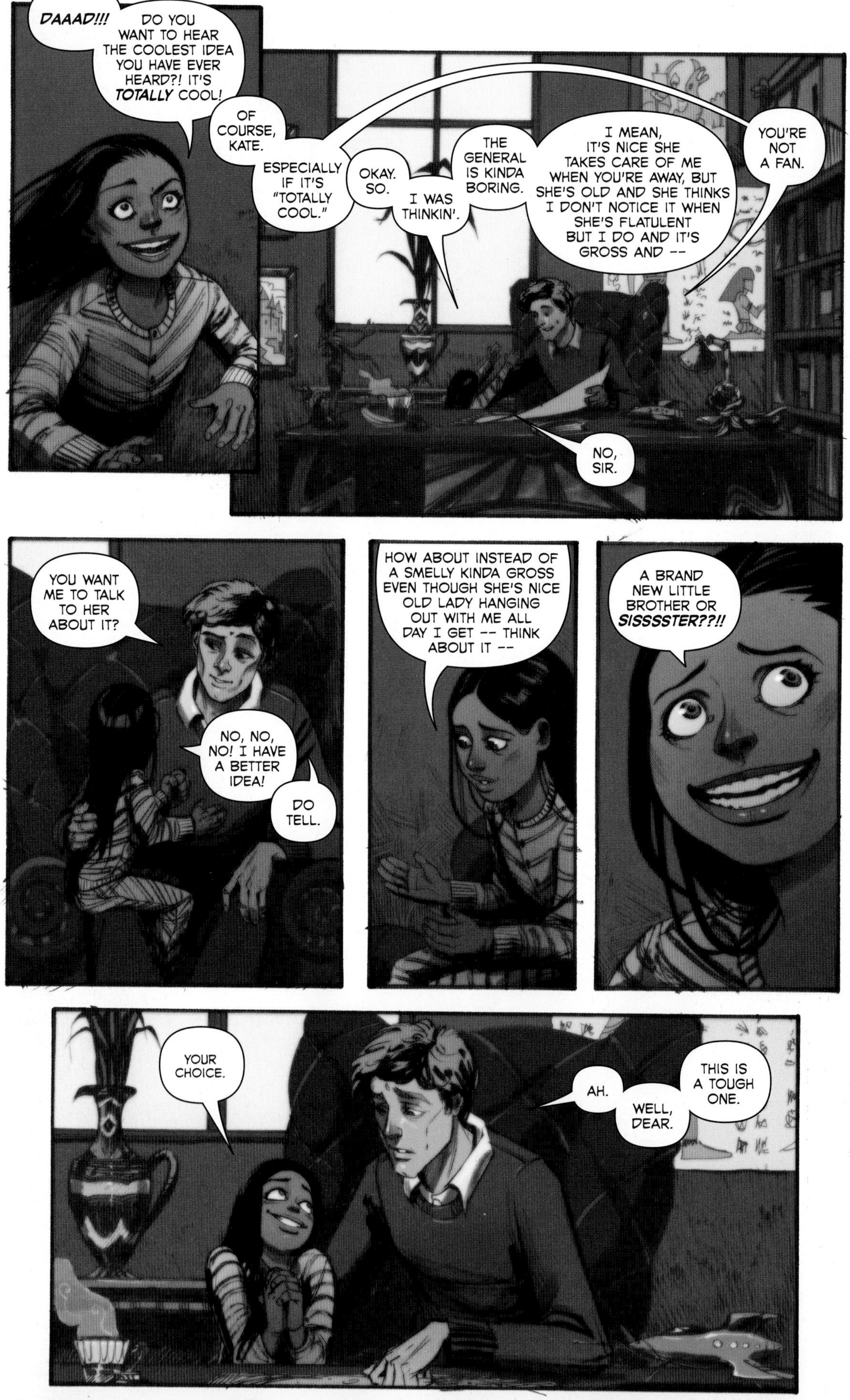
DAAAD!!! DO YOU WANT TO HEAR THE COOLEST IDEA YOU HAVE EVER HEARD?! IT'S TOTALLY COOL!
OF COURSE, KATE.
ESPECIALLY IF IT'S "TOTALLY COOL."
OKAY. SO.
I WAS THINKIN'.
THE GENERAL IS KINDA BORING.
I MEAN, IT'S NICE SHE TAKES CARE OF ME WHEN YOU'RE AWAY, BUT SHE'S OLD AND SHE THINKS I DON'T NOTICE IT WHEN SHE'S FLATULENT BUT I DO AND IT'S GROSS AND --
YOU'RE NOT A FAN.
NO, SIR.
YOU WANT ME TO TALK TO HER ABOUT IT?
NO, NO, NO! I HAVE A BETTER IDEA!
DO TELL.
HOW ABOUT INSTEAD OF A SMELLY KINDA GROSS EVEN THOUGH SHE'S NICE OLD LADY HANGING OUT WITH ME ALL DAY I GET -- THINK ABOUT IT --
A BRAND NEW LITTLE BROTHER OR SISSSSTER??!!
YOUR CHOICE.
AH.
WELL, DEAR.
THIS IS A TOUGH ONE.

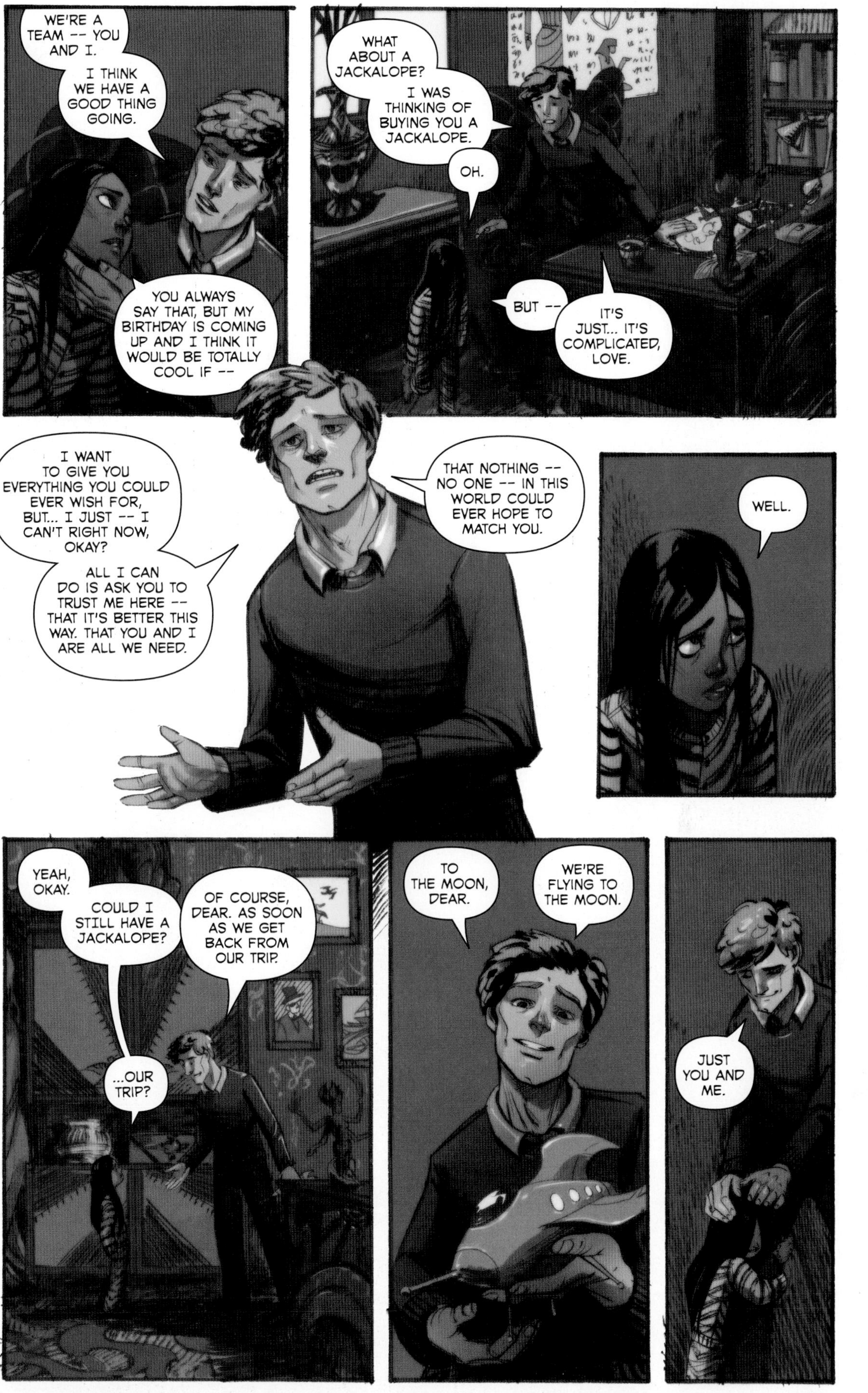
WE'RE A TEAM -- YOU AND I.
I THINK WE HAVE A GOOD THING GOING.
YOU ALWAYS SAY THAT, BUT MY BIRTHDAY IS COMING UP AND I THINK IT WOULD BE TOTALLY COOL IF --
WHAT ABOUT A JACKALOPE?
I WAS THINKING OF BUYING YOU A JACKALOPE.
OH.
BUT --
IT'S JUST... IT'S COMPLICATED, LOVE.
I WANT TO GIVE YOU EVERYTHING YOU COULD EVER WISH FOR, BUT... I JUST -- I CAN'T RIGHT NOW, OKAY?
ALL I CAN DO IS ASK YOU TO TRUST ME HERE -- THAT IT'S BETTER THIS WAY. THAT YOU AND I ARE ALL WE NEED.
THAT NOTHING -- NO ONE -- IN THIS WORLD COULD EVER HOPE TO MATCH YOU.
WELL.
YEAH, OKAY.
COULD I STILL HAVE A JACKALOPE?
OF COURSE, DEAR. AS SOON AS WE GET BACK FROM OUR TRIP.
...OUR TRIP?
TO THE MOON, DEAR.
WE'RE FLYING TO THE MOON.
JUST YOU AND ME.

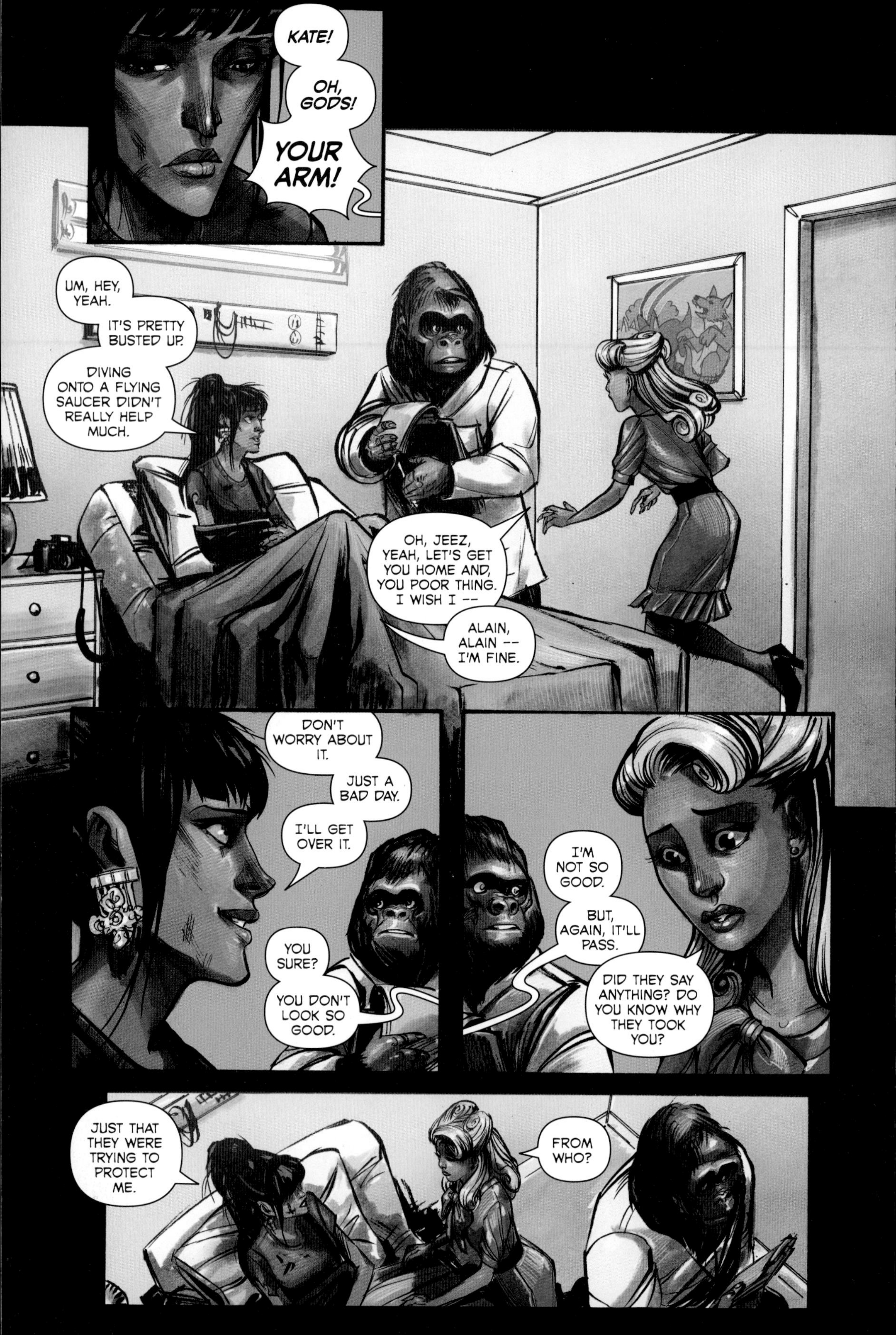
KATE!
OH, GODS!
YOUR ARM!
UM, HEY, YEAH.
IT'S PRETTY BUSTED UP.
DIVING ONTO A FLYING SAUCER DIDN'T REALLY HELP MUCH.
OH, JEEZ, YEAH, LET'S GET YOU HOME AND, YOU POOR THING. I WISH I --
ALAIN, ALAIN -- I'M FINE.
DON'T WORRY ABOUT IT.
JUST A BAD DAY.
I'LL GET OVER IT.
YOU SURE?
YOU DON'T LOOK SO GOOD.
I'M NOT SO GOOD.
BUT, AGAIN, IT'LL PASS.
DID THEY SAY ANYTHING? DO YOU KNOW WHY THEY TOOK YOU?
JUST THAT THEY WERE TRYING TO PROTECT ME.
FROM WHO?

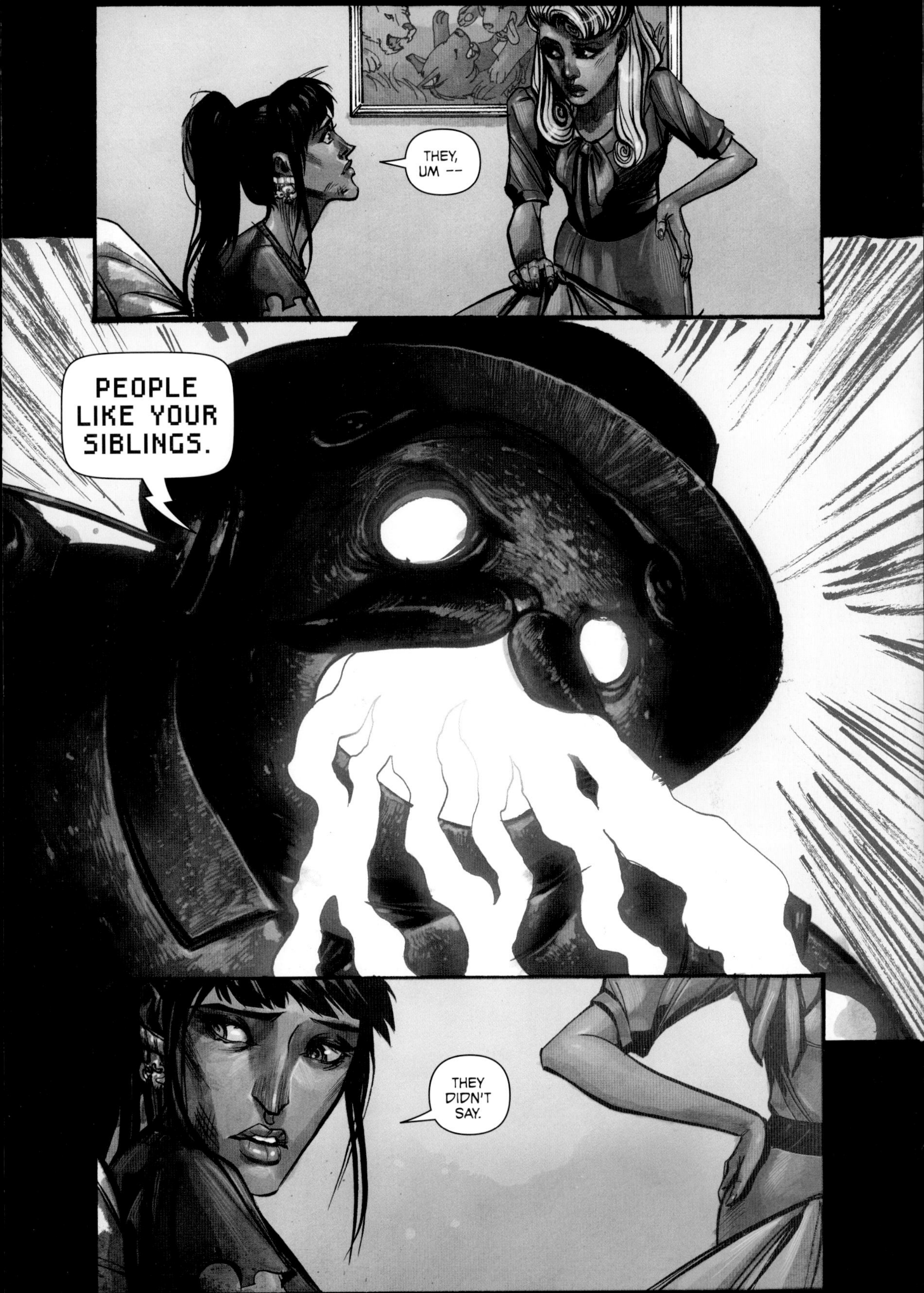
THEY, UM --
PEOPLE LIKE YOUR SIBLINGS.
THEY DIDN'T SAY.

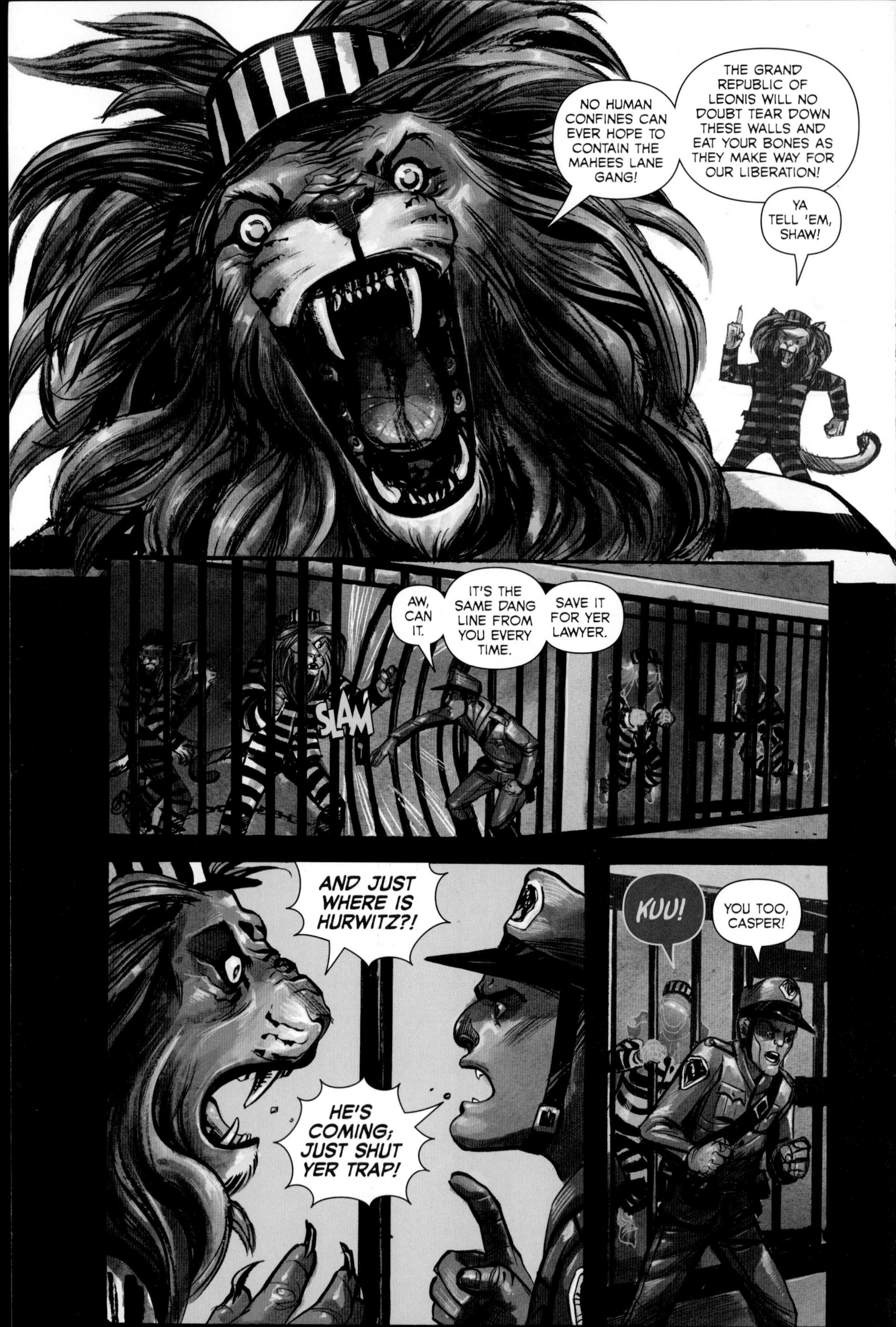
NO HUMAN CONFINES CAN EVER HOPE TO CONTAIN THE MAHEES LANE GANG!
THE GRAND REPUBLIC OF LEONIS WILL NO DOUBT TEAR DOWN THESE WALLS AND EAT YOUR BONES AS THEY MAKE WAY FOR OUR LIBERATION!
YA TELL 'EM, SHAW!
AW, CAN IT.
IT'S THE SAME DANG LINE FROM YOU EVERY TIME.
SAVE IT FOR YER LAWYER.
SLAM
AND JUST WHERE IS HURWITZ?!
HE'S COMING; JUST SHUT YER TRAP!
KUU!
YOU TOO, CASPER!

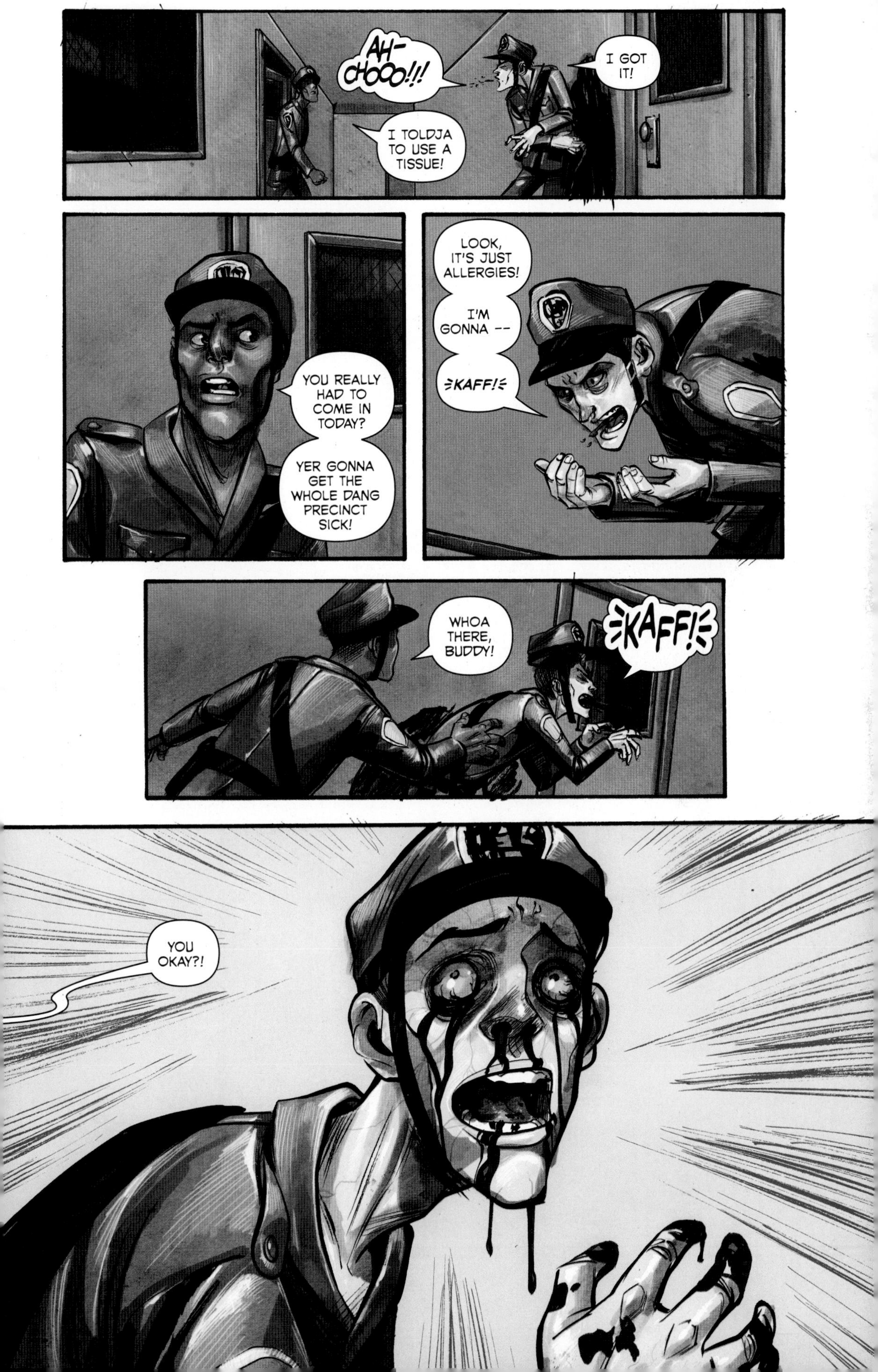
AH-CHOOO!!!
I GOT IT!
I TOLDJA TO USE A TISSUE!
YOU REALLY HAD TO COME IN TODAY?
YER GONNA GET THE WHOLE DANG PRECINCT SICK!
LOOK, IT'S JUST ALLERGIES!
I'M GONNA --
KAFF!
WHOA THERE, BUDDY!
KAFF!
YOU OKAY?!

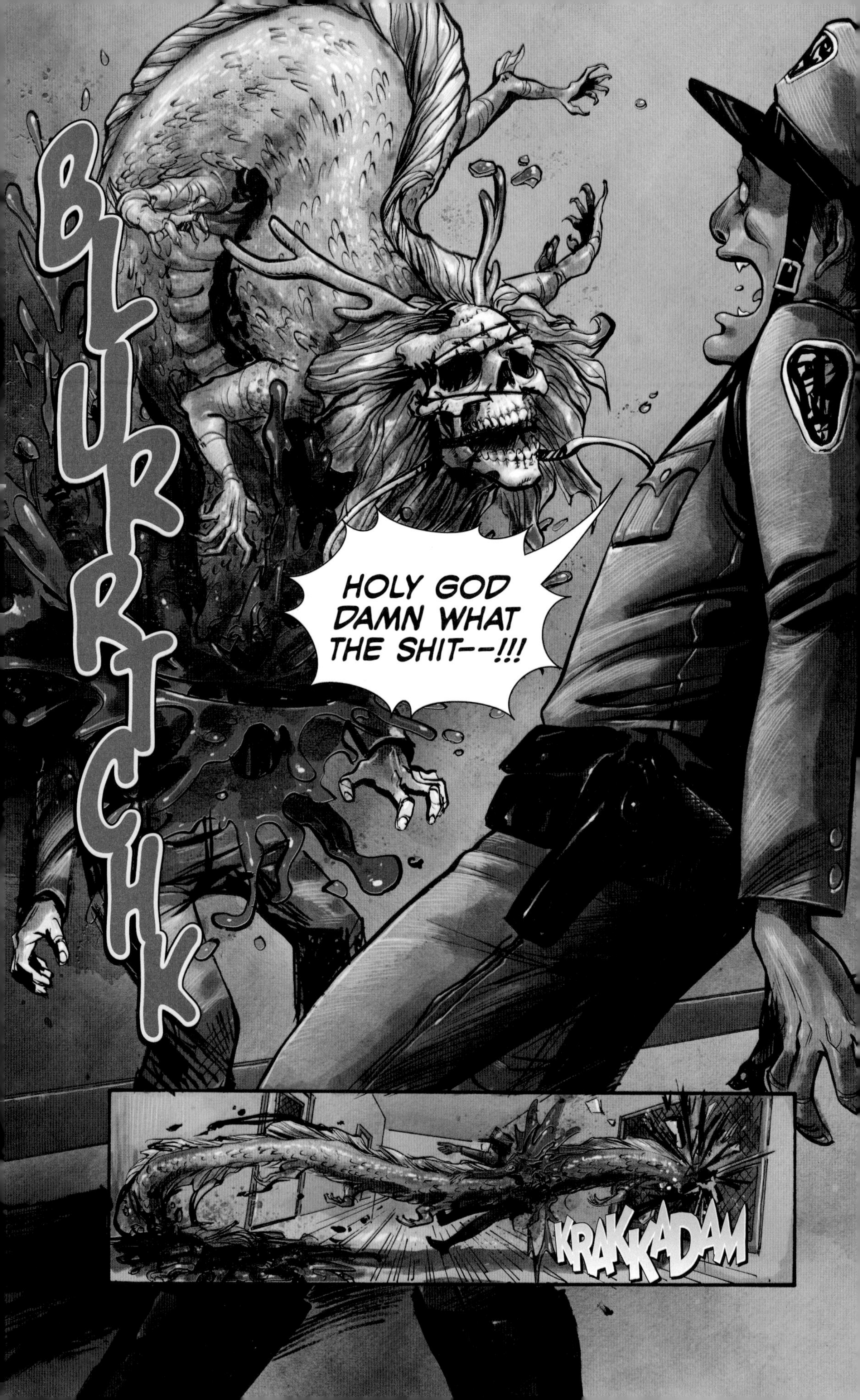
BLURRTCHK
HOLY GOD DAMN WHAT THE SHIT--!!!
KRAKKADAM

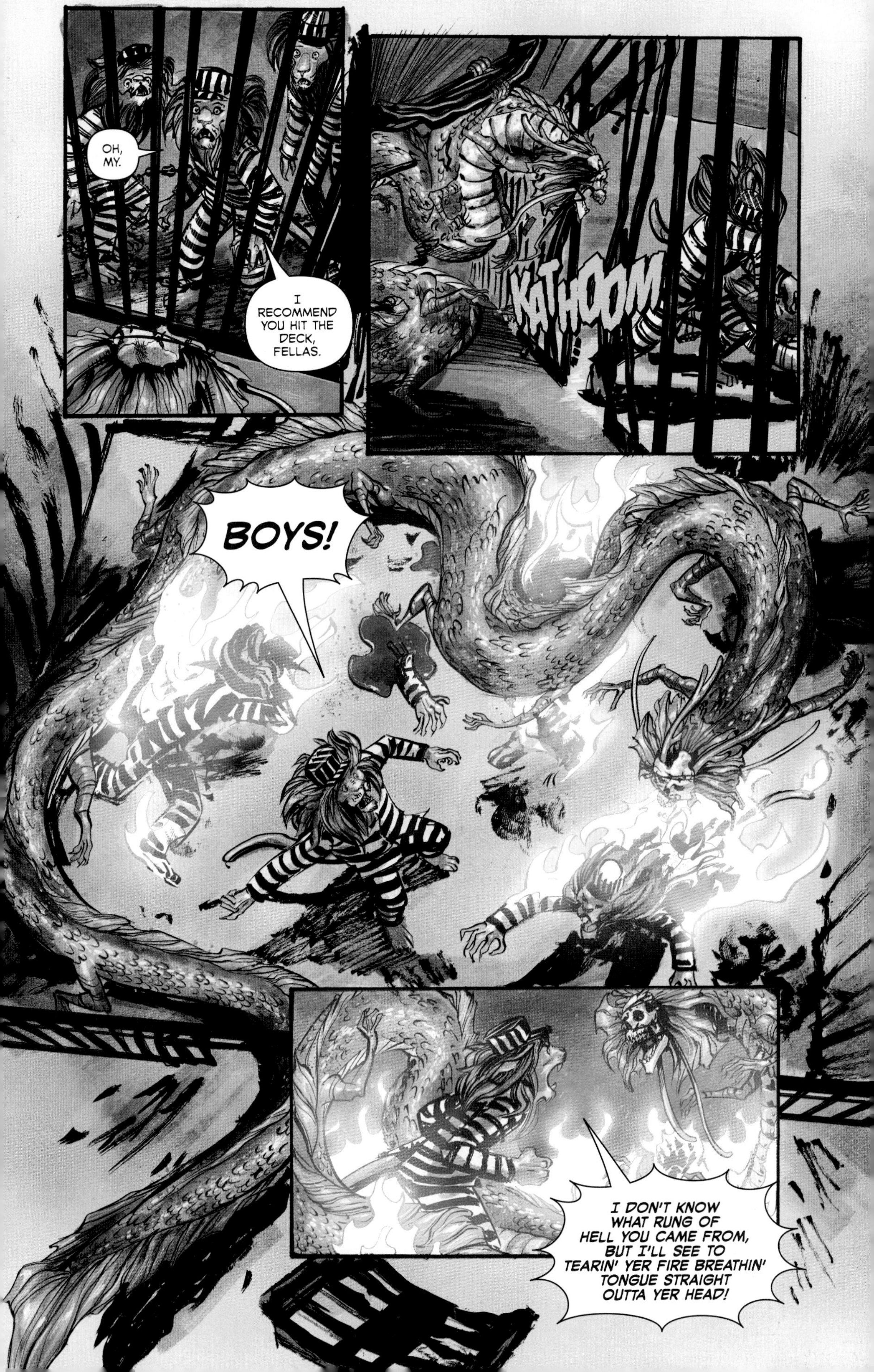
OH, MY.
I RECOMMEND YOU HIT THE DECK, FELLAS.
KATHOOM
BOYS!
I DON'T KNOW WHAT RUNG OF HELL YOU CAME FROM, BUT I'LL SEE TO TEARIN' YER FIRE BREATHIN' TONGUE STRAIGHT OUTTA YER HEAD!

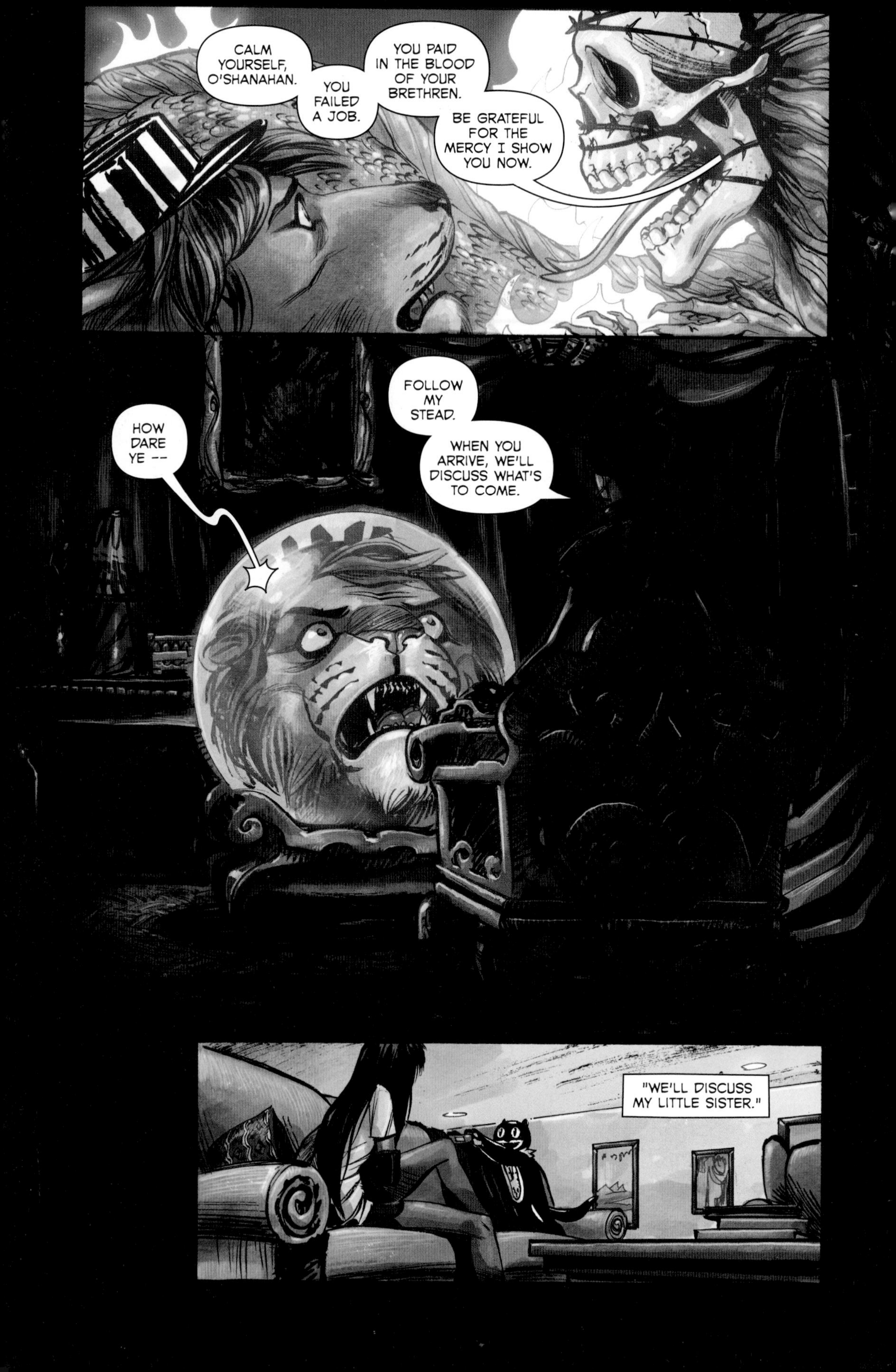
CALM YOURSELF, O'SHANAHAN.
YOU FAILED A JOB.
YOU PAID IN THE BLOOD OF YOUR BRETHREN.
BE GRATEFUL FOR THE MERCY I SHOW YOU NOW.
HOW DARE YE --
FOLLOW MY STEAD.
WHEN YOU ARRIVE, WE'LL DISCUSS WHAT'S TO COME.
"WE'LL DISCUSS MY LITTLE SISTER."

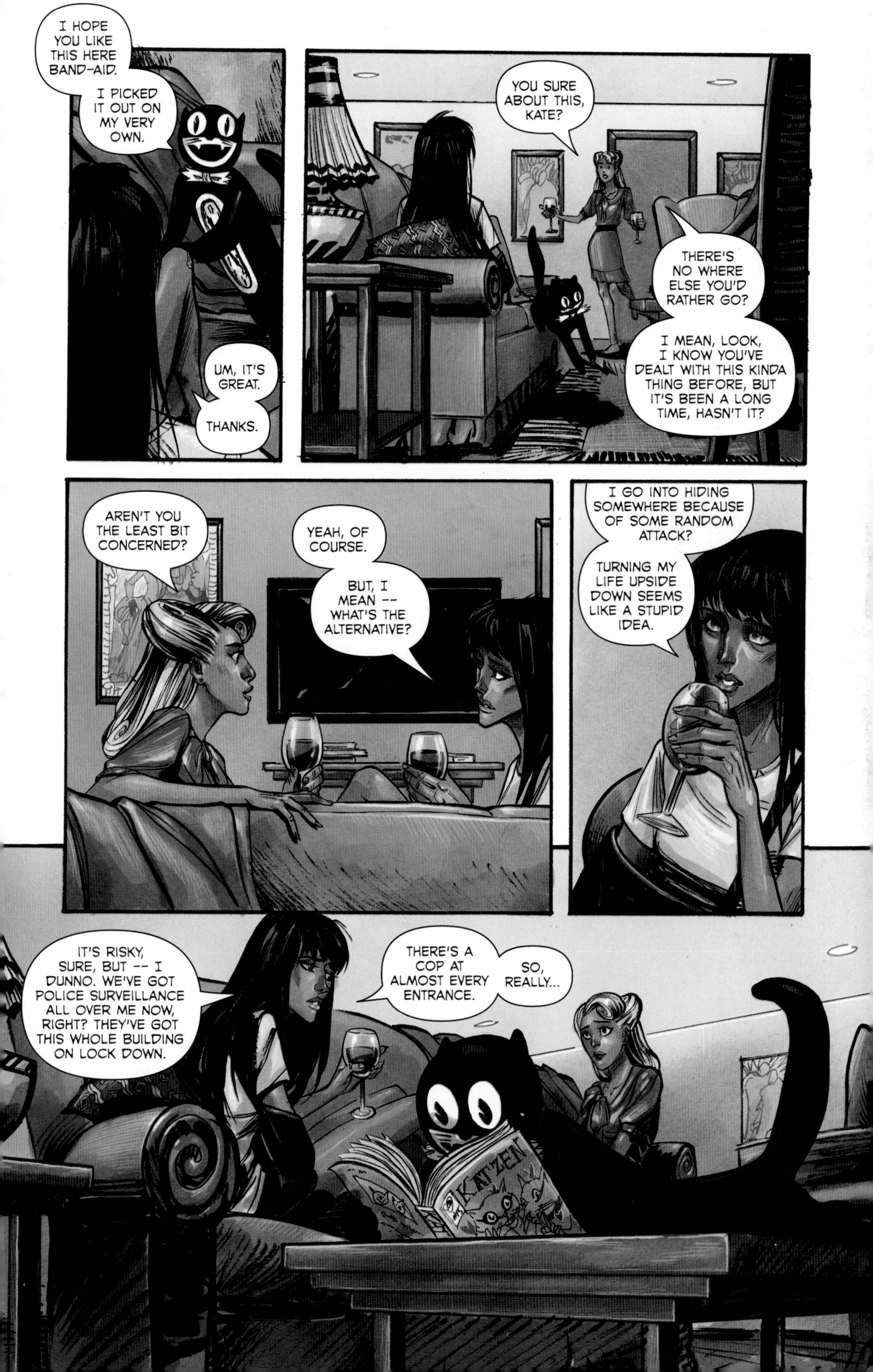

I HOPE YOU LIKE THIS HERE BAND-AID.
I PICKED IT OUT ON MY VERY OWN.
UM, IT'S GREAT.
THANKS.
YOU SURE ABOUT THIS, KATE?
THERE'S NO WHERE ELSE YOU'D RATHER GO?
I MEAN, LOOK, I KNOW YOU'VE DEALT WITH THIS KINDA THING BEFORE, BUT IT'S BEEN A LONG TIME, HASN'T IT?
AREN'T YOU THE LEAST BIT CONCERNED?
YEAH, OF COURSE.
BUT, I MEAN -- WHAT'S THE ALTERNATIVE?
I GO INTO HIDING SOMEWHERE BECAUSE OF SOME RANDOM ATTACK?
TURNING MY LIFE UPSIDE DOWN SEEMS LIKE A STUPID IDEA.
IT'S RISKY, SURE, BUT -- I DUNNO. WE'VE GOT POLICE SURVEILLANCE ALL OVER ME NOW, RIGHT? THEY'VE GOT THIS WHOLE BUILDING ON LOCK DOWN.
THERE'S A COP AT ALMOST EVERY ENTRANCE.
SO, REALLY...
KATZEN

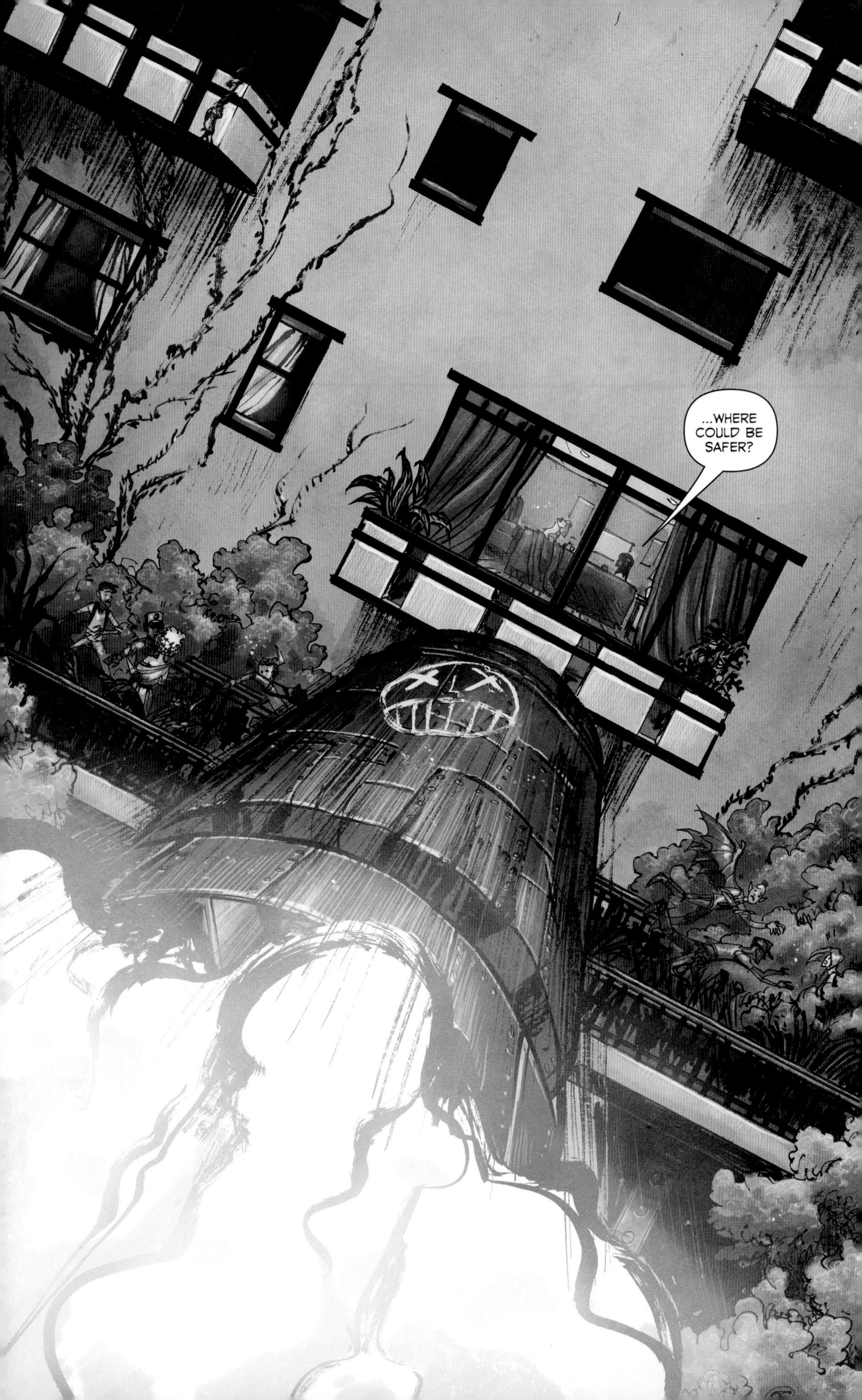
...WHERE COULD BE SAFER?

CHAPTER 3

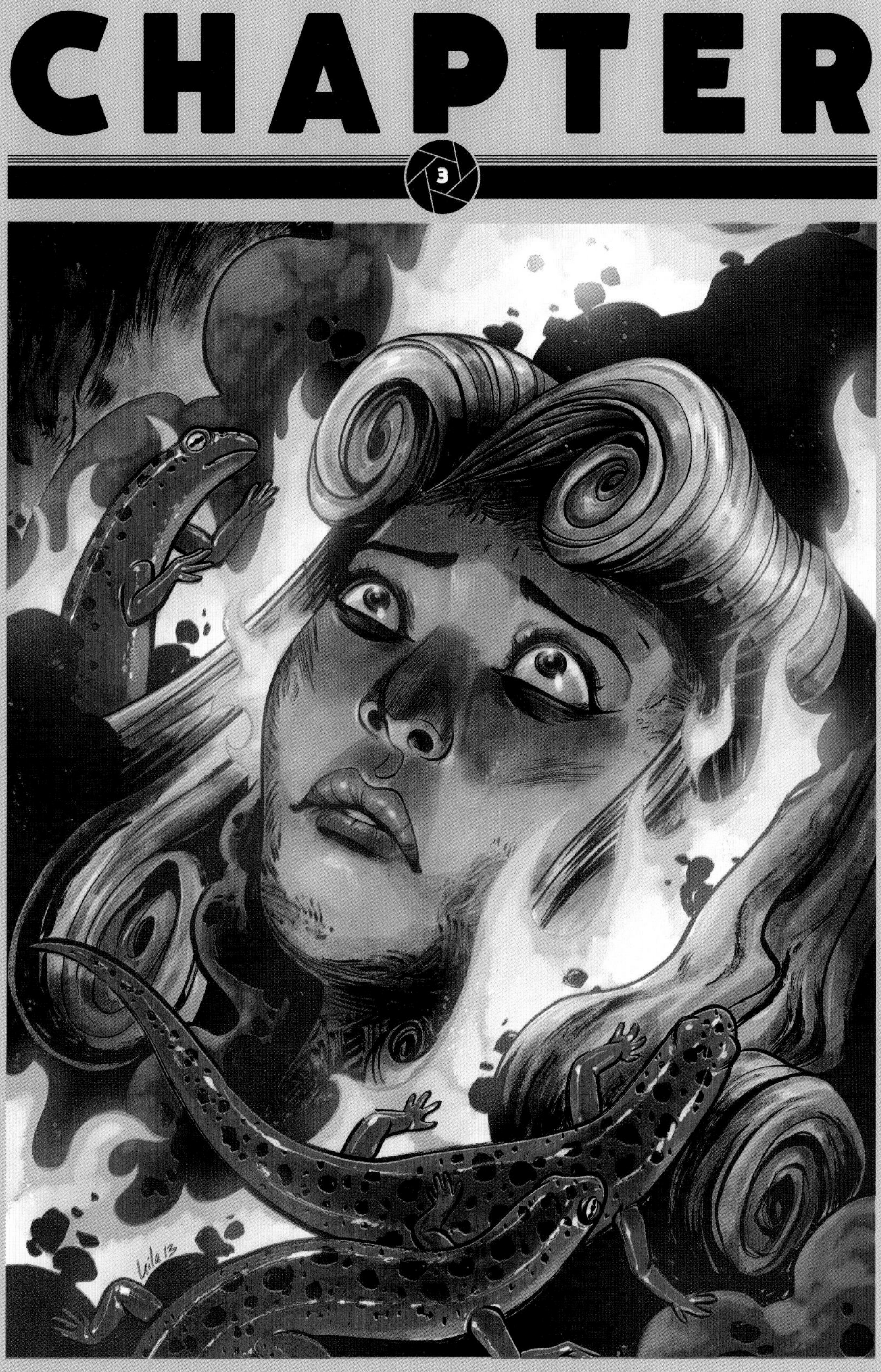

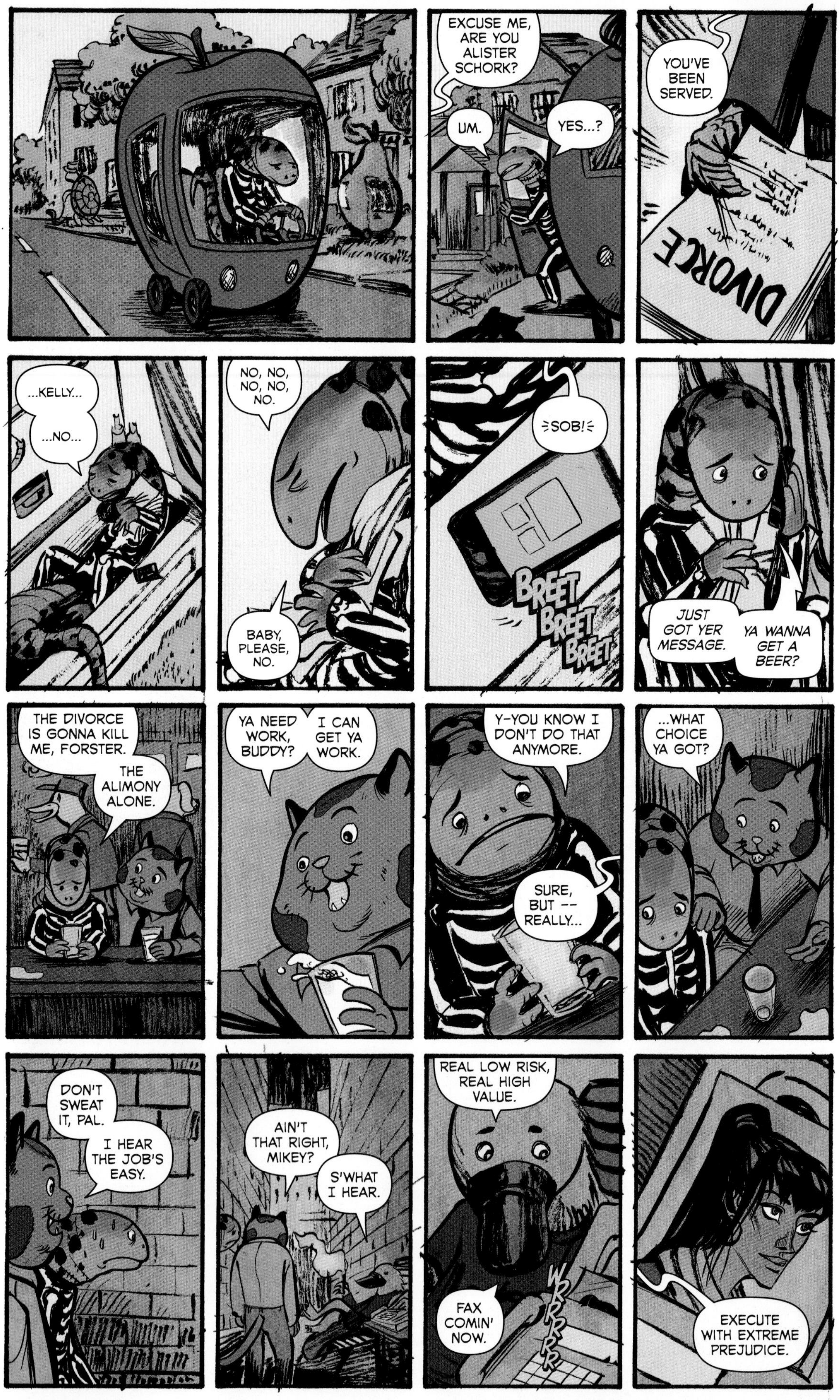
EXCUSE ME, ARE YOU ALISTER SCHORK?
UM.
YES...?
YOU'VE BEEN SERVED.
DIVORCE
...KELLY...
...NO...
NO, NO, NO, NO, NO.
BABY, PLEASE, NO.
SOB!
BREET BREET BREET
JUST GOT YER MESSAGE.
YA WANNA GET A BEER?
THE DIVORCE IS GONNA KILL ME, FORSTER.
THE ALIMONY ALONE.
YA NEED WORK, BUDDY?
I CAN GET YA WORK.
Y-YOU KNOW I DON'T DO THAT ANYMORE.
SURE, BUT -- REALLY...
...WHAT CHOICE YA GOT?
DON'T SWEAT IT, PAL.
I HEAR THE JOB'S EASY.
AIN'T THAT RIGHT, MIKEY?
S'WHAT I HEAR.
REAL LOW RISK, REAL HIGH VALUE.
FAX COMIN' NOW.
WRRRR
EXECUTE WITH EXTREME PREJUDICE.

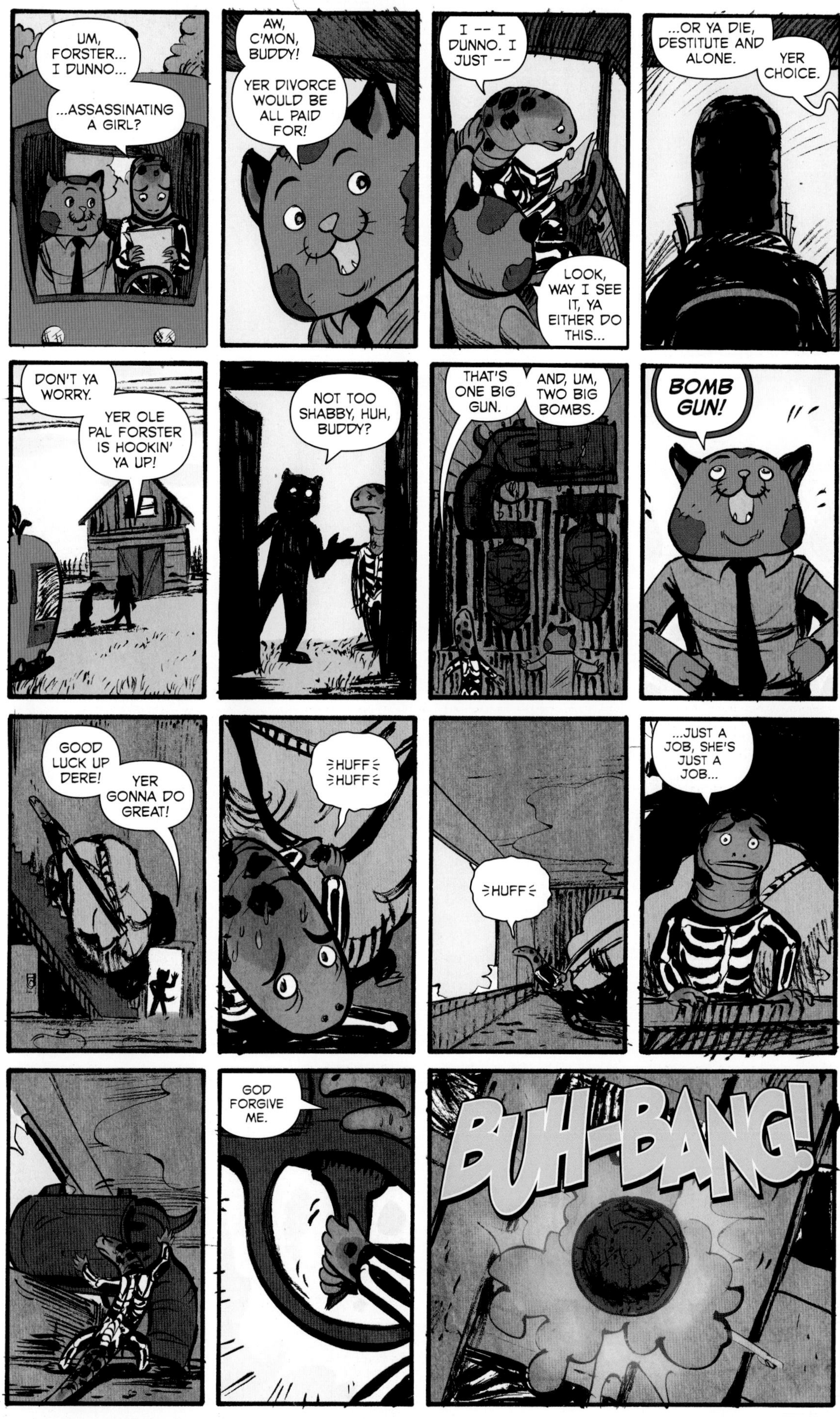
UM, FORSTER... I DUNNO...
...ASSASSINATING A GIRL?
AW, C'MON, BUDDY!
YER DIVORCE WOULD BE ALL PAID FOR!
I -- I DUNNO. I JUST --
LOOK, WAY I SEE IT, YA EITHER DO THIS...
...OR YA DIE, DESTITUTE AND ALONE.
YER CHOICE.
DON'T YA WORRY.
YER OLE PAL FORSTER IS HOOKIN' YA UP!
NOT TOO SHABBY, HUH, BUDDY?
THAT'S ONE BIG GUN.
AND, UM, TWO BIG BOMBS.
BOMB GUN!
GOOD LUCK UP DERE!
YER GONNA DO GREAT!
HUFF HUFF
HUFF
...JUST A JOB, SHE'S JUST A JOB...
GOD FORGIVE ME.
BUH-BANG!

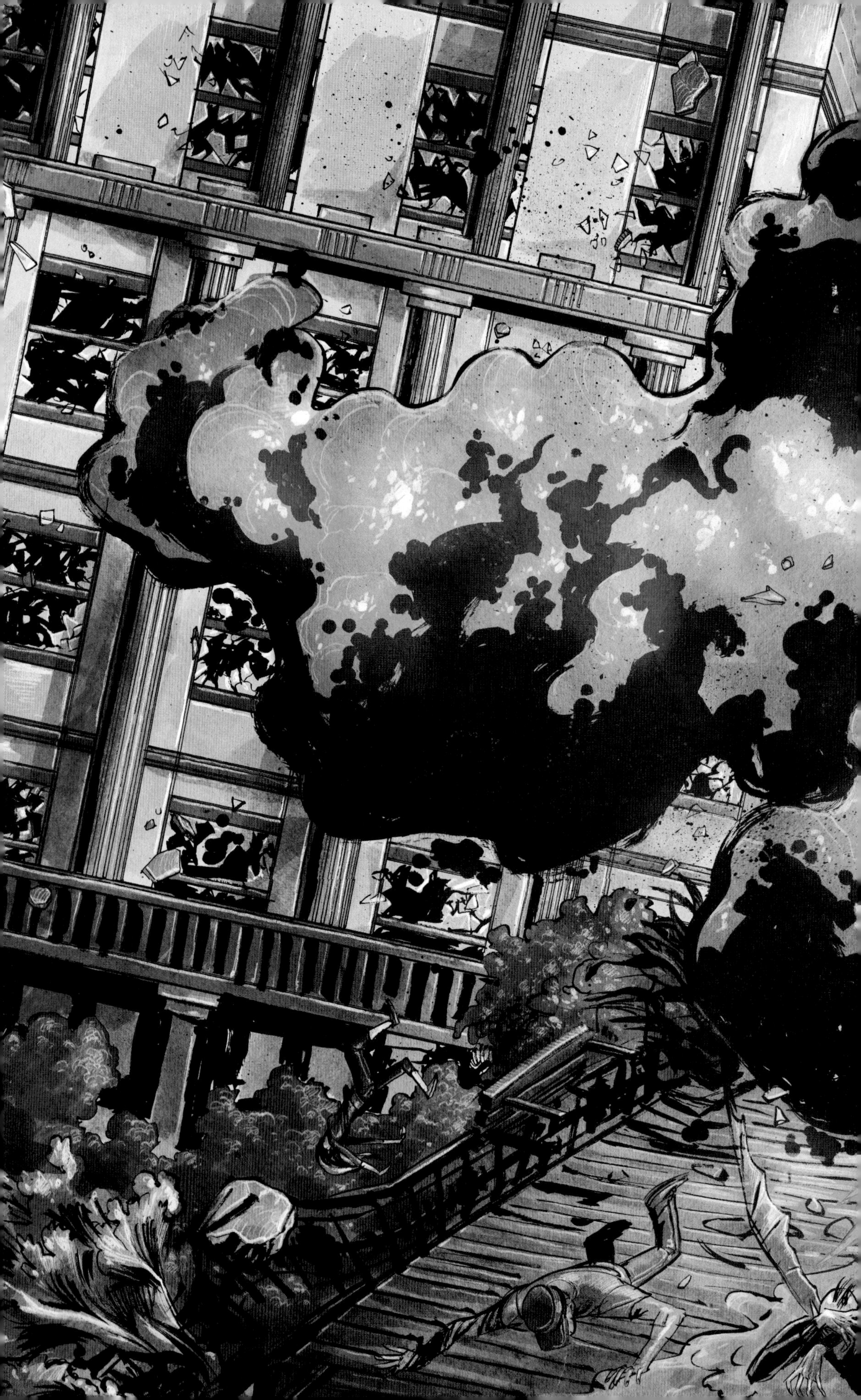

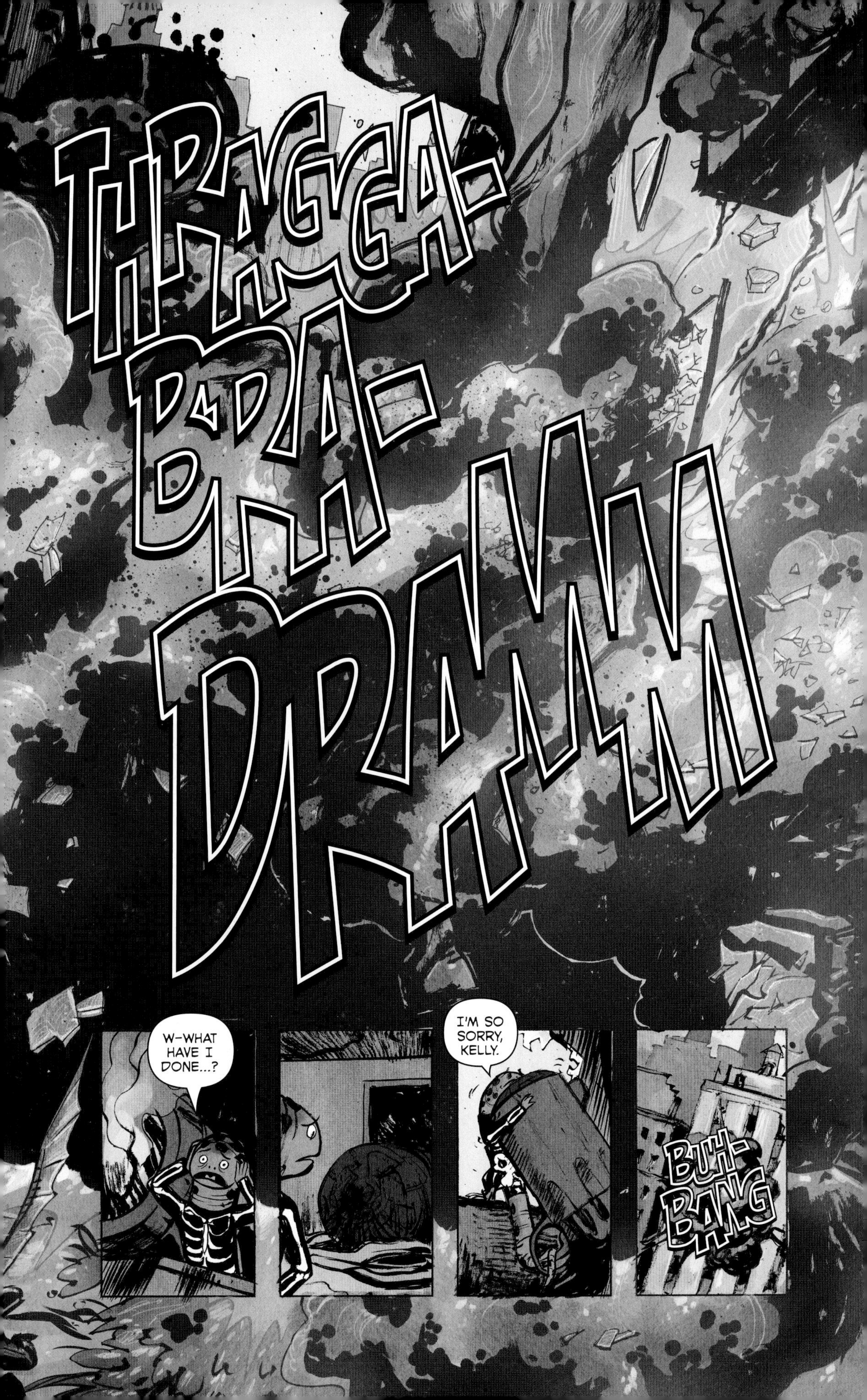
THRAGGGA-
BRA-
DRAMM
W-WHAT HAVE I DONE...?
I'M SO SORRY, KELLY.
BUH-BANG

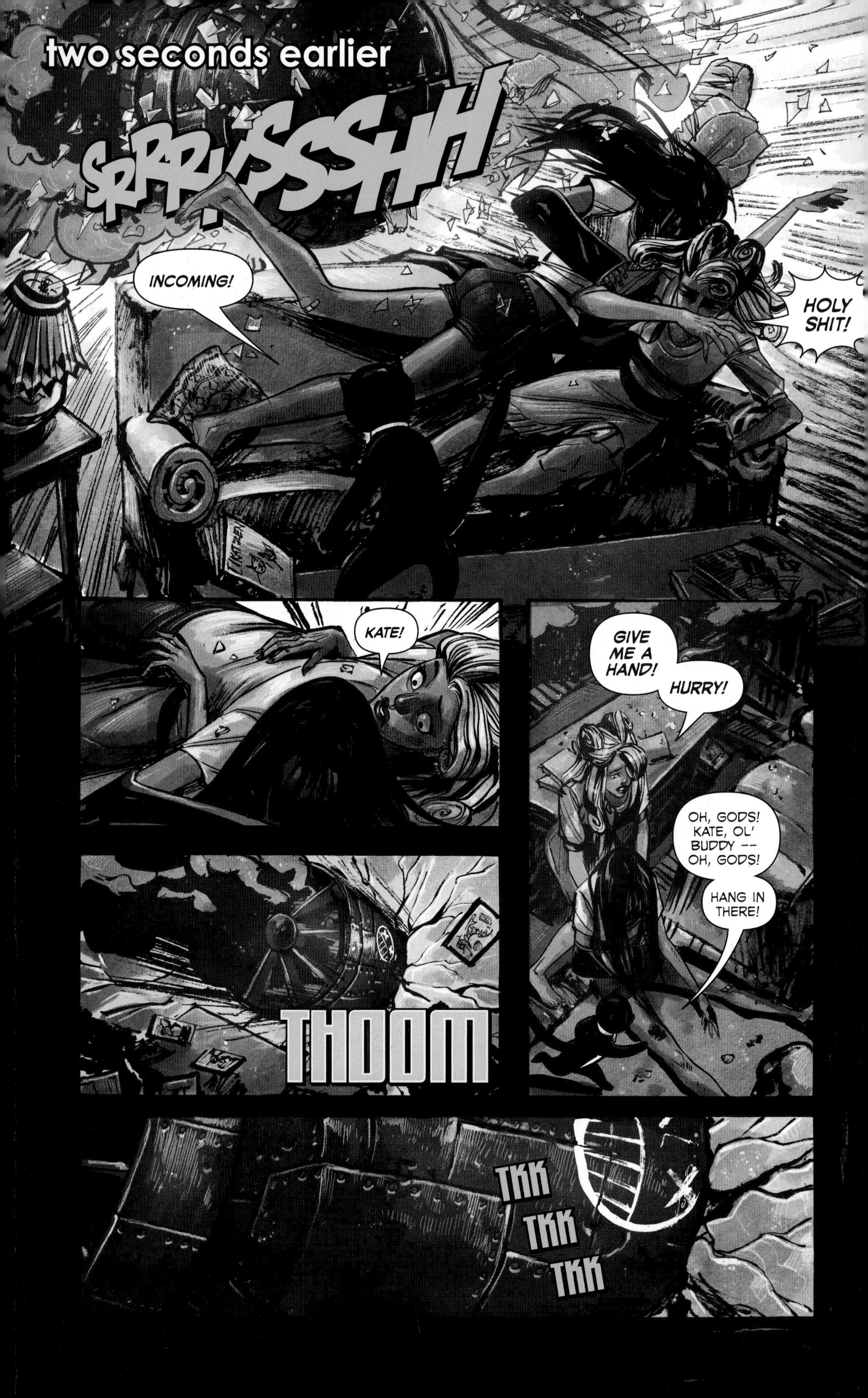
two seconds earlier
SKRRSSSHH
INCOMING!
HOLY SHIT!
KATE!
THOOM
GIVE ME A HAND!
HURRY!
OH, GODS! KATE, OL' BUDDY -- OH, GODS!
HANG IN THERE!
TKK
TKK
TKK

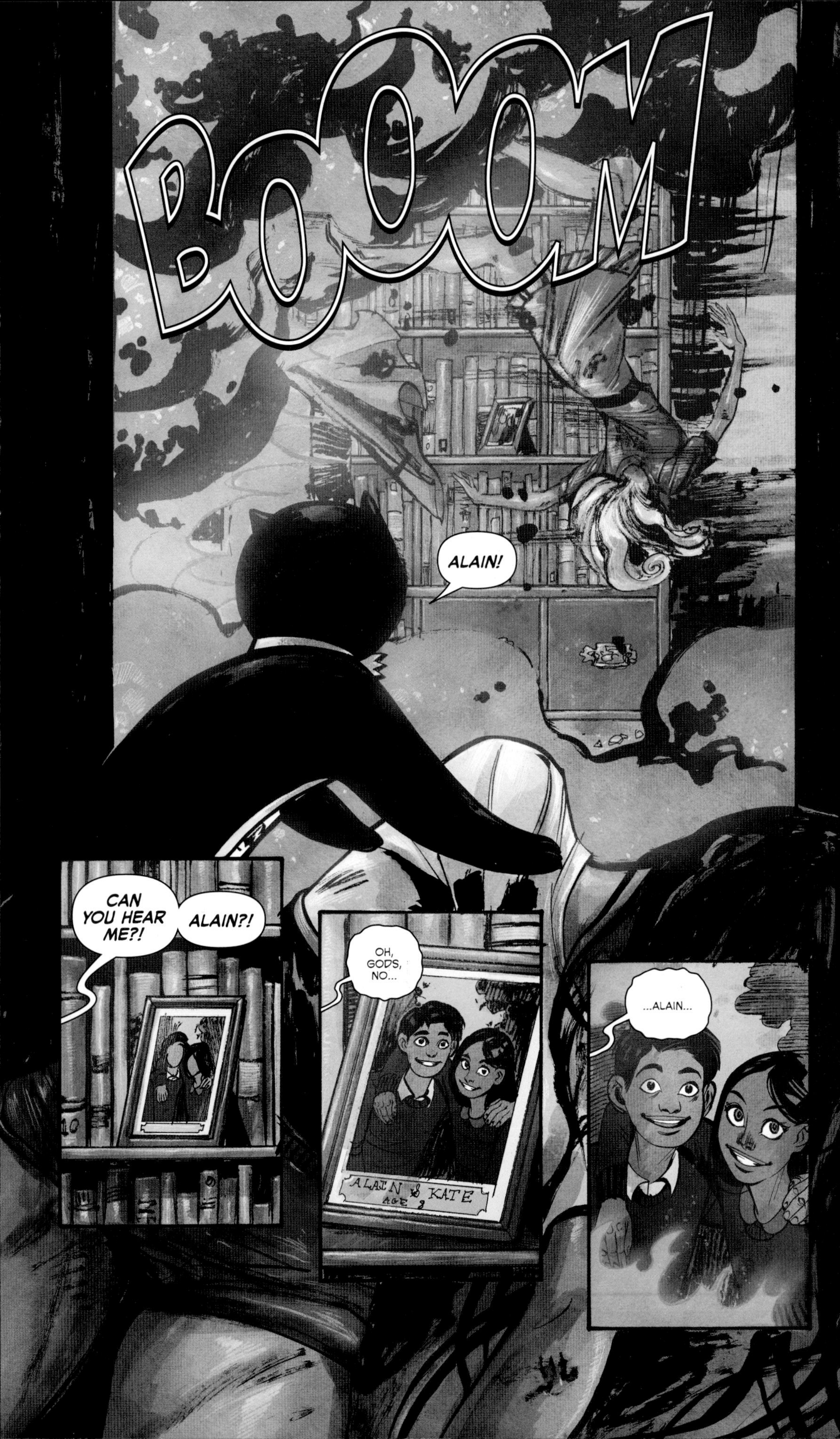
BOOOM
ALAIN!
CAN YOU HEAR ME?!
ALAIN?!
OH, GODS, NO...
ALAIN & KATE AGE 2
...ALAIN...

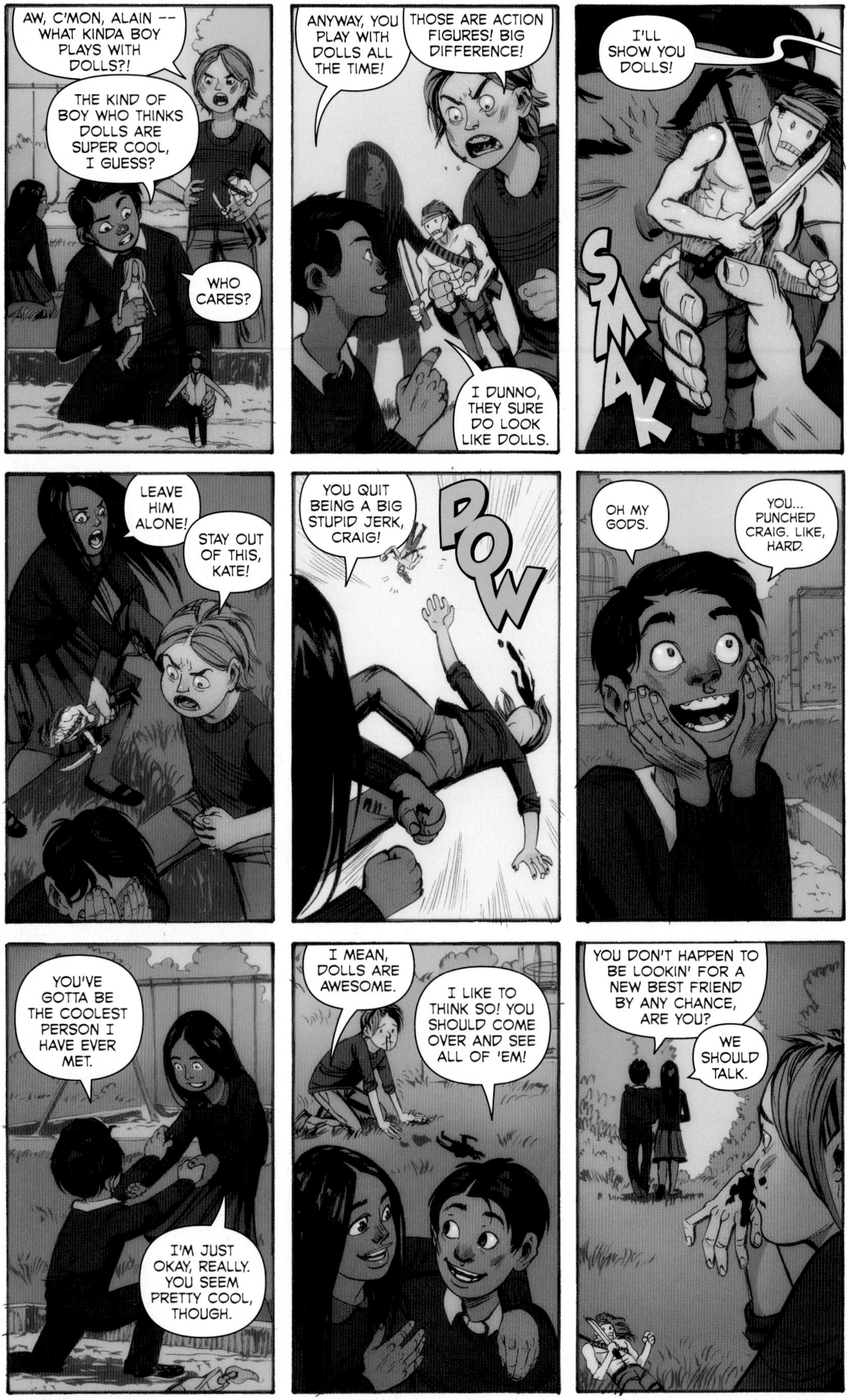
AW, C'MON, ALAIN -- WHAT KINDA BOY PLAYS WITH DOLLS?!
THE KIND OF BOY WHO THINKS DOLLS ARE SUPER COOL, I GUESS?
WHO CARES?
ANYWAY, YOU PLAY WITH DOLLS ALL THE TIME!
THOSE ARE ACTION FIGURES! BIG DIFFERENCE!
I DUNNO, THEY SURE DO LOOK LIKE DOLLS.
I'LL SHOW YOU DOLLS!
SMAK
LEAVE HIM ALONE!
STAY OUT OF THIS, KATE!
YOU QUIT BEING A BIG STUPID JERK, CRAIG!
POW
OH MY GODS.
YOU... PUNCHED CRAIG. LIKE, HARD.
YOU'VE GOTTA BE THE COOLEST PERSON I HAVE EVER MET.
I'M JUST OKAY, REALLY. YOU SEEM PRETTY COOL, THOUGH.
I MEAN, DOLLS ARE AWESOME.
I LIKE TO THINK SO! YOU SHOULD COME OVER AND SEE ALL OF 'EM!
YOU DON'T HAPPEN TO BE LOOKIN' FOR A NEW BEST FRIEND BY ANY CHANCE, ARE YOU?
WE SHOULD TALK.

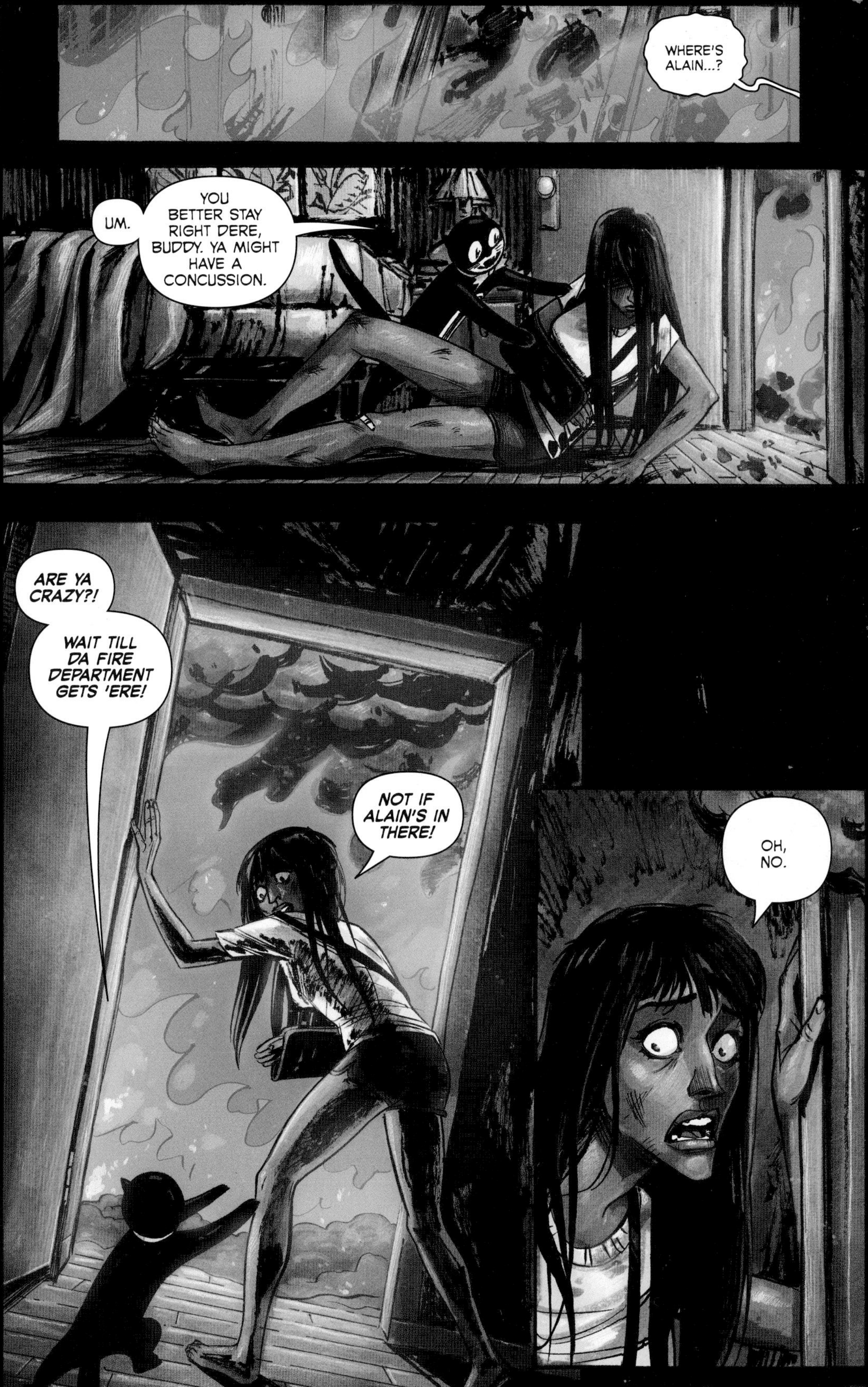
WHERE'S ALAIN...?
UM.
YOU BETTER STAY RIGHT DERE, BUDDY. YA MIGHT HAVE A CONCUSSION.
ARE YA CRAZY?!
WAIT TILL DA FIRE DEPARTMENT GETS 'ERE!
NOT IF ALAIN'S IN THERE!
OH, NO.

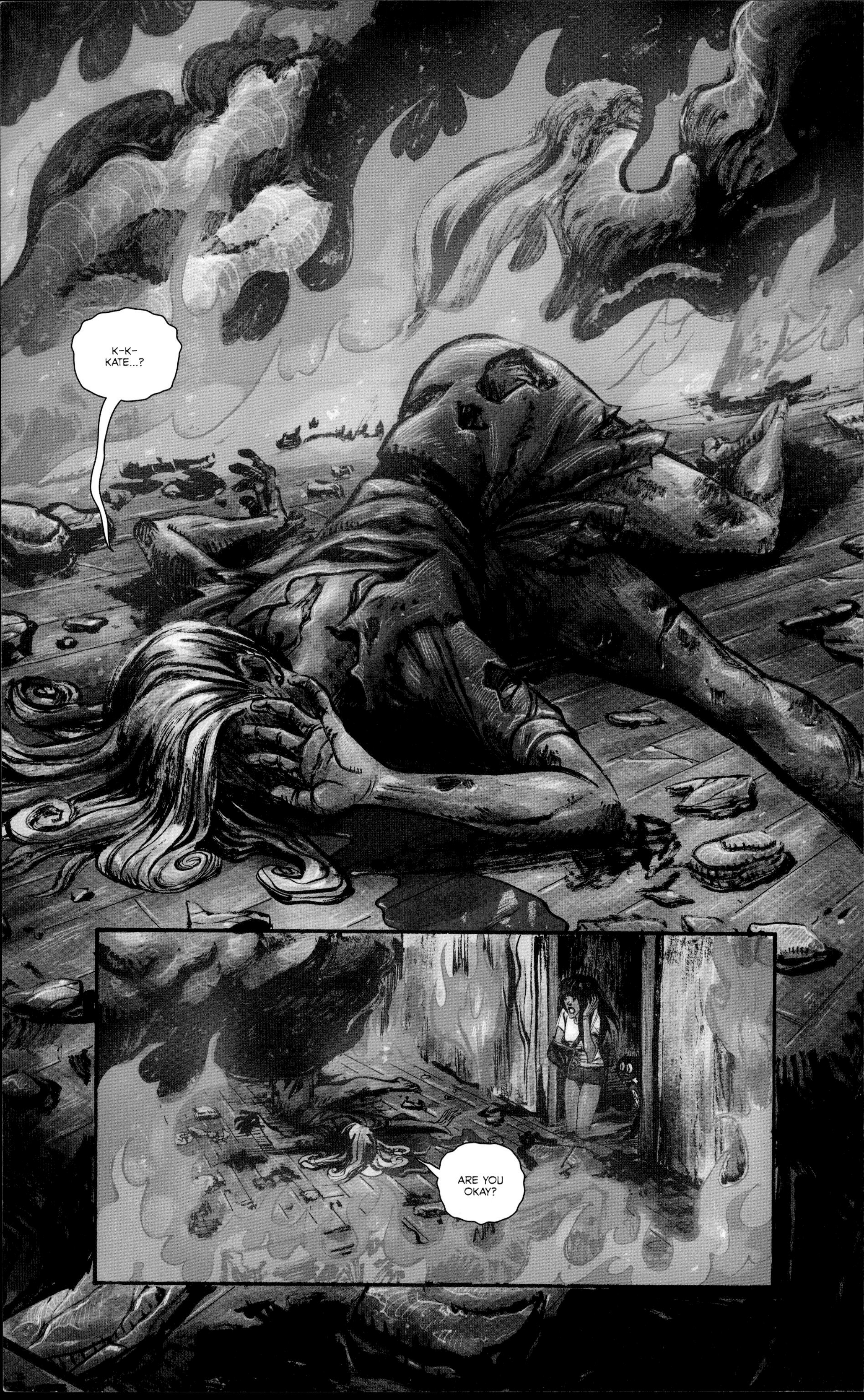
K-K-
KATE...?
ARE YOU
OKAY?

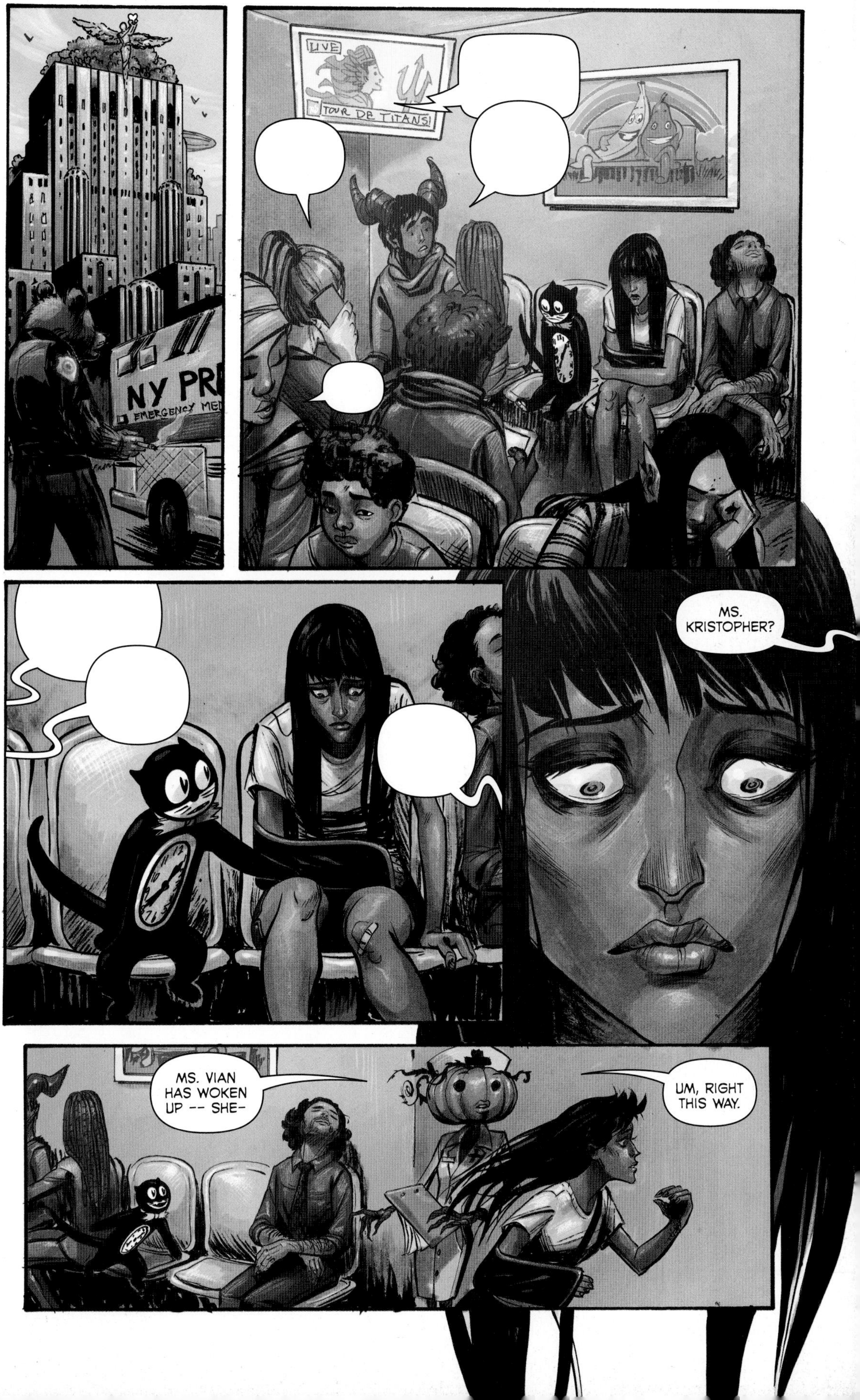
LIVE
TOUR DE TITANS!
NY PR
EMERGENCY MED
MS. KRISTOPHER?
MS. VIAN HAS WOKEN UP -- SHE-
UM, RIGHT THIS WAY.

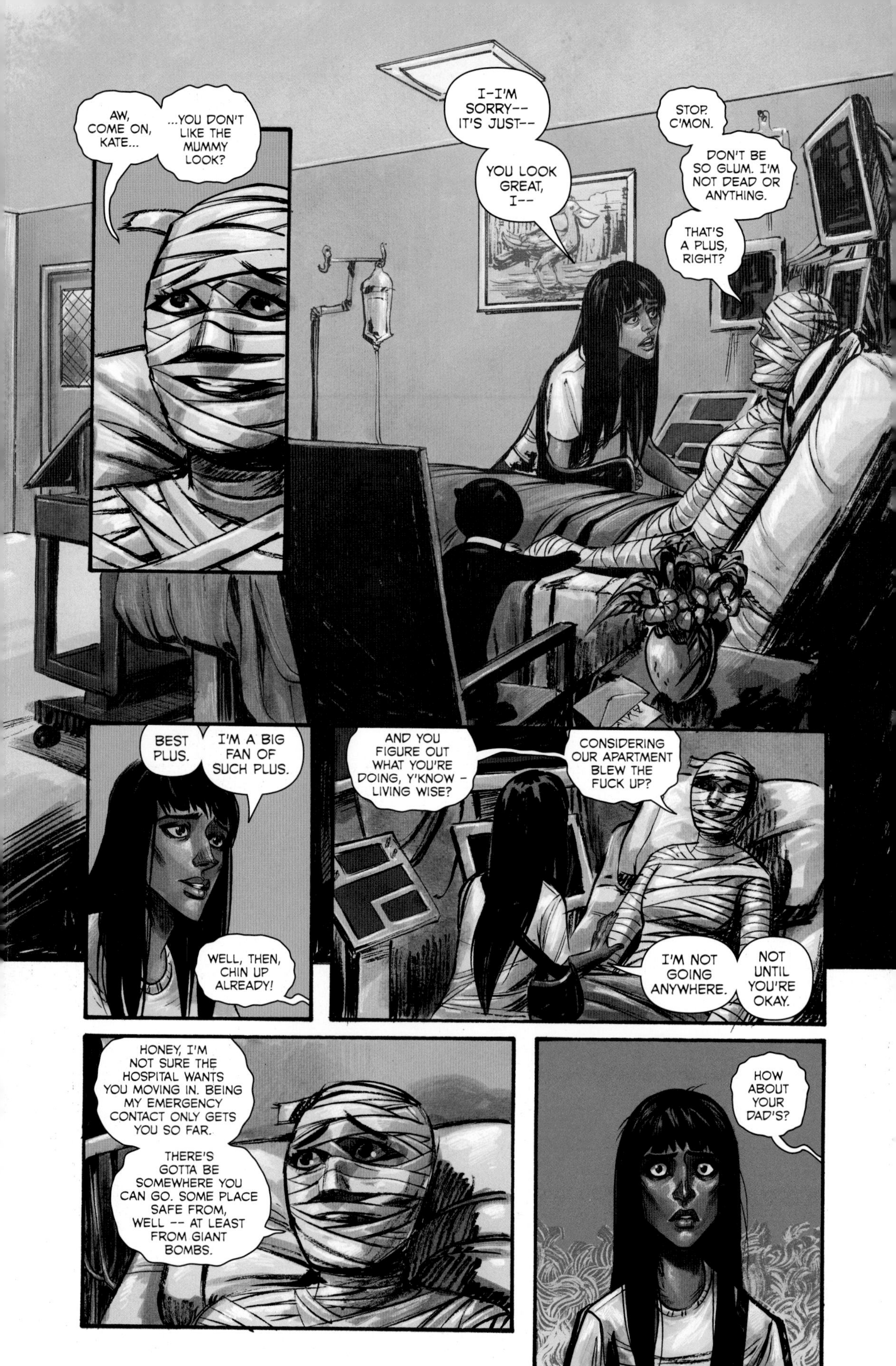
AW, COME ON, KATE...
...YOU DON'T LIKE THE MUMMY LOOK?
I-I'M SORRY-- IT'S JUST--
YOU LOOK GREAT, I--
STOP. C'MON.
DON'T BE SO GLUM. I'M NOT DEAD OR ANYTHING.
THAT'S A PLUS, RIGHT?
BEST PLUS.
I'M A BIG FAN OF SUCH PLUS.
WELL, THEN, CHIN UP ALREADY!
AND YOU FIGURE OUT WHAT YOU'RE DOING, Y'KNOW - LIVING WISE?
CONSIDERING OUR APARTMENT BLEW THE FUCK UP?
I'M NOT GOING ANYWHERE.
NOT UNTIL YOU'RE OKAY.
HONEY, I'M NOT SURE THE HOSPITAL WANTS YOU MOVING IN. BEING MY EMERGENCY CONTACT ONLY GETS YOU SO FAR.
THERE'S GOTTA BE SOMEWHERE YOU CAN GO. SOME PLACE SAFE FROM, WELL -- AT LEAST FROM GIANT BOMBS.
HOW ABOUT YOUR DAD'S?

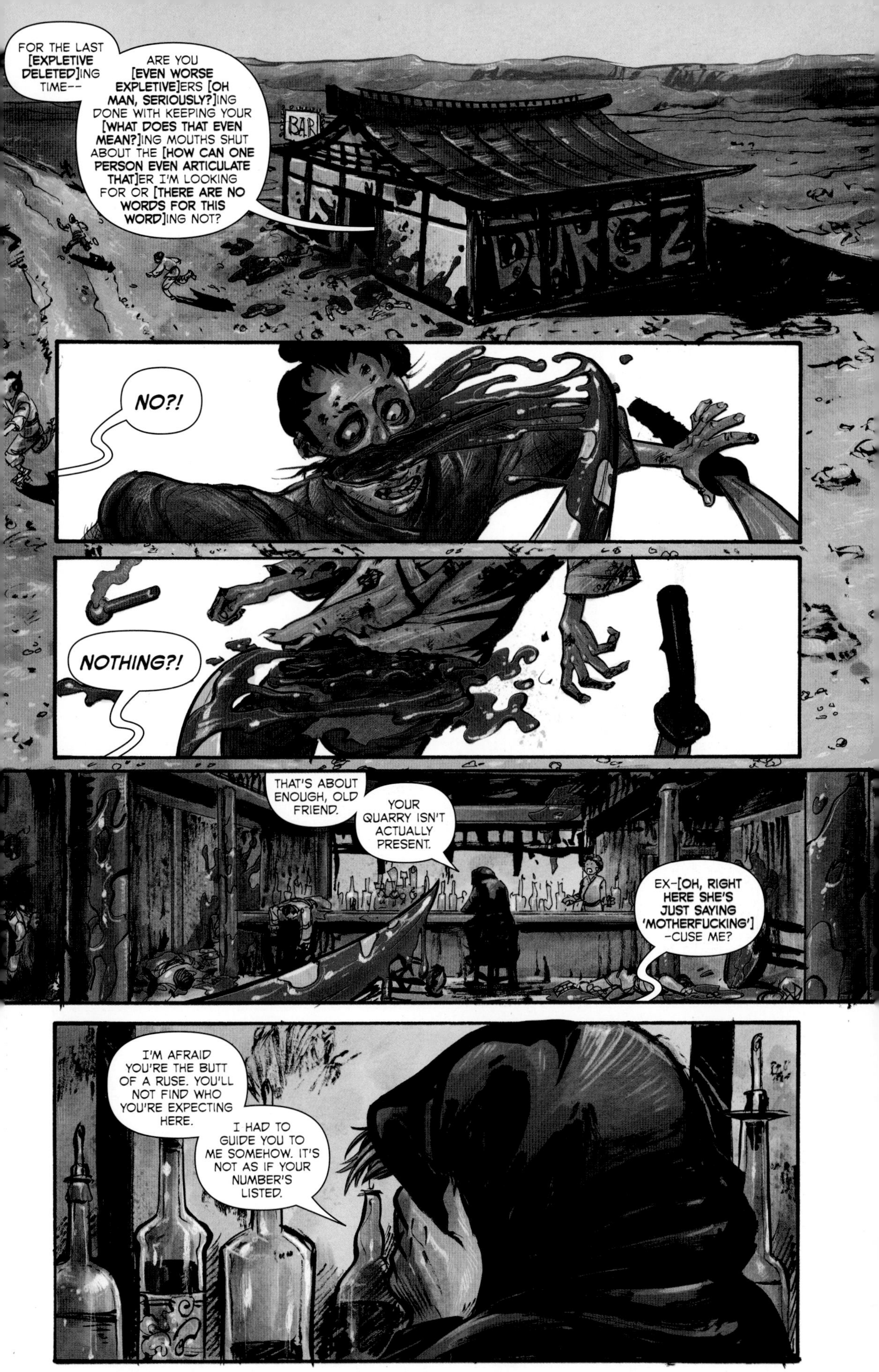
FOR THE LAST [EXPLETIVE DELETED]ING TIME--
ARE YOU [EVEN WORSE EXPLETIVE]ERS [OH MAN, SERIOUSLY?]ING DONE WITH KEEPING YOUR [WHAT DOES THAT EVEN MEAN?]ING MOUTHS SHUT ABOUT THE [HOW CAN ONE PERSON EVEN ARTICULATE THAT]ER I'M LOOKING FOR OR [THERE ARE NO WORDS FOR THIS WORD]ING NOT?
BAR
NO?!
NOTHING?!
THAT'S ABOUT ENOUGH, OLD FRIEND.
YOUR QUARRY ISN'T ACTUALLY PRESENT.
EX-[OH, RIGHT HERE SHE'S JUST SAYING 'MOTHERFUCKING'] -CUSE ME?
I'M AFRAID YOU'RE THE BUTT OF A RUSE. YOU'LL NOT FIND WHO YOU'RE EXPECTING HERE.
I HAD TO GUIDE YOU TO ME SOMEHOW. IT'S NOT AS IF YOUR NUMBER'S LISTED.

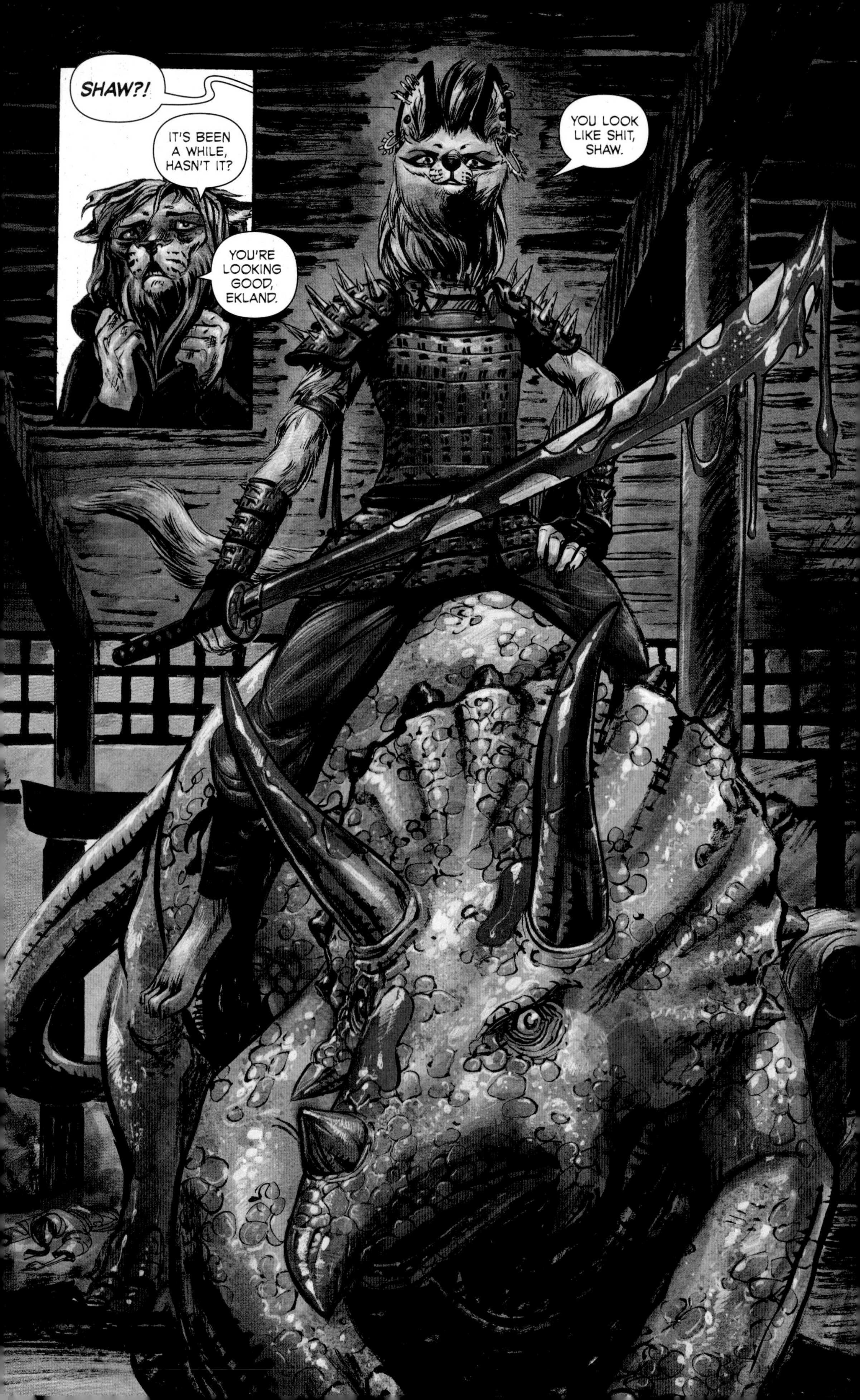
SHAW?!
IT'S BEEN A WHILE, HASN'T IT?
YOU'RE LOOKING GOOD, EKLAND.
YOU LOOK LIKE SHIT, SHAW.

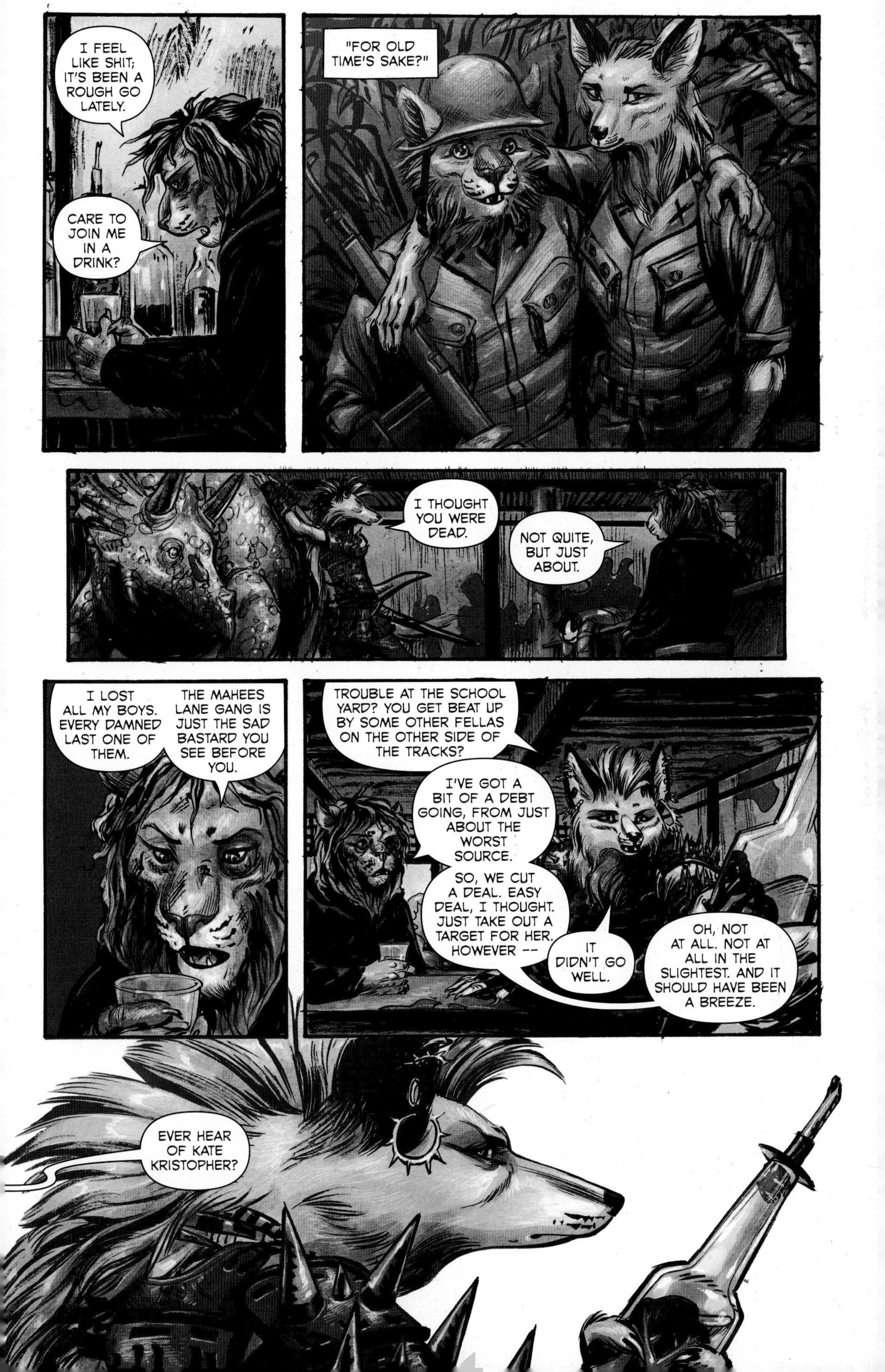
I FEEL LIKE SHIT; IT'S BEEN A ROUGH GO LATELY.
CARE TO JOIN ME IN A DRINK?
"FOR OLD TIME'S SAKE?"
I THOUGHT YOU WERE DEAD.
NOT QUITE, BUT JUST ABOUT.
I LOST ALL MY BOYS. EVERY DAMNED LAST ONE OF THEM.
THE MAHEES LANE GANG IS JUST THE SAD BASTARD YOU SEE BEFORE YOU.
TROUBLE AT THE SCHOOL YARD? YOU GET BEAT UP BY SOME OTHER FELLAS ON THE OTHER SIDE OF THE TRACKS?
I'VE GOT A BIT OF A DEBT GOING, FROM JUST ABOUT THE WORST SOURCE.
SO, WE CUT A DEAL. EASY DEAL, I THOUGHT. JUST TAKE OUT A TARGET FOR HER. HOWEVER --
IT DIDN'T GO WELL.
OH, NOT AT ALL. NOT AT ALL IN THE SLIGHTEST. AND IT SHOULD HAVE BEEN A BREEZE.
EVER HEAR OF KATE KRISTOPHER?

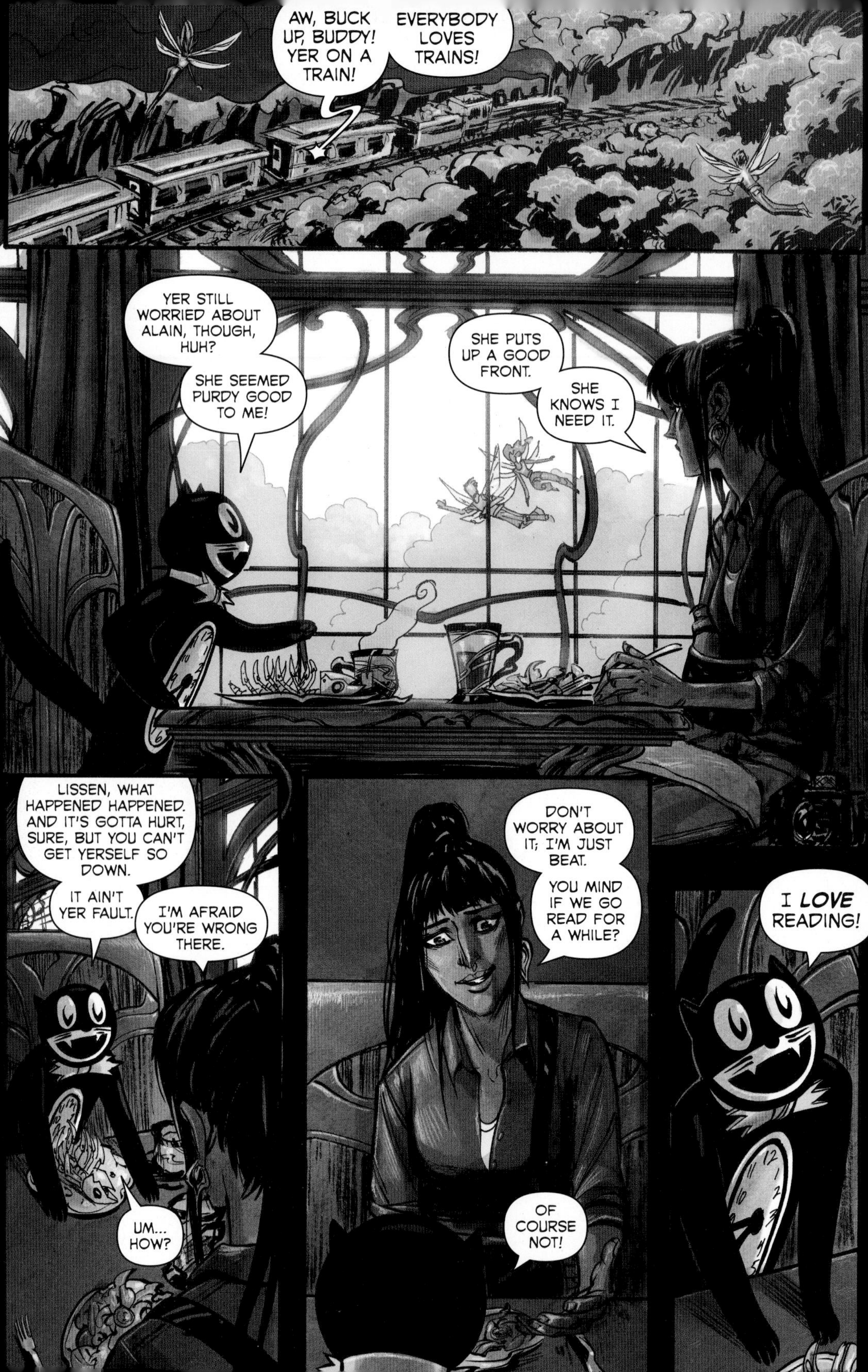
AW, BUCK UP, BUDDY! YER ON A TRAIN!
EVERYBODY LOVES TRAINS!
YER STILL WORRIED ABOUT ALAIN, THOUGH, HUH?
SHE SEEMED PURDY GOOD TO ME!
SHE PUTS UP A GOOD FRONT.
SHE KNOWS I NEED IT.
LISSEN, WHAT HAPPENED HAPPENED. AND IT'S GOTTA HURT, SURE, BUT YOU CAN'T GET YERSELF SO DOWN.
IT AIN'T YER FAULT.
I'M AFRAID YOU'RE WRONG THERE.
UM... HOW?
DON'T WORRY ABOUT IT; I'M JUST BEAT.
YOU MIND IF WE GO READ FOR A WHILE?
OF COURSE NOT!
I LOVE READING!

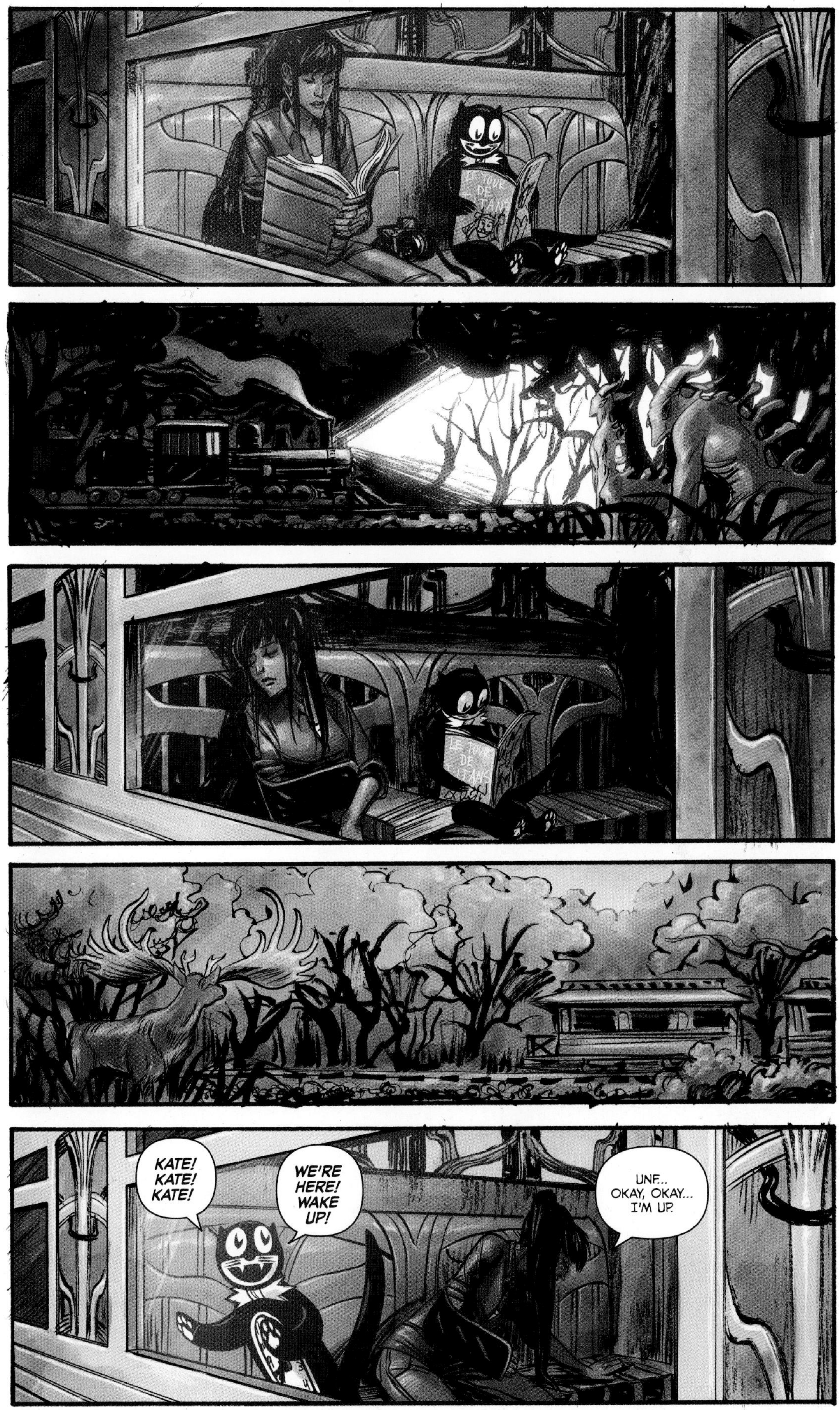
LE TOUR DE TITANS
LE TOUR DE TITANS
KATE! KATE! KATE!
WE'RE HERE! WAKE UP!
UNF... OKAY, OKAY... I'M UP.

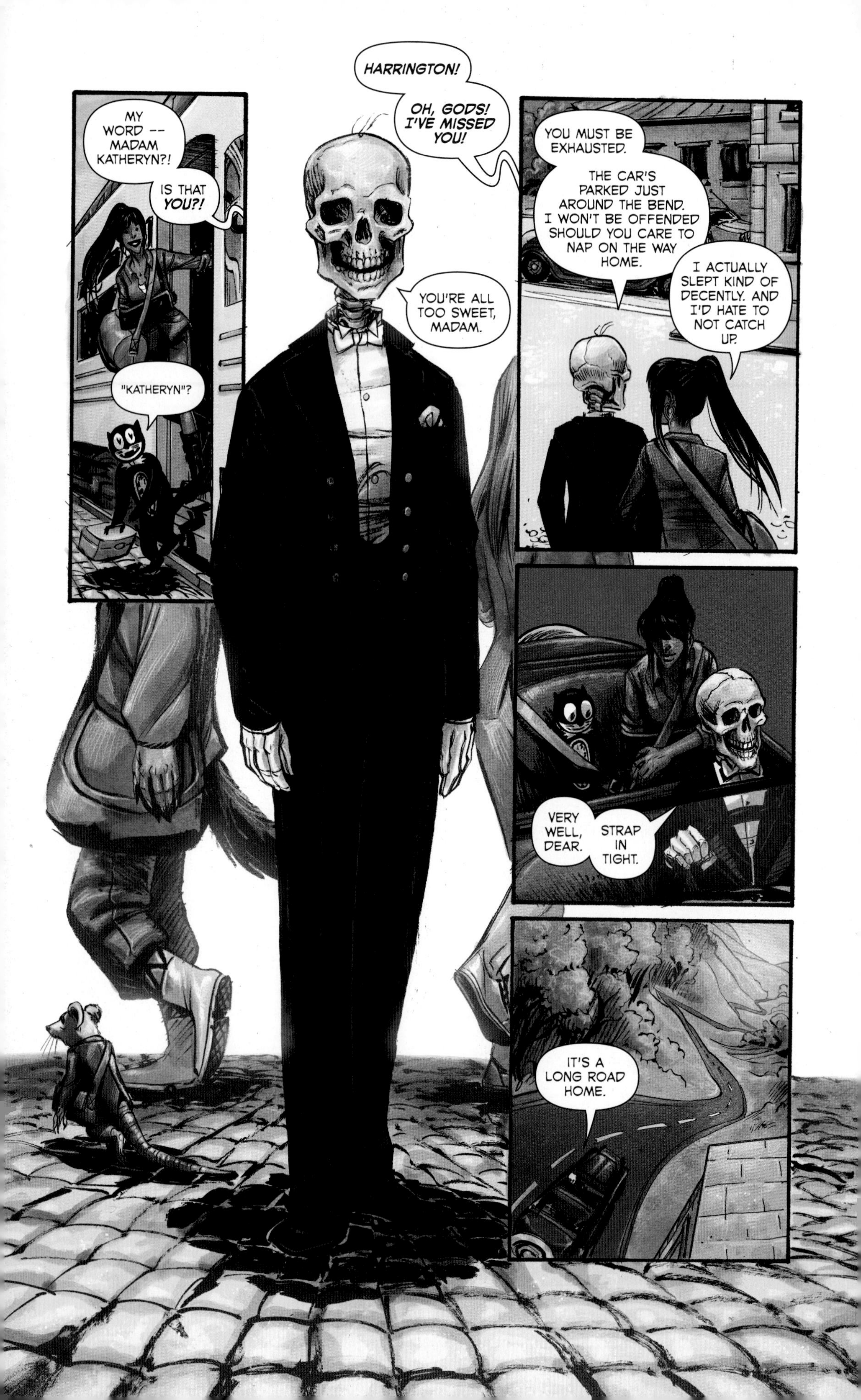
MY WORD -- MADAM KATHERYN?!
IS THAT YOU?!
"KATHERYN"?
HARRINGTON!
OH, GODS! I'VE MISSED YOU!
YOU'RE ALL TOO SWEET, MADAM.
YOU MUST BE EXHAUSTED.
THE CAR'S PARKED JUST AROUND THE BEND. I WON'T BE OFFENDED SHOULD YOU CARE TO NAP ON THE WAY HOME.
I ACTUALLY SLEPT KIND OF DECENTLY. AND I'D HATE TO NOT CATCH UP.
VERY WELL, DEAR.
STRAP IN TIGHT.
IT'S A LONG ROAD HOME.

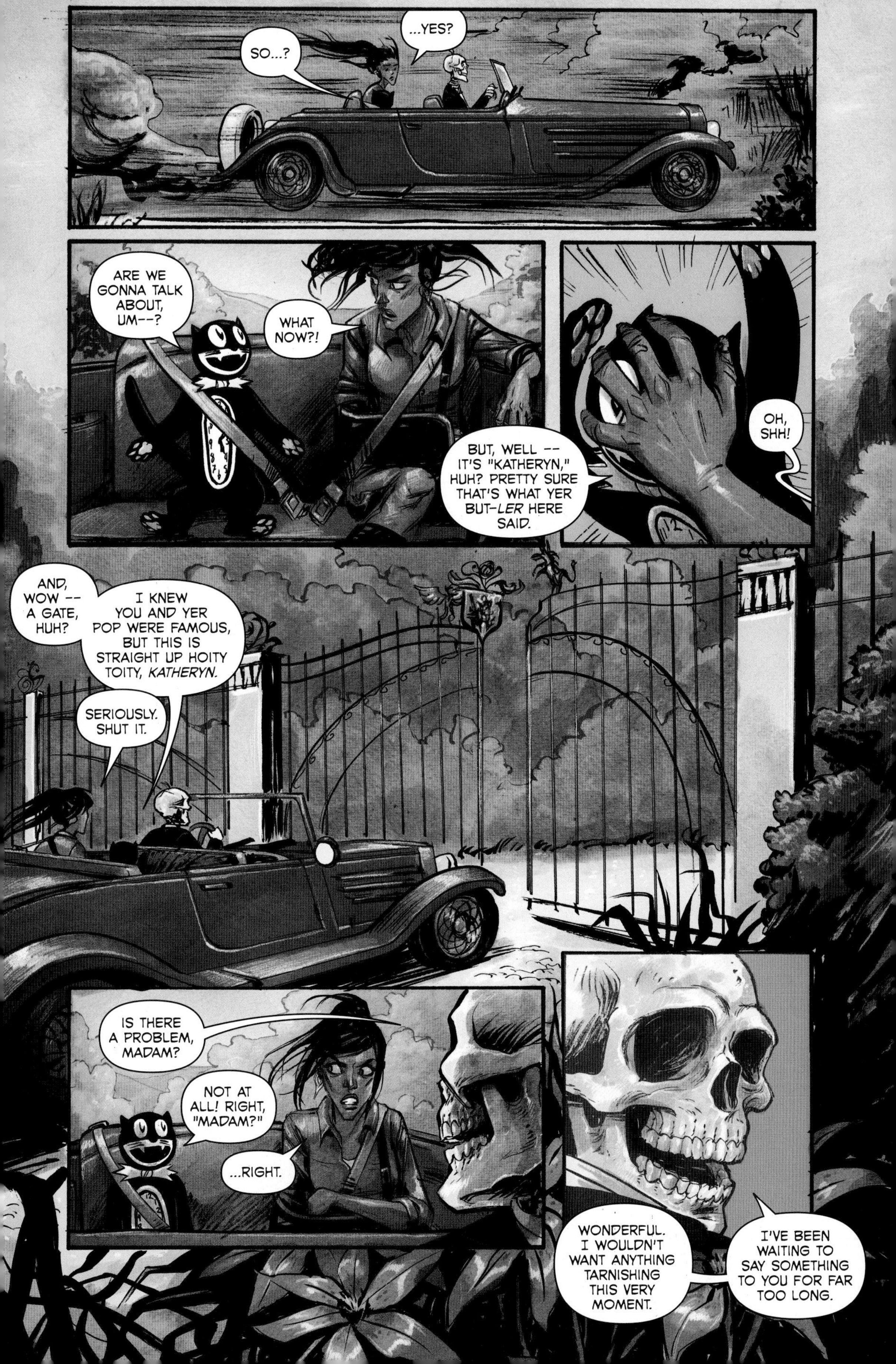

SO...?
...YES?
ARE WE GONNA TALK ABOUT, UM--?
WHAT NOW?!
BUT, WELL -- IT'S "KATHERYN," HUH? PRETTY SURE THAT'S WHAT YER BUT-LER HERE SAID.
OH, SHH!
AND, WOW -- A GATE, HUH?
I KNEW YOU AND YER POP WERE FAMOUS, BUT THIS IS STRAIGHT UP HOITY TOITY, KATHERYN.
SERIOUSLY. SHUT IT.
IS THERE A PROBLEM, MADAM?
NOT AT ALL! RIGHT, "MADAM?"
...RIGHT.
WONDERFUL. I WOULDN'T WANT ANYTHING TARNISHING THIS VERY MOMENT.
I'VE BEEN WAITING TO SAY SOMETHING TO YOU FOR FAR TOO LONG.

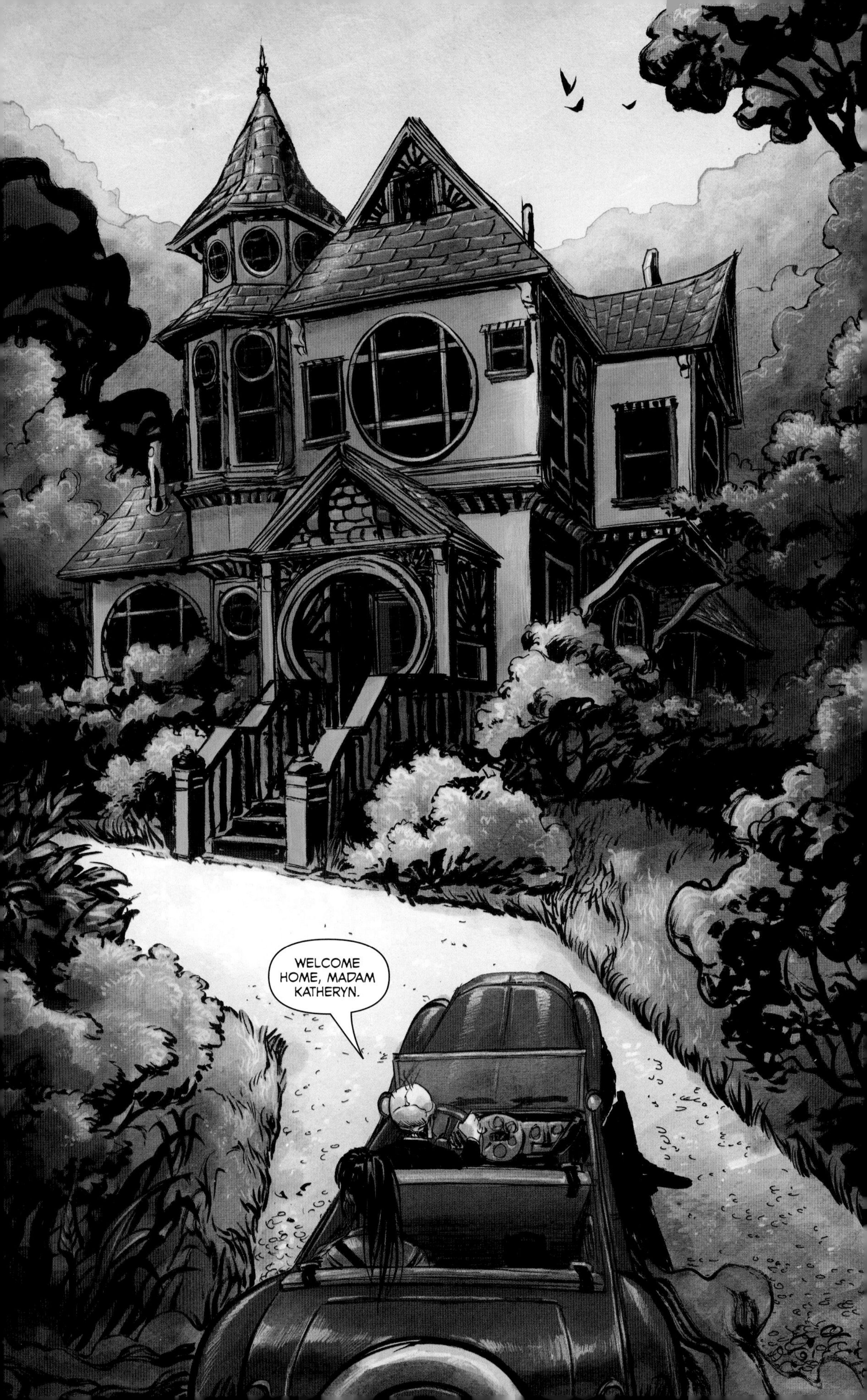
WELCOME HOME, MADAM KATHERYN.

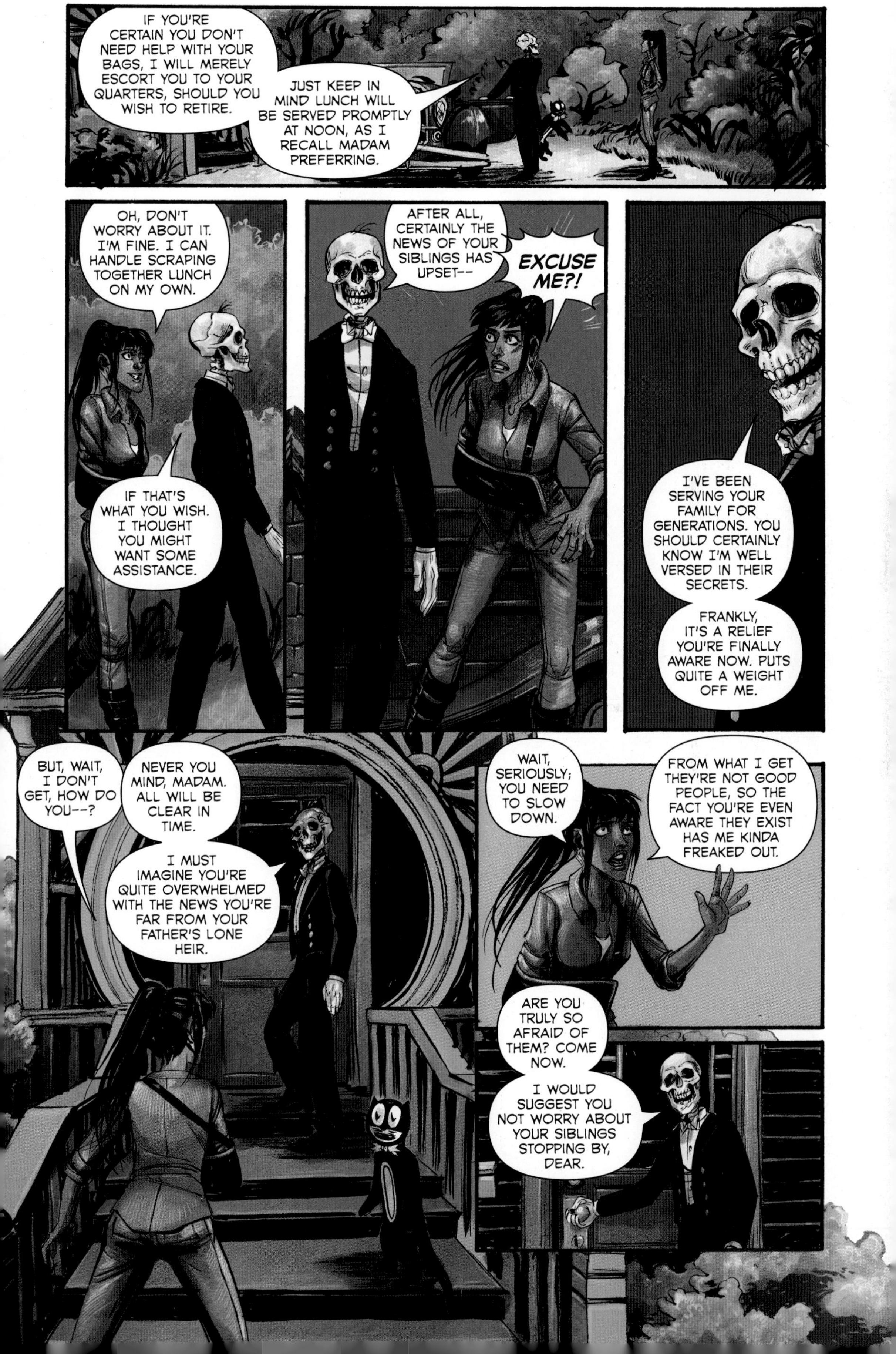
IF YOU'RE CERTAIN YOU DON'T NEED HELP WITH YOUR BAGS, I WILL MERELY ESCORT YOU TO YOUR QUARTERS, SHOULD YOU WISH TO RETIRE.
JUST KEEP IN MIND LUNCH WILL BE SERVED PROMPTLY AT NOON, AS I RECALL MADAM PREFERRING.
OH, DON'T WORRY ABOUT IT. I'M FINE. I CAN HANDLE SCRAPING TOGETHER LUNCH ON MY OWN.
IF THAT'S WHAT YOU WISH. I THOUGHT YOU MIGHT WANT SOME ASSISTANCE.
AFTER ALL, CERTAINLY THE NEWS OF YOUR SIBLINGS HAS UPSET--
EXCUSE ME?!
I'VE BEEN SERVING YOUR FAMILY FOR GENERATIONS. YOU SHOULD CERTAINLY KNOW I'M WELL VERSED IN THEIR SECRETS.
FRANKLY, IT'S A RELIEF YOU'RE FINALLY AWARE NOW. PUTS QUITE A WEIGHT OFF ME.
BUT, WAIT, I DON'T GET, HOW DO YOU--?
NEVER YOU MIND, MADAM. ALL WILL BE CLEAR IN TIME.
I MUST IMAGINE YOU'RE QUITE OVERWHELMED WITH THE NEWS YOU'RE FAR FROM YOUR FATHER'S LONE HEIR.
WAIT, SERIOUSLY; YOU NEED TO SLOW DOWN.
FROM WHAT I GET THEY'RE NOT GOOD PEOPLE, SO THE FACT YOU'RE EVEN AWARE THEY EXIST HAS ME KINDA FREAKED OUT.
ARE YOU TRULY SO AFRAID OF THEM? COME NOW.
I WOULD SUGGEST YOU NOT WORRY ABOUT YOUR SIBLINGS STOPPING BY, DEAR.

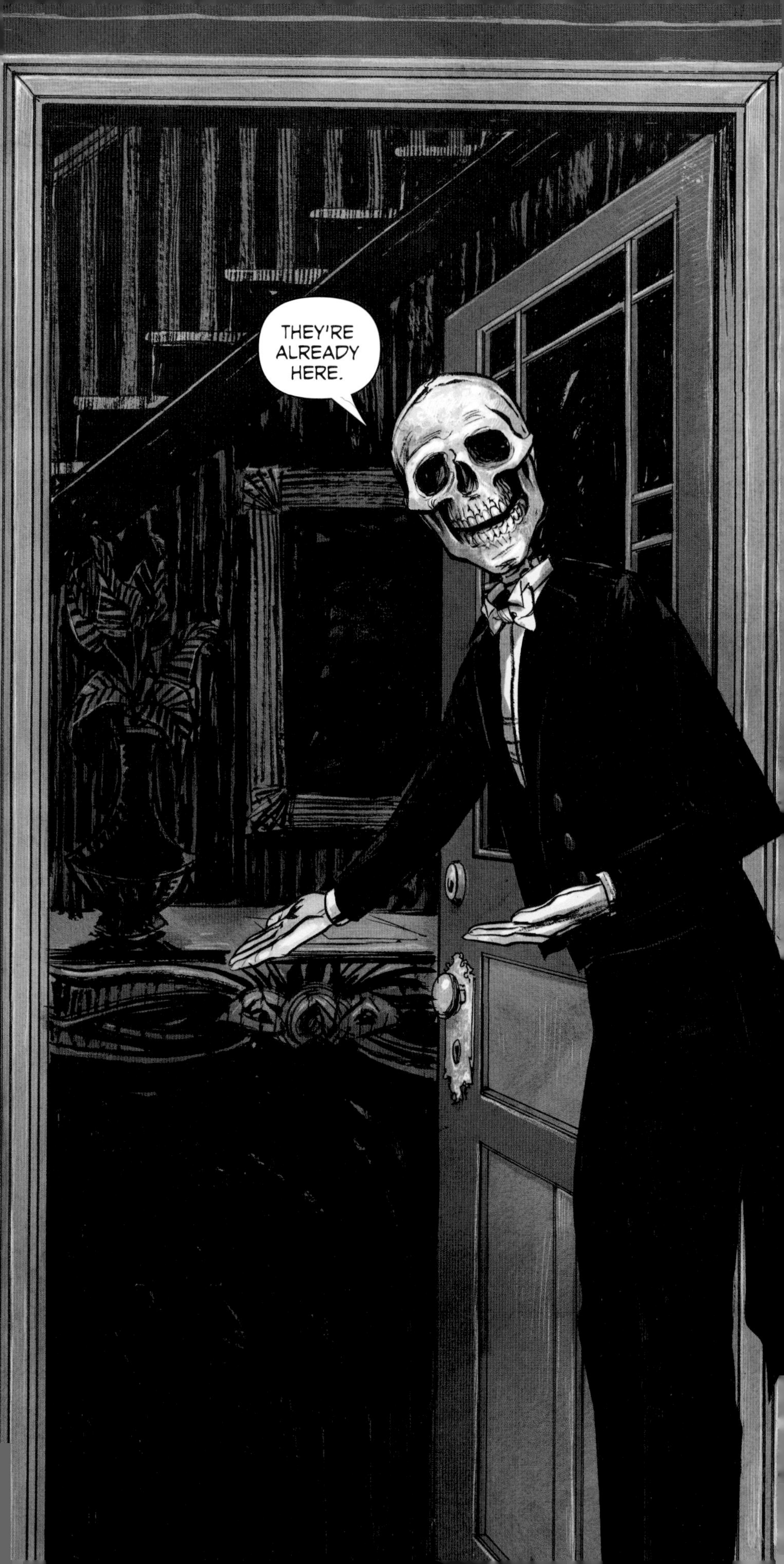
THEY'RE ALREADY HERE.

CHAPTER

4

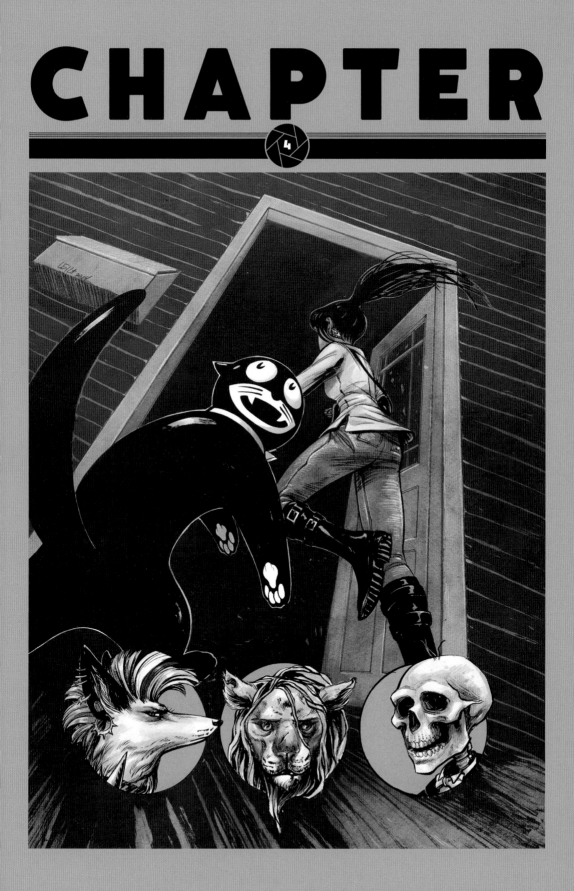

REGINALD HARRINGTON WAS
A BITTER YOUNG BOY...

...WHO GREW INTO
A BITTER OLD MAN.

HE WATCHED THE WORLD
GO BY WITHOUT HIM, YET
SHOWED NO REMORSE.

HAPPINESS CAME ONLY IN
THE STRICTEST SOLITUDE.

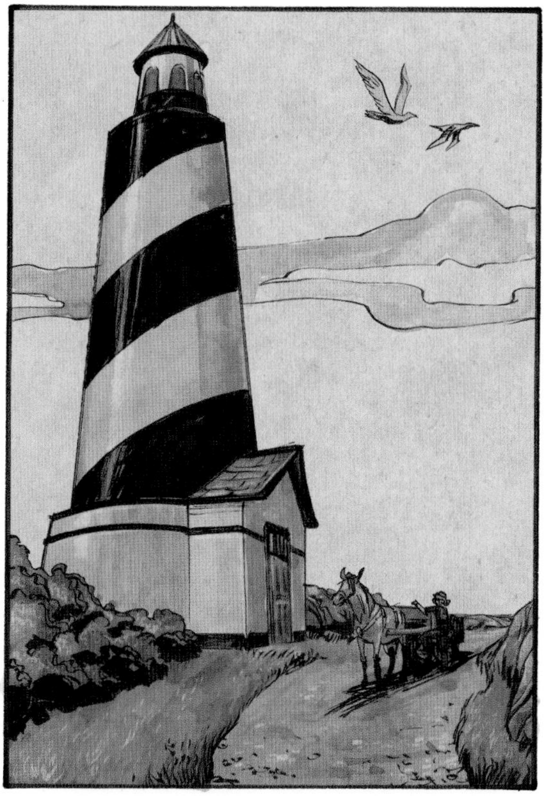

AT THE AGE OF SIXTY, REGINALD SPENT HIS LIFE SAVINGS ON MOVING TO THE COAST, FAR AWAY FROM ANY OTHER LIVING BEING.

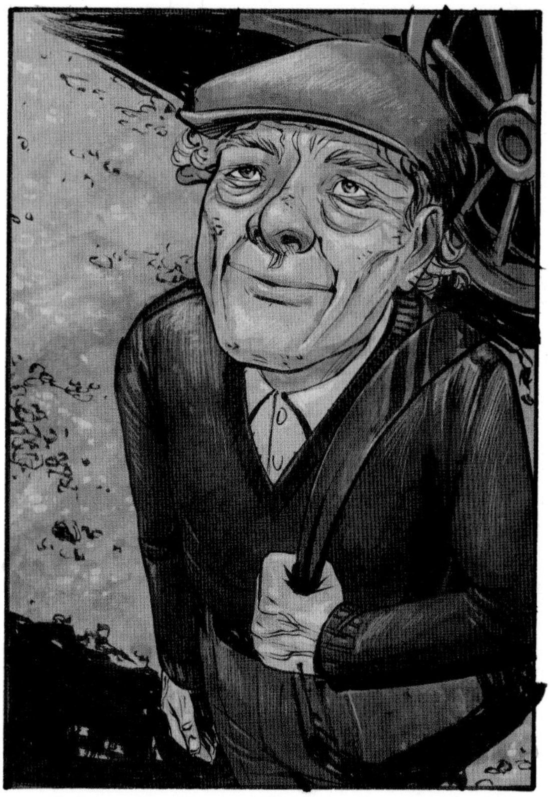

IT WAS TRANQUIL, IDYLLIC - WHAT HE HAD LONGED FOR OVER DECADES.

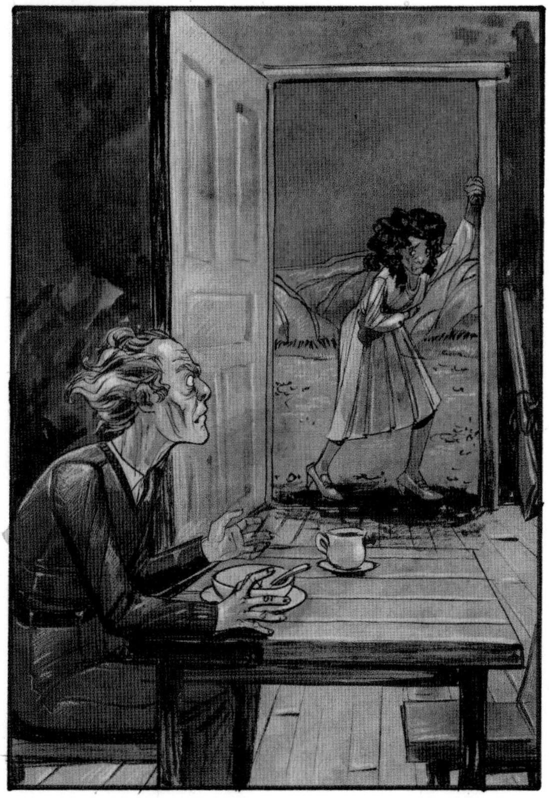

THEN ONE DAY HIS QUIET EXISTENCE SHATTERED, AS A DYING WOMAN CAME TO HIS DOOR.

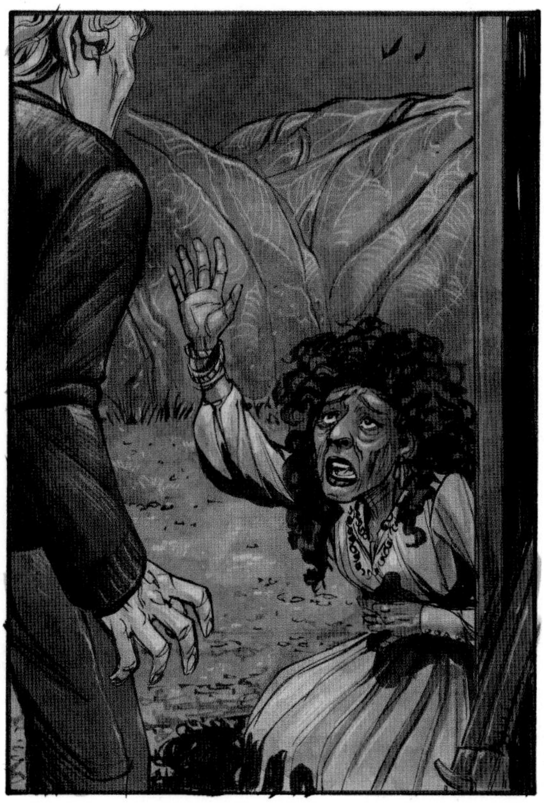

SHE WAS SHOT, IN NEED OF ASSISTANCE, DESPERATE FOR REFUGE.

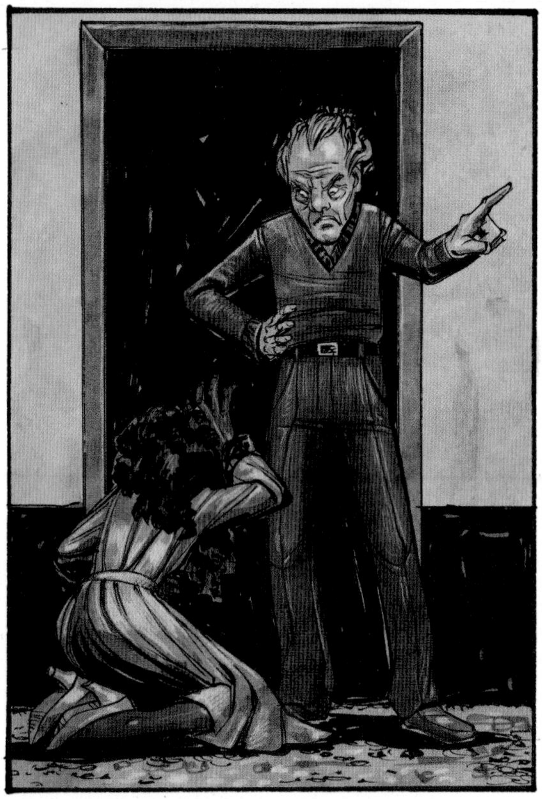

REGINALD OFFERED THE OLD WOMAN ONLY A SIMPLE, "NO."

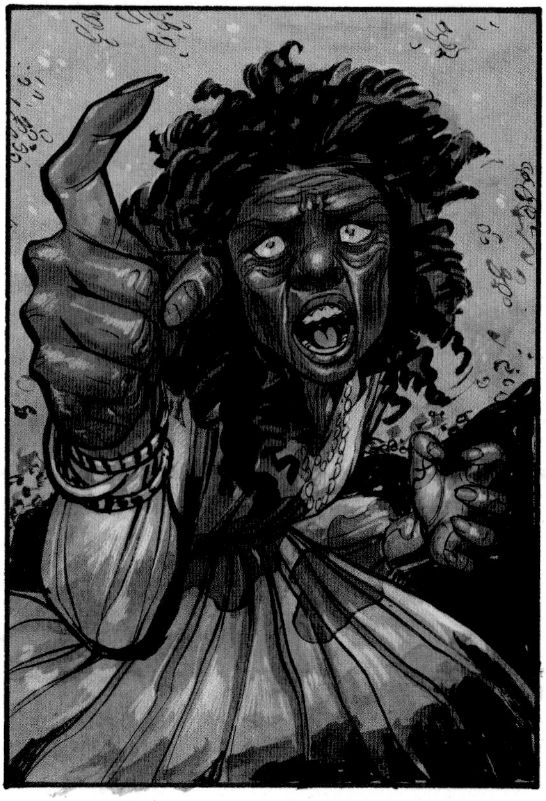

"TURN ME AWAY AND I CURSE YOU TO SERVE MY HEIRS WITHOUT END," SHE THREATENED.

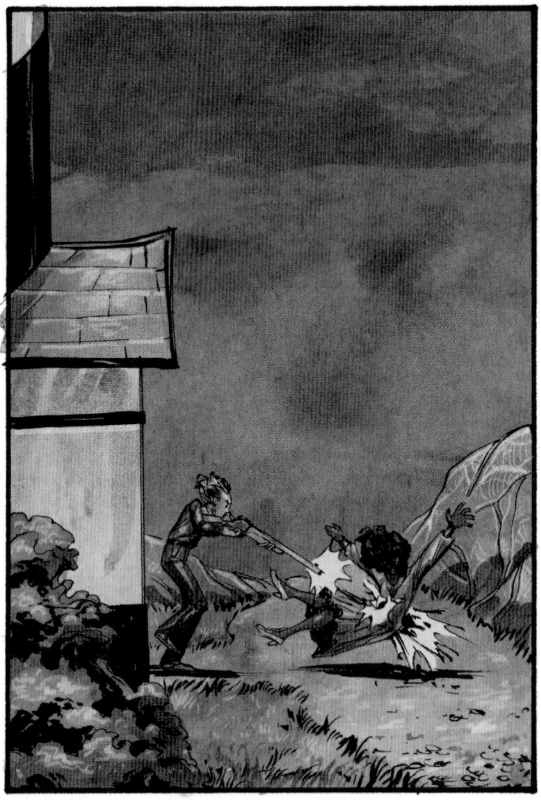

YET REGINALD GAVE NO QUARTER.

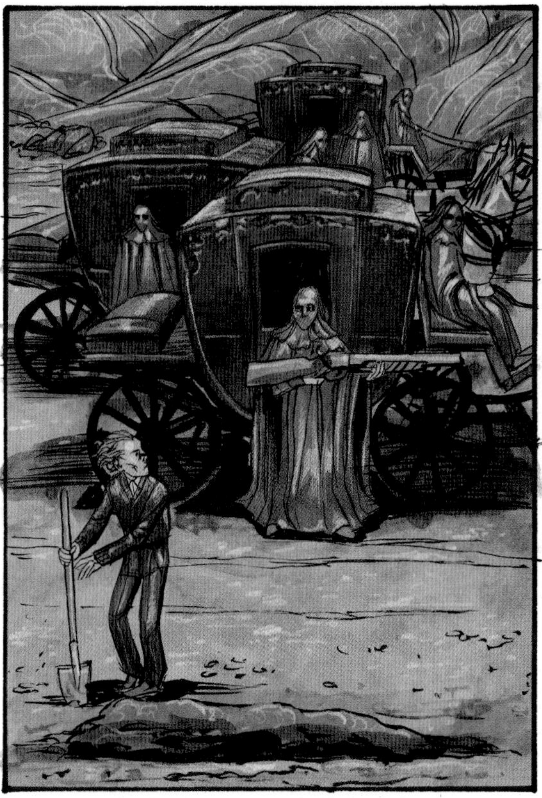

HE MET HER EXTENDED FAMILY MERE DAYS LATER.

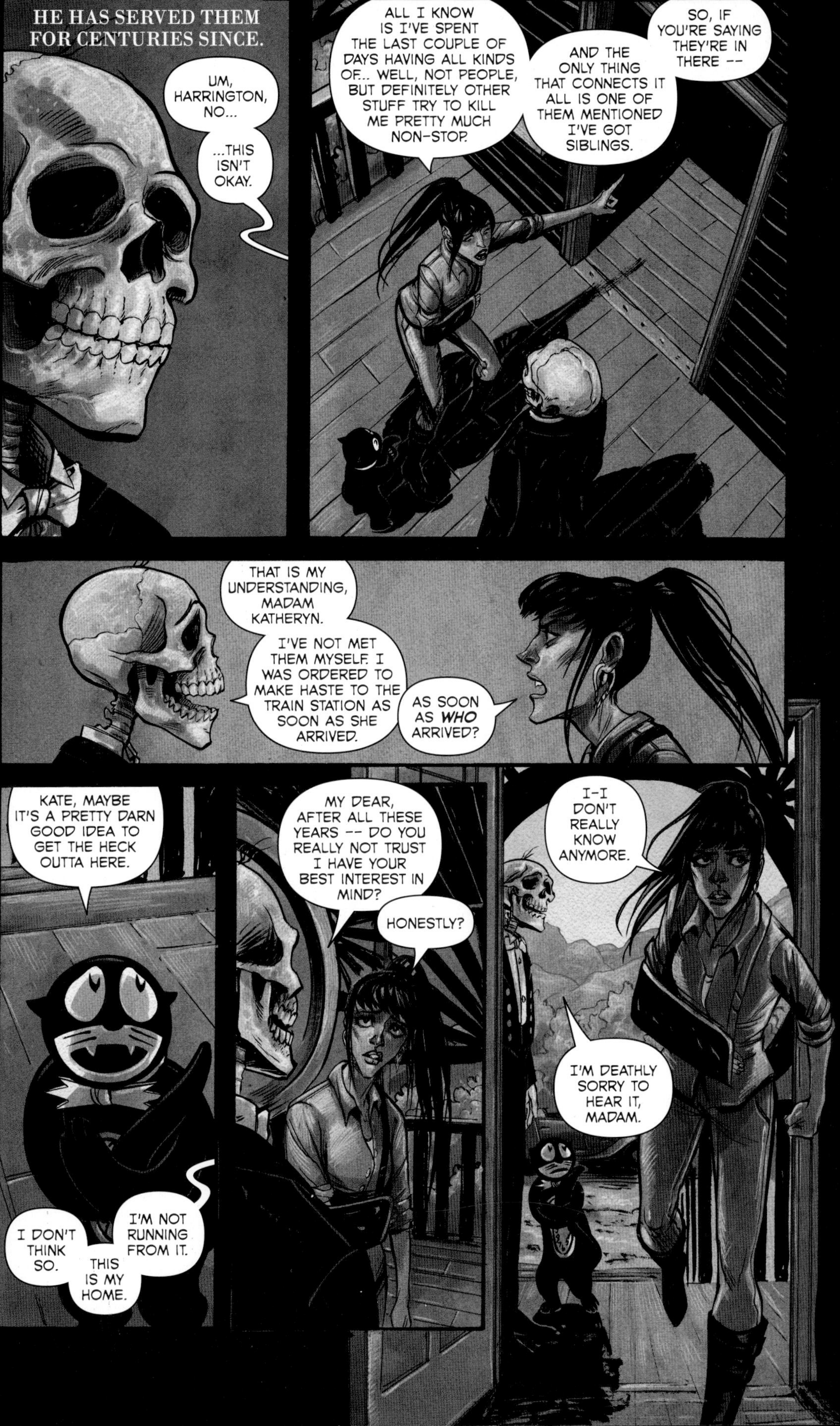
HE HAS SERVED THEM FOR CENTURIES SINCE.
UM, HARRINGTON, NO...
...THIS ISN'T OKAY.
ALL I KNOW IS I'VE SPENT THE LAST COUPLE OF DAYS HAVING ALL KINDS OF... WELL, NOT PEOPLE, BUT DEFINITELY OTHER STUFF TRY TO KILL ME PRETTY MUCH NON-STOP.
AND THE ONLY THING THAT CONNECTS IT ALL IS ONE OF THEM MENTIONED I'VE GOT SIBLINGS.
SO, IF YOU'RE SAYING THEY'RE IN THERE --
THAT IS MY UNDERSTANDING, MADAM KATHERYN.
I'VE NOT MET THEM MYSELF. I WAS ORDERED TO MAKE HASTE TO THE TRAIN STATION AS SOON AS SHE ARRIVED.
AS SOON AS *WHO* ARRIVED?
KATE, MAYBE IT'S A PRETTY DARN GOOD IDEA TO GET THE HECK OUTTA HERE.
I DON'T THINK SO.
I'M NOT RUNNING FROM IT.
THIS IS MY HOME.
MY DEAR, AFTER ALL THESE YEARS -- DO YOU REALLY NOT TRUST I HAVE YOUR BEST INTEREST IN MIND?
HONESTLY?
I-I DON'T REALLY KNOW ANYMORE.
I'M DEATHLY SORRY TO HEAR IT, MADAM.

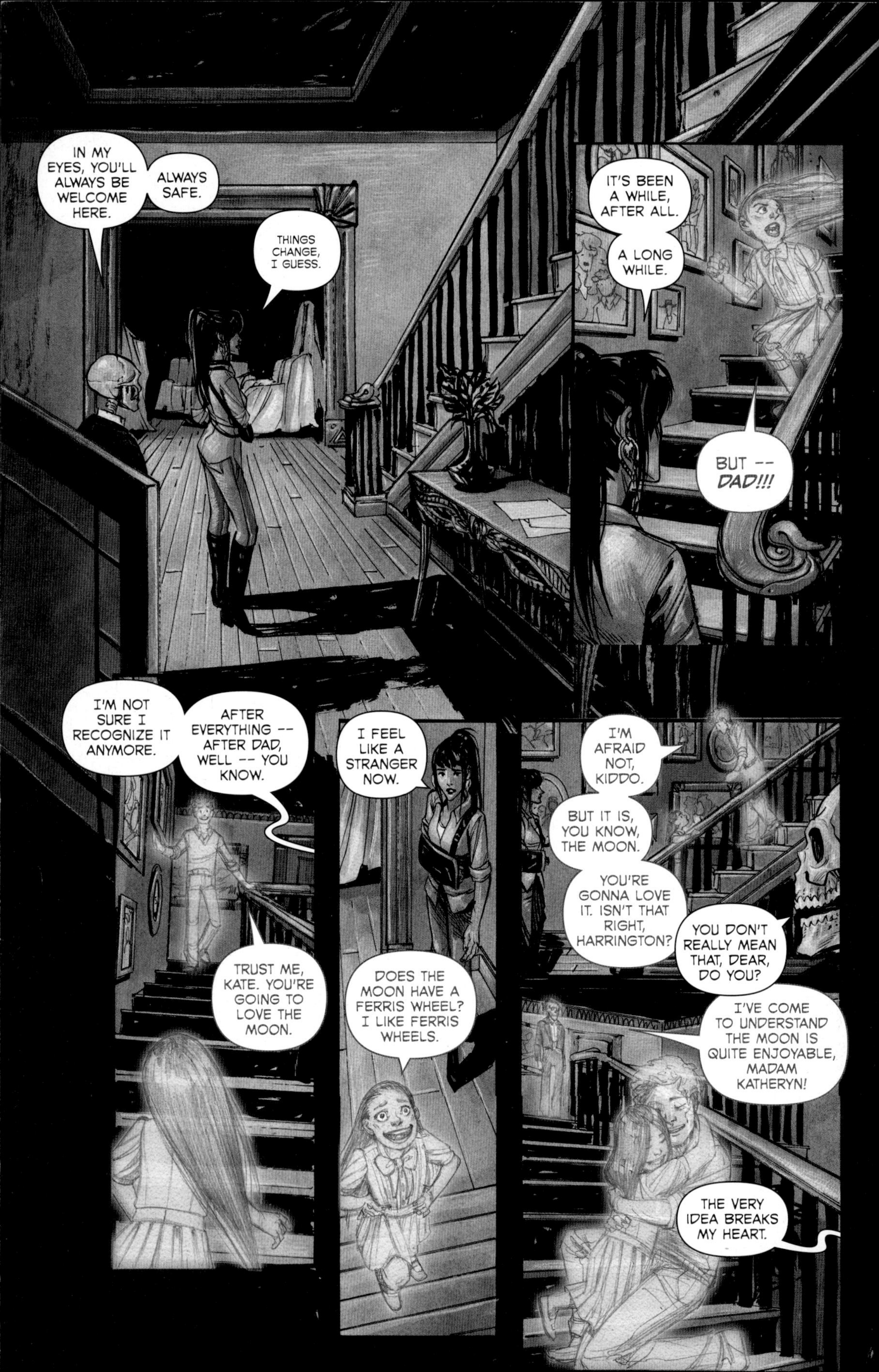
IN MY EYES, YOU'LL ALWAYS BE WELCOME HERE.
ALWAYS SAFE.
THINGS CHANGE, I GUESS.
IT'S BEEN A WHILE, AFTER ALL.
A LONG WHILE.
BUT -- DAD!!!
I'M NOT SURE I RECOGNIZE IT ANYMORE.
AFTER EVERYTHING -- AFTER DAD, WELL -- YOU KNOW.
TRUST ME, KATE. YOU'RE GOING TO LOVE THE MOON.
I FEEL LIKE A STRANGER NOW.
DOES THE MOON HAVE A FERRIS WHEEL? I LIKE FERRIS WHEELS.
I'M AFRAID NOT, KIDDO.
BUT IT IS, YOU KNOW, THE MOON.
YOU'RE GONNA LOVE IT. ISN'T THAT RIGHT, HARRINGTON?
YOU DON'T REALLY MEAN THAT, DEAR, DO YOU?
I'VE COME TO UNDERSTAND THE MOON IS QUITE ENJOYABLE, MADAM KATHERYN!
THE VERY IDEA BREAKS MY HEART.

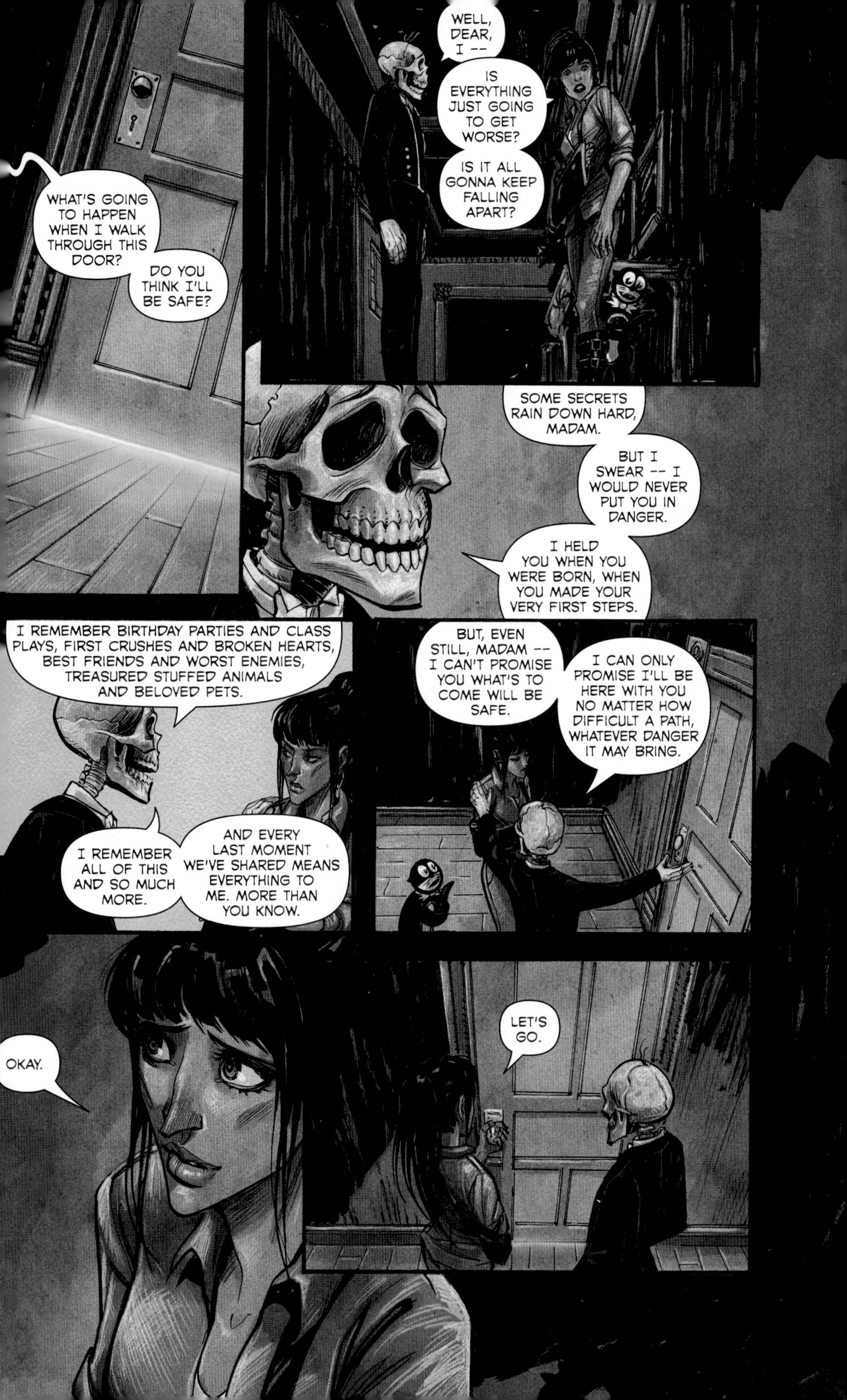
WHAT'S GOING TO HAPPEN WHEN I WALK THROUGH THIS DOOR?
DO YOU THINK I'LL BE SAFE?
WELL, DEAR, I --
IS EVERYTHING JUST GOING TO GET WORSE?
IS IT ALL GONNA KEEP FALLING APART?
SOME SECRETS RAIN DOWN HARD, MADAM.
BUT I SWEAR -- I WOULD NEVER PUT YOU IN DANGER.
I HELD YOU WHEN YOU WERE BORN, WHEN YOU MADE YOUR VERY FIRST STEPS.
I REMEMBER BIRTHDAY PARTIES AND CLASS PLAYS, FIRST CRUSHES AND BROKEN HEARTS, BEST FRIENDS AND WORST ENEMIES, TREASURED STUFFED ANIMALS AND BELOVED PETS.
I REMEMBER ALL OF THIS AND SO MUCH MORE.
AND EVERY LAST MOMENT WE'VE SHARED MEANS EVERYTHING TO ME. MORE THAN YOU KNOW.
BUT, EVEN STILL, MADAM -- I CAN'T PROMISE YOU WHAT'S TO COME WILL BE SAFE.
I CAN ONLY PROMISE I'LL BE HERE WITH YOU NO MATTER HOW DIFFICULT A PATH, WHATEVER DANGER IT MAY BRING.
OKAY.
LET'S GO.

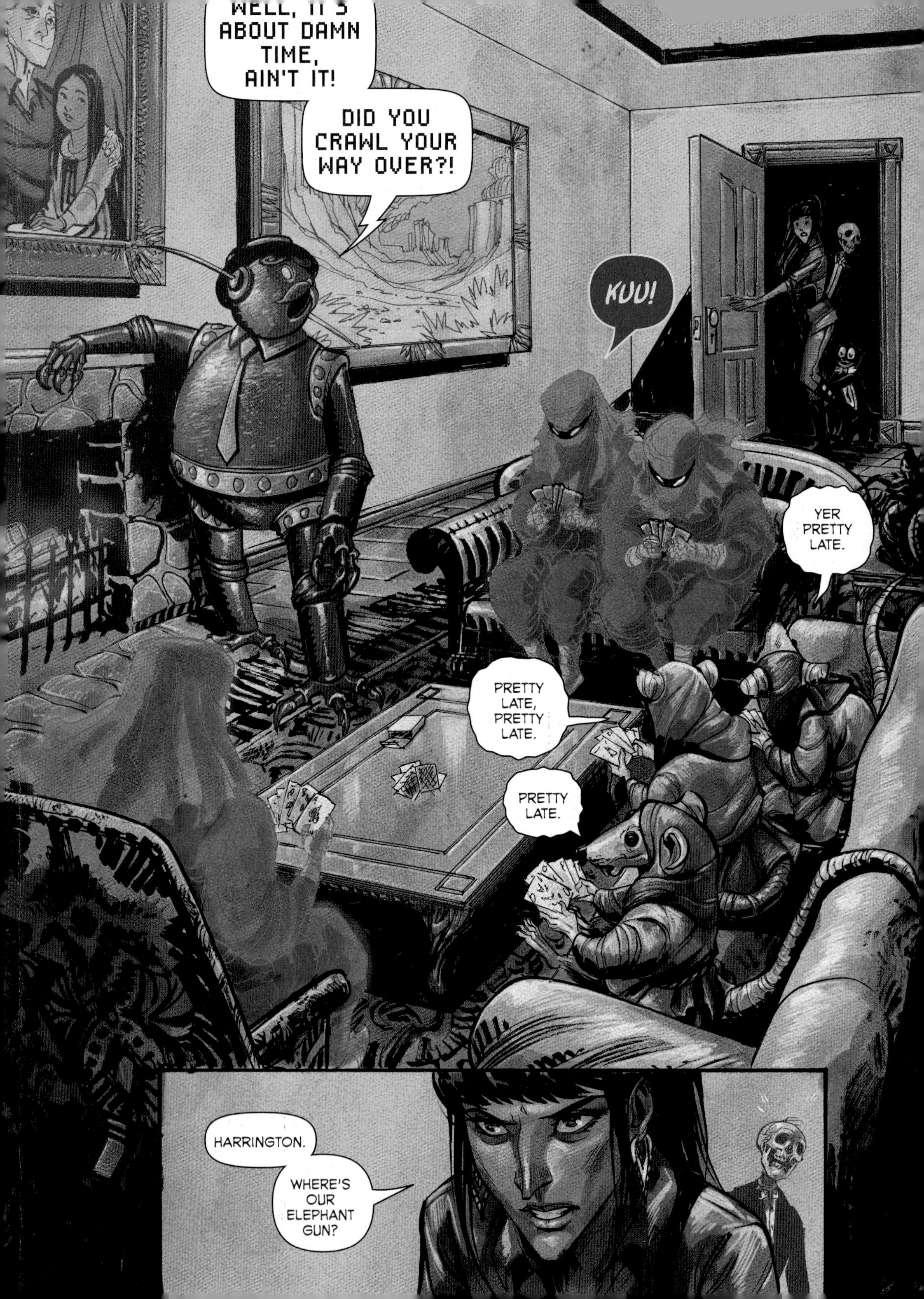
WELL, IT'S ABOUT DAMN TIME, AIN'T IT!
DID YOU CRAWL YOUR WAY OVER?!
KUU!
YER PRETTY LATE.
PRETTY LATE, PRETTY LATE.
PRETTY LATE.
HARRINGTON.
WHERE'S OUR ELEPHANT GUN?

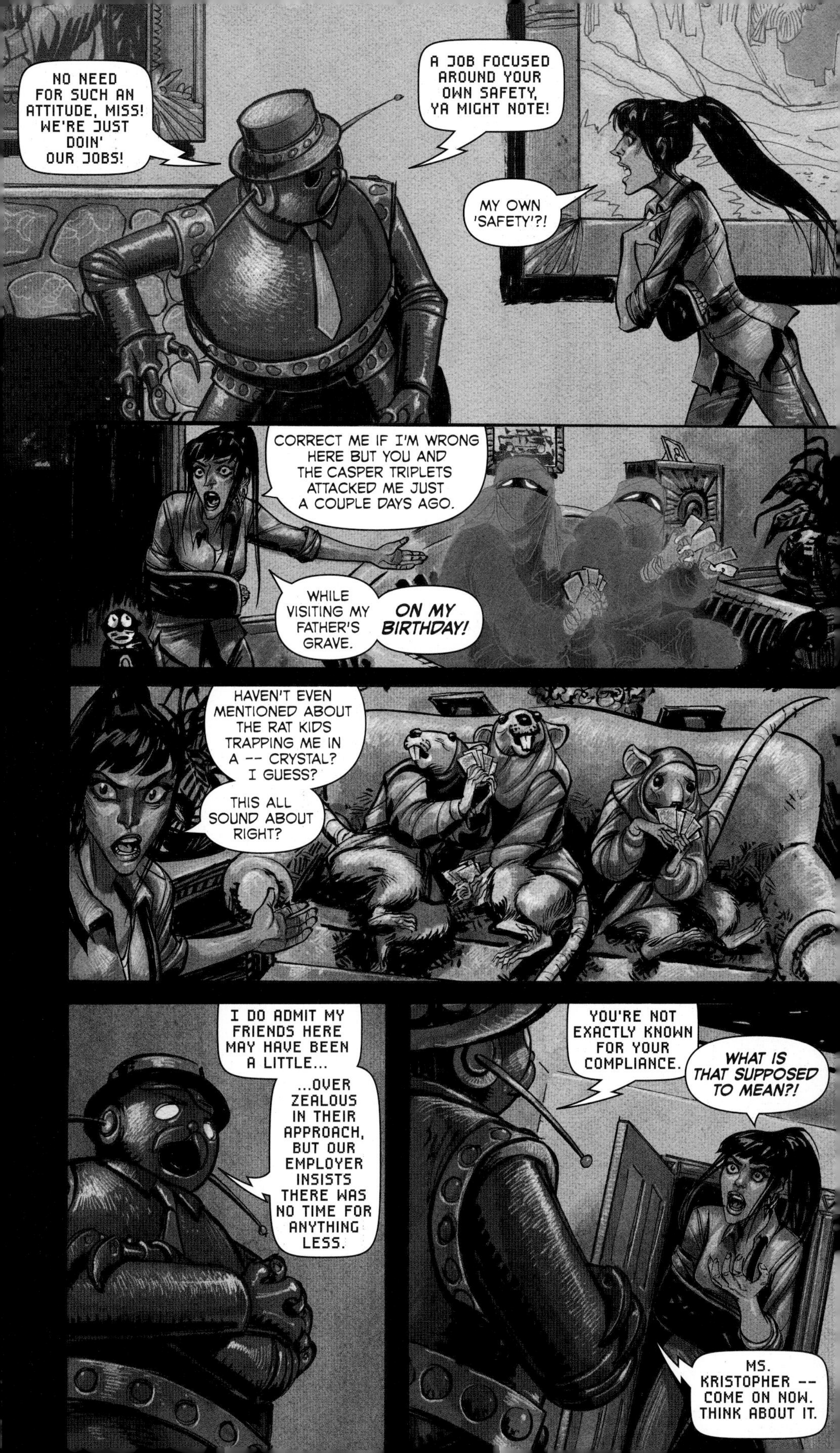
NO NEED FOR SUCH AN ATTITUDE, MISS! WE'RE JUST DOIN' OUR JOBS!
A JOB FOCUSED AROUND YOUR OWN SAFETY, YA MIGHT NOTE!
MY OWN 'SAFETY'?!
CORRECT ME IF I'M WRONG HERE BUT YOU AND THE CASPER TRIPLETS ATTACKED ME JUST A COUPLE DAYS AGO.
WHILE VISITING MY FATHER'S GRAVE.
ON MY BIRTHDAY!
HAVEN'T EVEN MENTIONED ABOUT THE RAT KIDS TRAPPING ME IN A -- CRYSTAL? I GUESS?
THIS ALL SOUND ABOUT RIGHT?
I DO ADMIT MY FRIENDS HERE MAY HAVE BEEN A LITTLE...
...OVER ZEALOUS IN THEIR APPROACH, BUT OUR EMPLOYER INSISTS THERE WAS NO TIME FOR ANYTHING LESS.
YOU'RE NOT EXACTLY KNOWN FOR YOUR COMPLIANCE.
WHAT IS THAT SUPPOSED TO MEAN?!
MS. KRISTOPHER -- COME ON NOW. THINK ABOUT IT.

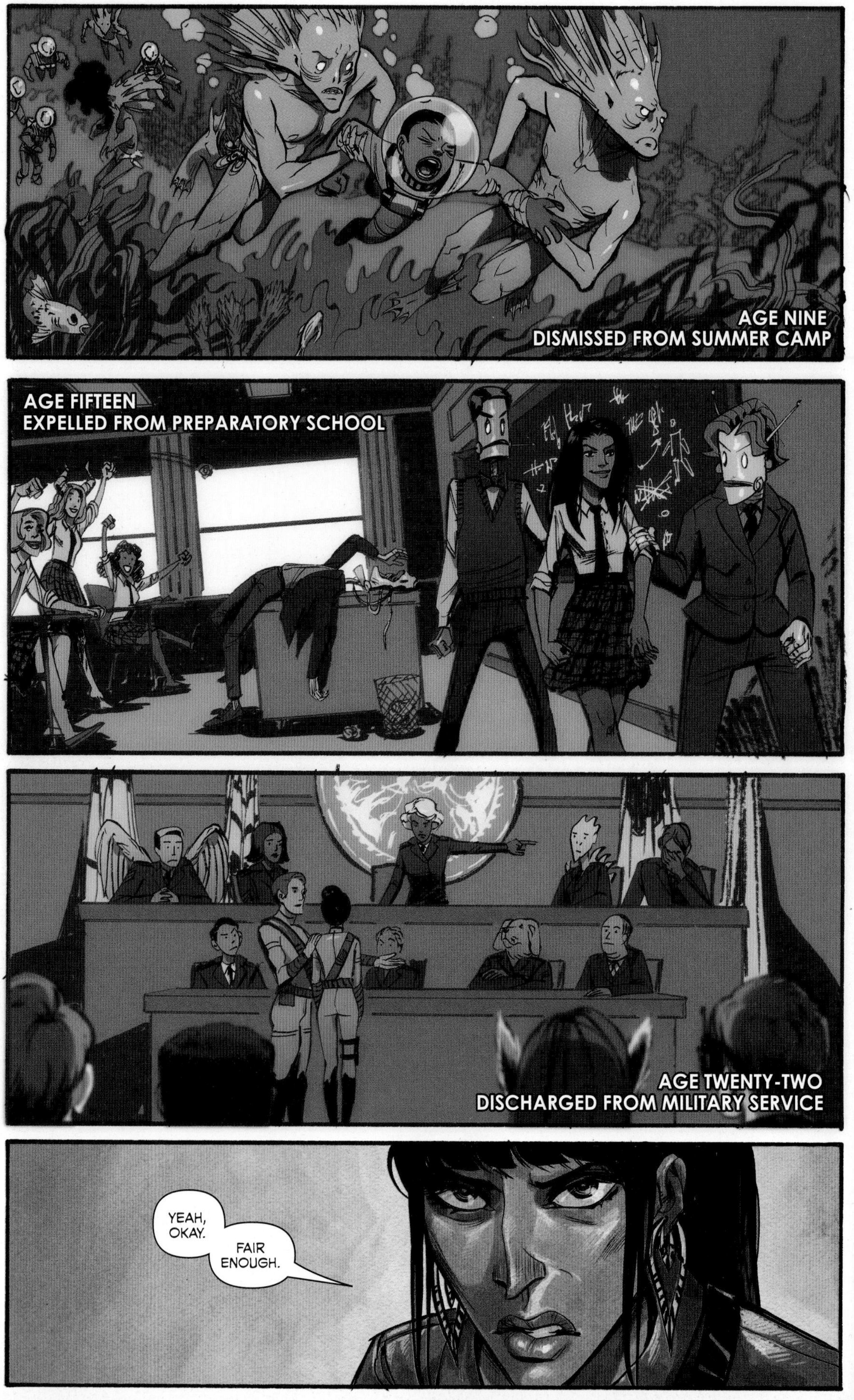
AGE NINE
DISMISSED FROM SUMMER CAMP
AGE FIFTEEN
EXPELLED FROM PREPARATORY SCHOOL
AGE TWENTY-TWO
DISCHARGED FROM MILITARY SERVICE
YEAH, OKAY.
FAIR ENOUGH.

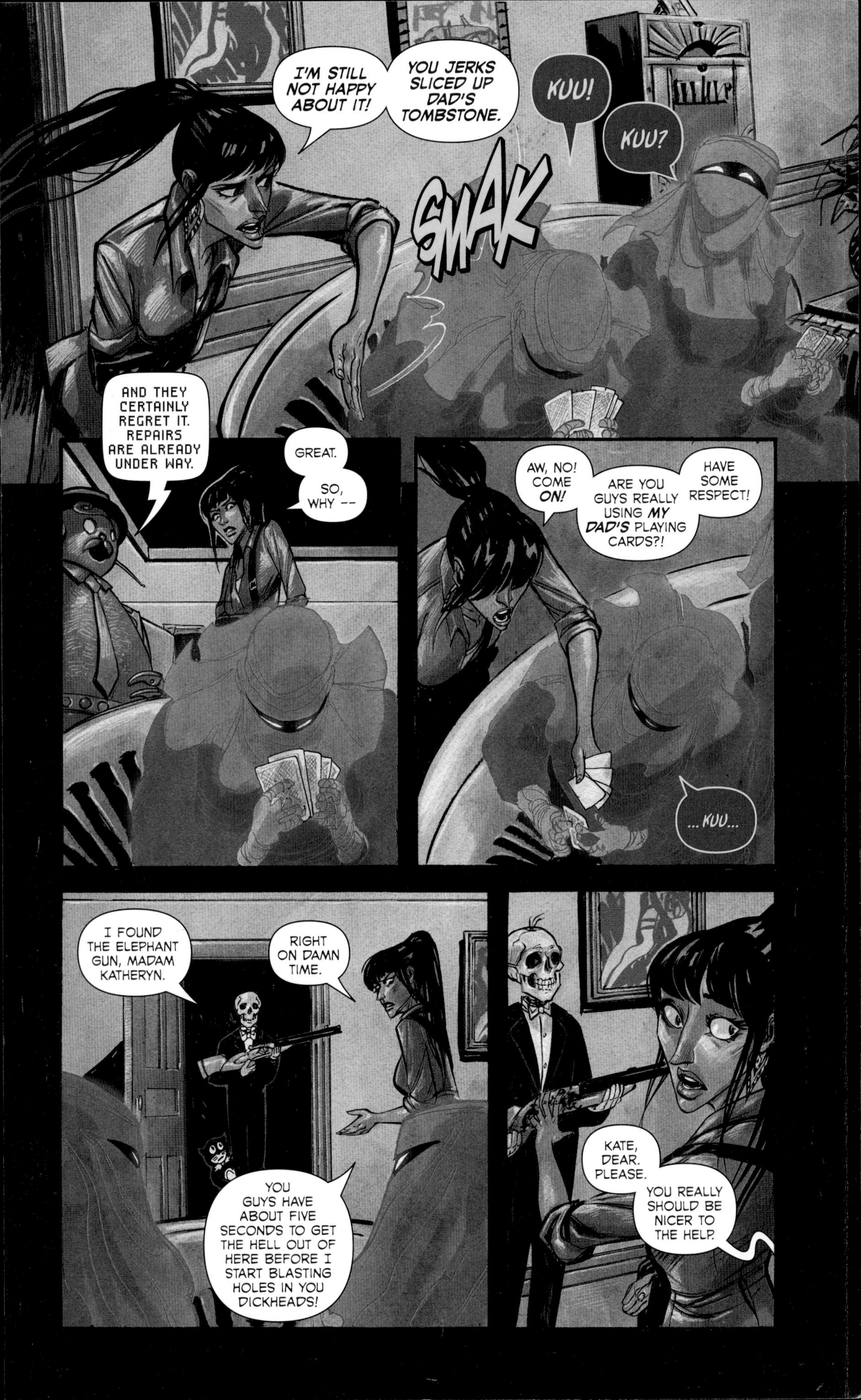
I'M STILL NOT HAPPY ABOUT IT!
YOU JERKS SLICED UP DAD'S TOMBSTONE.
KUU!
KUU?
SMAK
AND THEY CERTAINLY REGRET IT. REPAIRS ARE ALREADY UNDER WAY.
GREAT.
SO, WHY --
AW, NO! COME ON!
ARE YOU GUYS REALLY USING MY DAD'S PLAYING CARDS?!
HAVE SOME RESPECT!
...KUU...
I FOUND THE ELEPHANT GUN, MADAM KATHERYN.
RIGHT ON DAMN TIME.
YOU GUYS HAVE ABOUT FIVE SECONDS TO GET THE HELL OUT OF HERE BEFORE I START BLASTING HOLES IN YOU DICKHEADS!
KATE, DEAR. PLEASE.
YOU REALLY SHOULD BE NICER TO THE HELP.

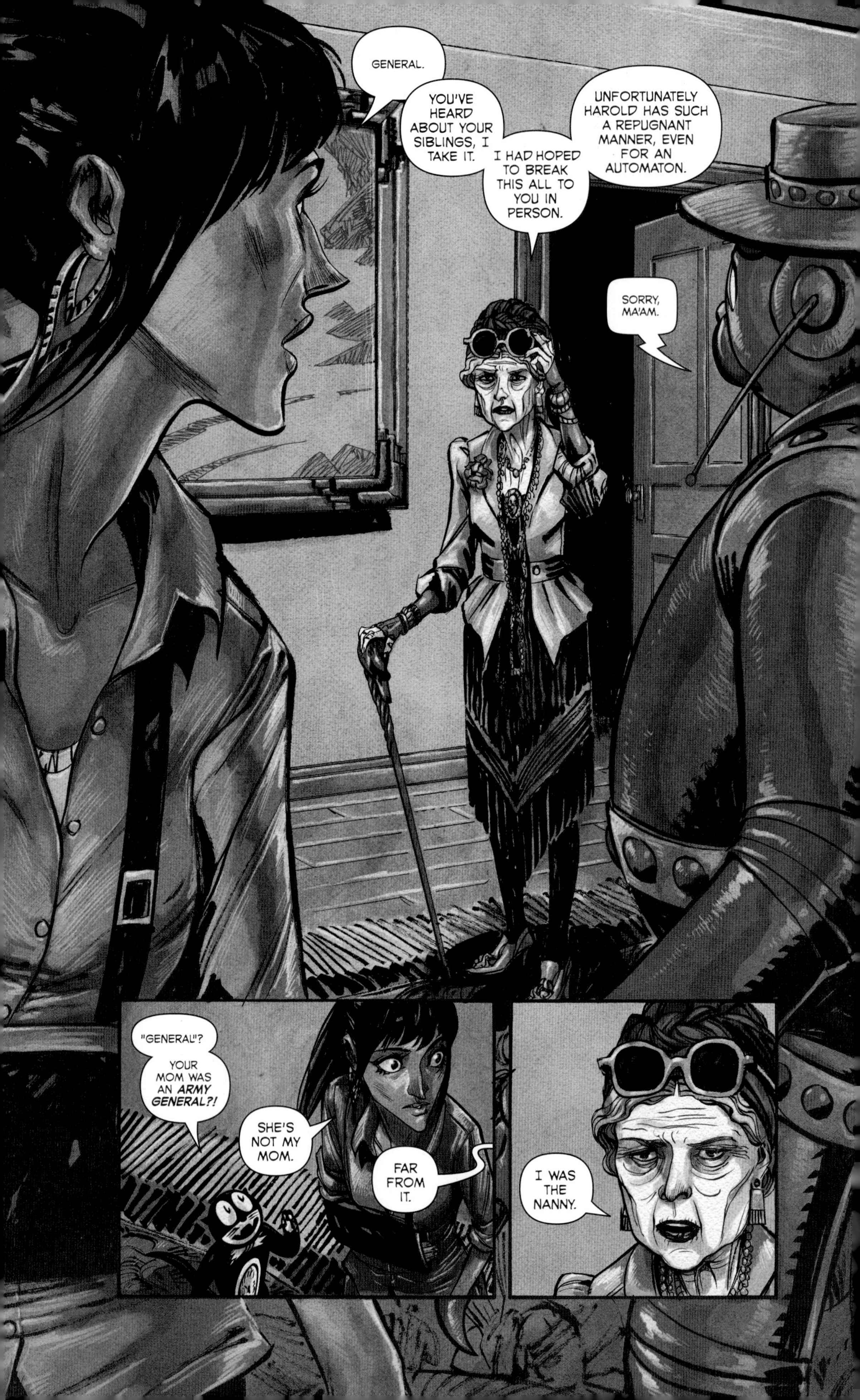
GENERAL.
YOU'VE HEARD ABOUT YOUR SIBLINGS, I TAKE IT.
I HAD HOPED TO BREAK THIS ALL TO YOU IN PERSON.
UNFORTUNATELY HAROLD HAS SUCH A REPUGNANT MANNER, EVEN FOR AN AUTOMATON.
SORRY, MA'AM.
"GENERAL"?
YOUR MOM WAS AN *ARMY GENERAL?!*
SHE'S NOT MY MOM.
FAR FROM IT.
I WAS THE NANNY.

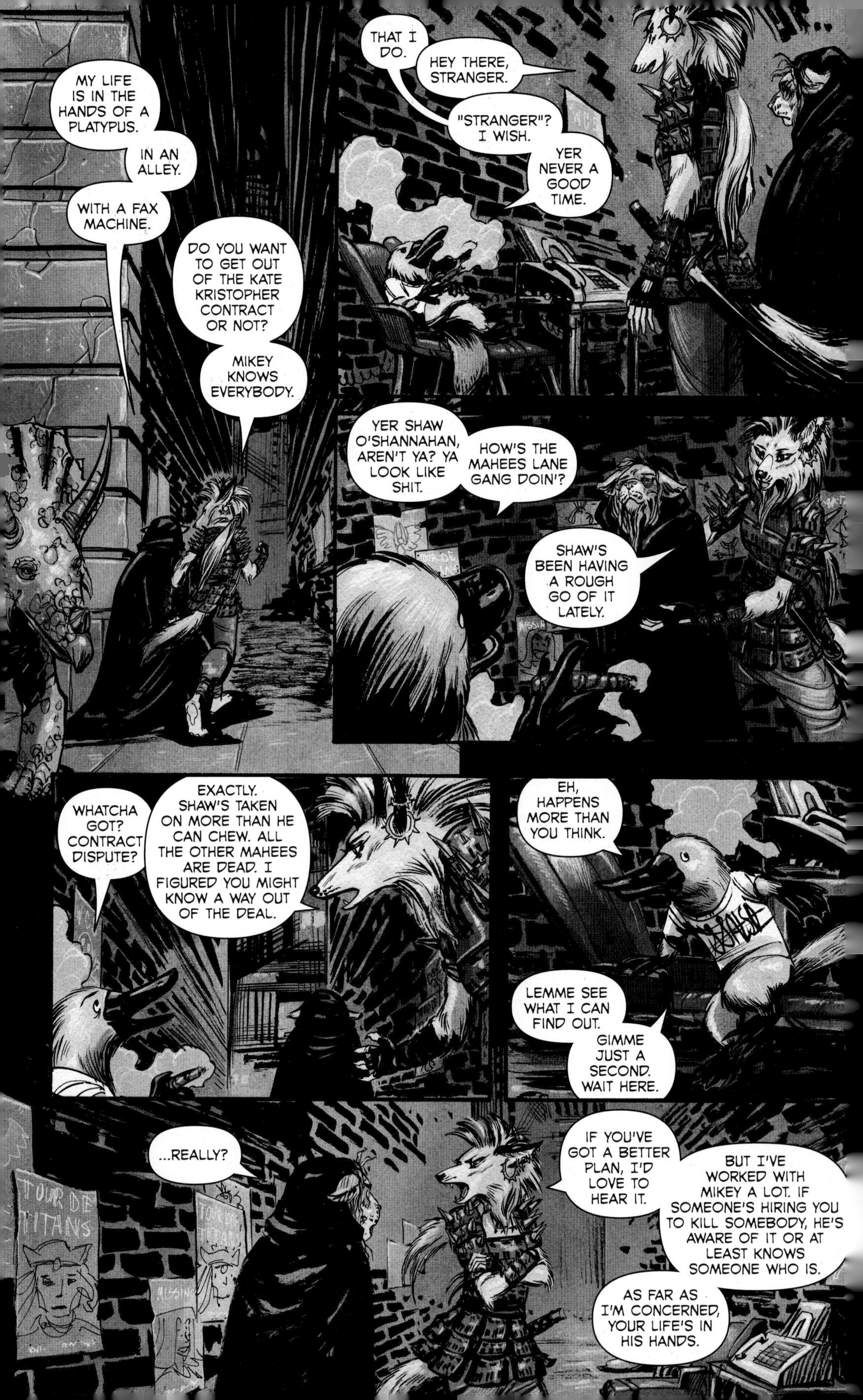
MY LIFE IS IN THE HANDS OF A PLATYPUS.
IN AN ALLEY.
WITH A FAX MACHINE.
DO YOU WANT TO GET OUT OF THE KATE KRISTOPHER CONTRACT OR NOT?
MIKEY KNOWS EVERYBODY.
HEY THERE, STRANGER.
THAT I DO.
"STRANGER"? I WISH.
YER NEVER A GOOD TIME.
YER SHAW O'SHANNAHAN, AREN'T YA? YA LOOK LIKE SHIT.
HOW'S THE MAHEES LANE GANG DOIN'?
SHAW'S BEEN HAVING A ROUGH GO OF IT LATELY.
WHATCHA GOT? CONTRACT DISPUTE?
EXACTLY. SHAW'S TAKEN ON MORE THAN HE CAN CHEW. ALL THE OTHER MAHEES ARE DEAD. I FIGURED YOU MIGHT KNOW A WAY OUT OF THE DEAL.
EH, HAPPENS MORE THAN YOU THINK.
LEMME SEE WHAT I CAN FIND OUT.
GIMME JUST A SECOND. WAIT HERE.
...REALLY?
IF YOU'VE GOT A BETTER PLAN, I'D LOVE TO HEAR IT.
BUT I'VE WORKED WITH MIKEY A LOT. IF SOMEONE'S HIRING YOU TO KILL SOMEBODY, HE'S AWARE OF IT OR AT LEAST KNOWS SOMEONE WHO IS.
AS FAR AS I'M CONCERNED, YOUR LIFE'S IN HIS HANDS.
TOUR DE TITANS
TOUR DE TITANS
MISSING

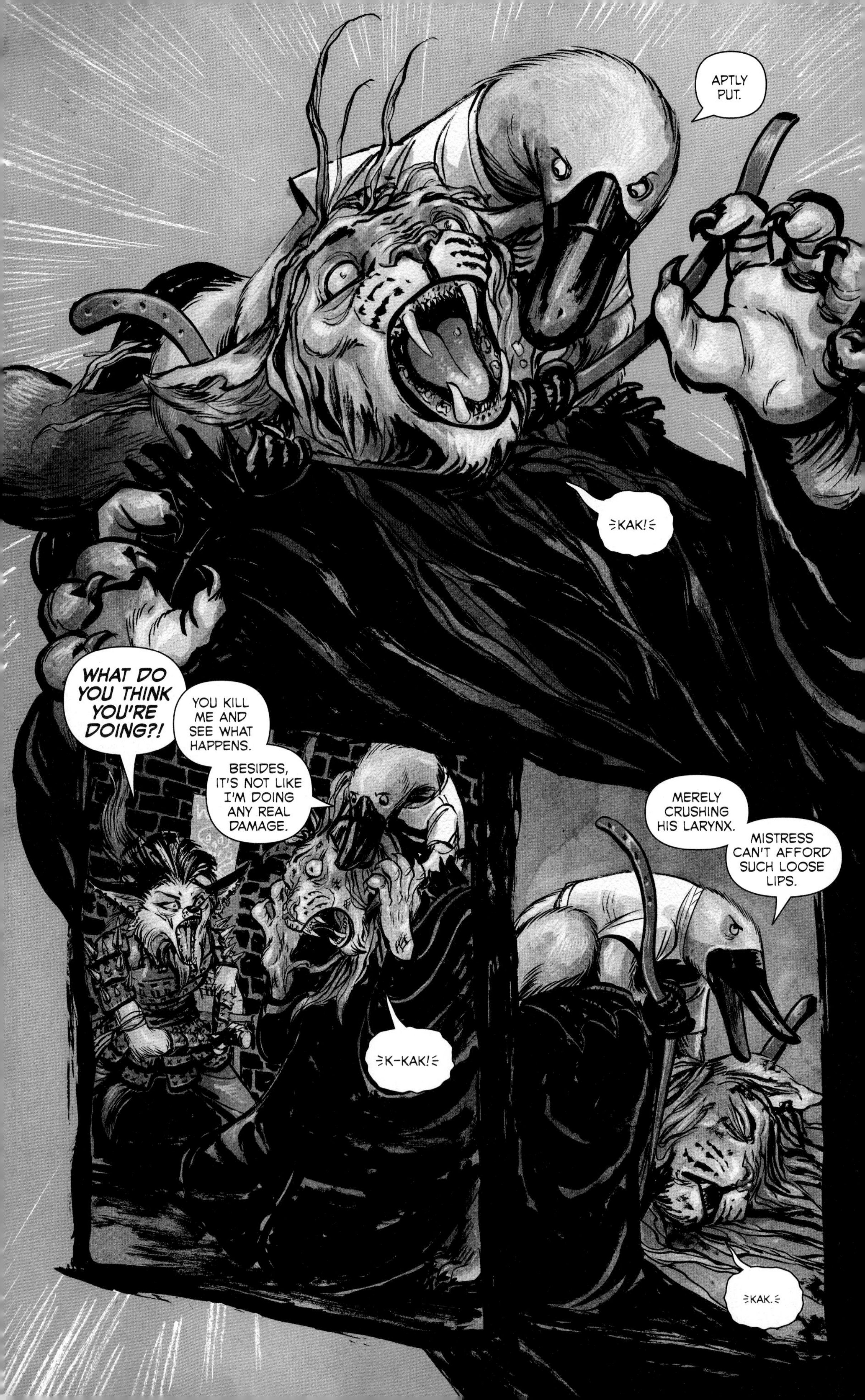
APTLY PUT.
KAK!
WHAT DO YOU THINK YOU'RE DOING?!
YOU KILL ME AND SEE WHAT HAPPENS.
BESIDES, IT'S NOT LIKE I'M DOING ANY REAL DAMAGE.
K-KAK!
MERELY CRUSHING HIS LARYNX.
MISTRESS CAN'T AFFORD SUCH LOOSE LIPS.
KAK.

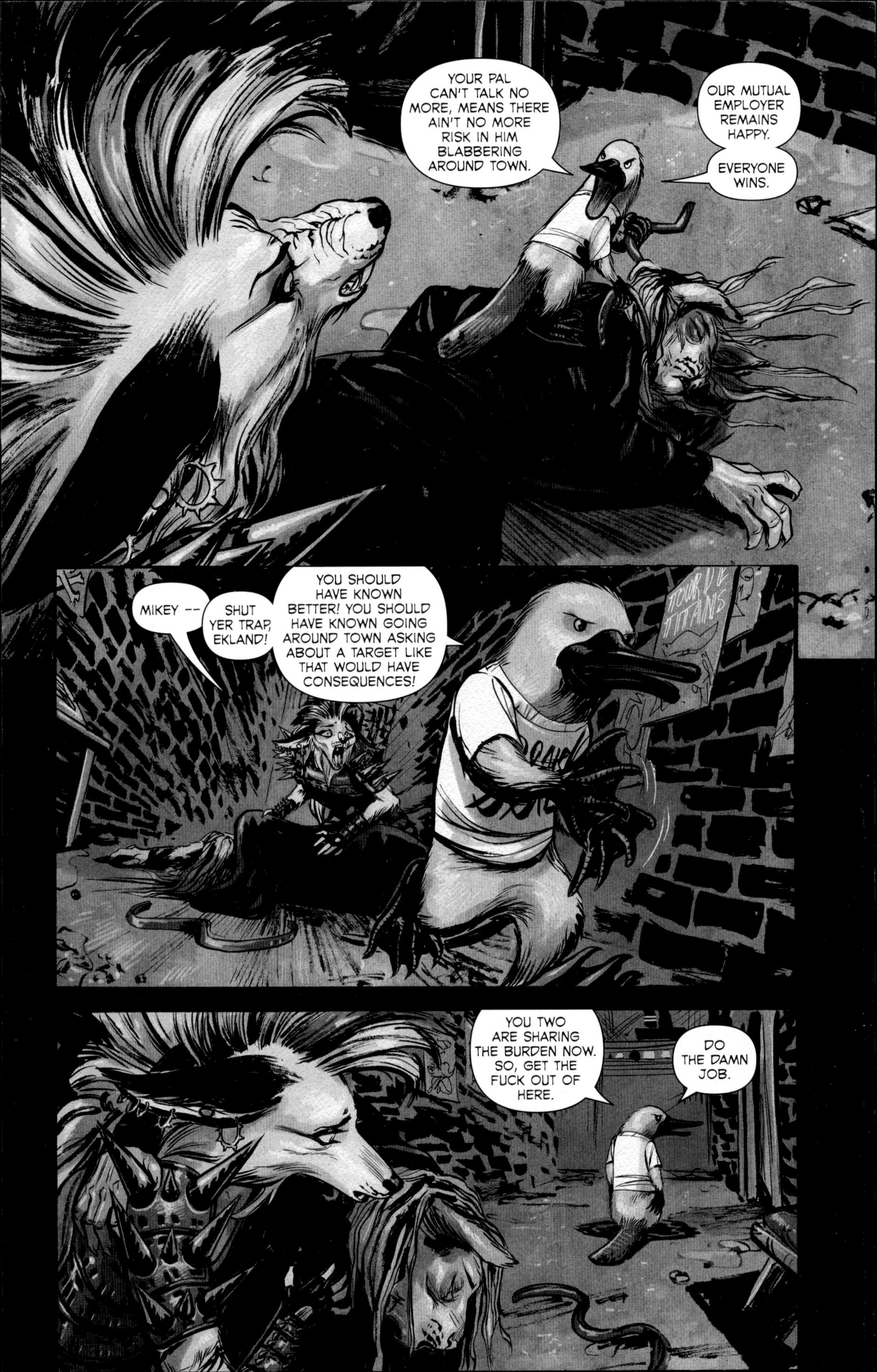
YOUR PAL CAN'T TALK NO MORE, MEANS THERE AIN'T NO MORE RISK IN HIM BLABBERING AROUND TOWN.
OUR MUTUAL EMPLOYER REMAINS HAPPY.
EVERYONE WINS.
MIKEY --
SHUT YER TRAP, EKLAND!
YOU SHOULD HAVE KNOWN BETTER! YOU SHOULD HAVE KNOWN GOING AROUND TOWN ASKING ABOUT A TARGET LIKE THAT WOULD HAVE CONSEQUENCES!
YOU TWO ARE SHARING THE BURDEN NOW. SO, GET THE FUCK OUT OF HERE.
DO THE DAMN JOB.

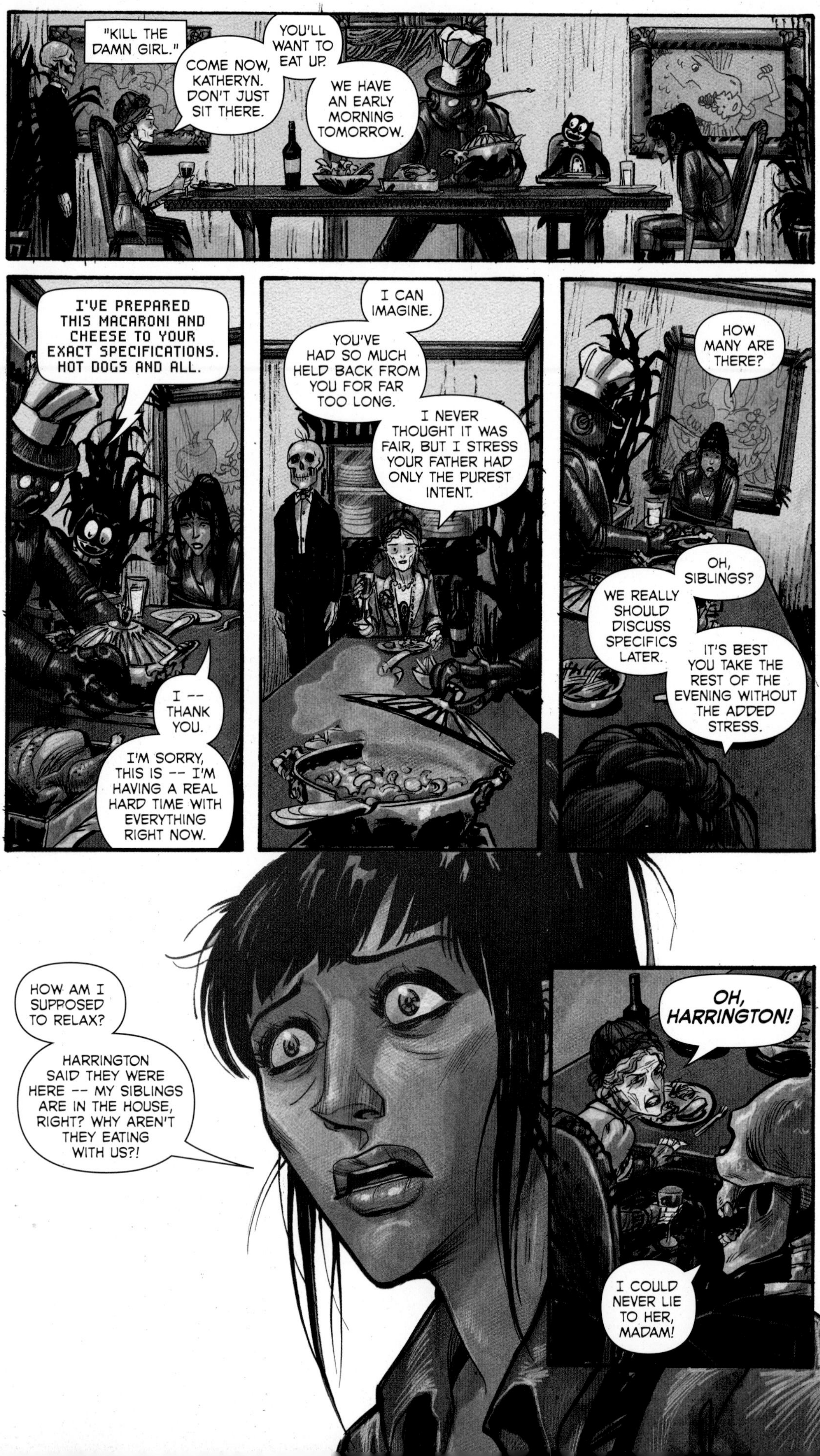
"KILL THE DAMN GIRL."
COME NOW, KATHERYN. DON'T JUST SIT THERE.
YOU'LL WANT TO EAT UP.
WE HAVE AN EARLY MORNING TOMORROW.
I'VE PREPARED THIS MACARONI AND CHEESE TO YOUR EXACT SPECIFICATIONS. HOT DOGS AND ALL.
I -- THANK YOU.
I'M SORRY, THIS IS -- I'M HAVING A REAL HARD TIME WITH EVERYTHING RIGHT NOW.
I CAN IMAGINE.
YOU'VE HAD SO MUCH HELD BACK FROM YOU FOR FAR TOO LONG.
I NEVER THOUGHT IT WAS FAIR, BUT I STRESS YOUR FATHER HAD ONLY THE PUREST INTENT.
HOW MANY ARE THERE?
OH, SIBLINGS?
WE REALLY SHOULD DISCUSS SPECIFICS LATER.
IT'S BEST YOU TAKE THE REST OF THE EVENING WITHOUT THE ADDED STRESS.
HOW AM I SUPPOSED TO RELAX?
HARRINGTON SAID THEY WERE HERE -- MY SIBLINGS ARE IN THE HOUSE, RIGHT? WHY AREN'T THEY EATING WITH US?!
OH, HARRINGTON!
I COULD NEVER LIE TO HER, MADAM!

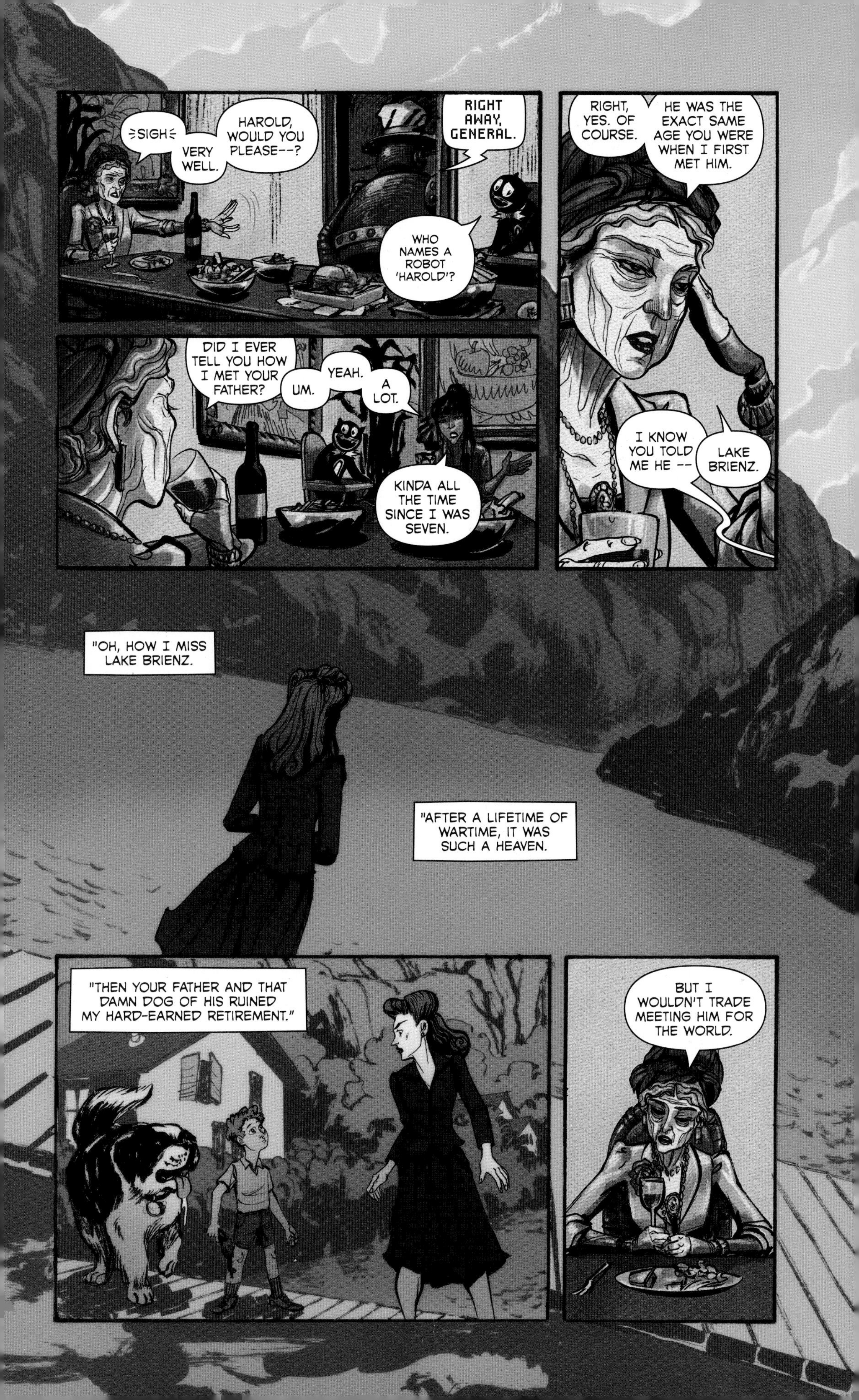
≈SIGH≈
VERY WELL.
HAROLD, WOULD YOU PLEASE--?
RIGHT AWAY, GENERAL.
WHO NAMES A ROBOT 'HAROLD'?
RIGHT, YES. OF COURSE.
HE WAS THE EXACT SAME AGE YOU WERE WHEN I FIRST MET HIM.
DID I EVER TELL YOU HOW I MET YOUR FATHER?
UM.
YEAH.
A LOT.
KINDA ALL THE TIME SINCE I WAS SEVEN.
I KNOW YOU TOLD ME HE --
LAKE BRIENZ.
"OH, HOW I MISS LAKE BRIENZ.
"AFTER A LIFETIME OF WARTIME, IT WAS SUCH A HEAVEN.
"THEN YOUR FATHER AND THAT DAMN DOG OF HIS RUINED MY HARD-EARNED RETIREMENT."
BUT I WOULDN'T TRADE MEETING HIM FOR THE WORLD.

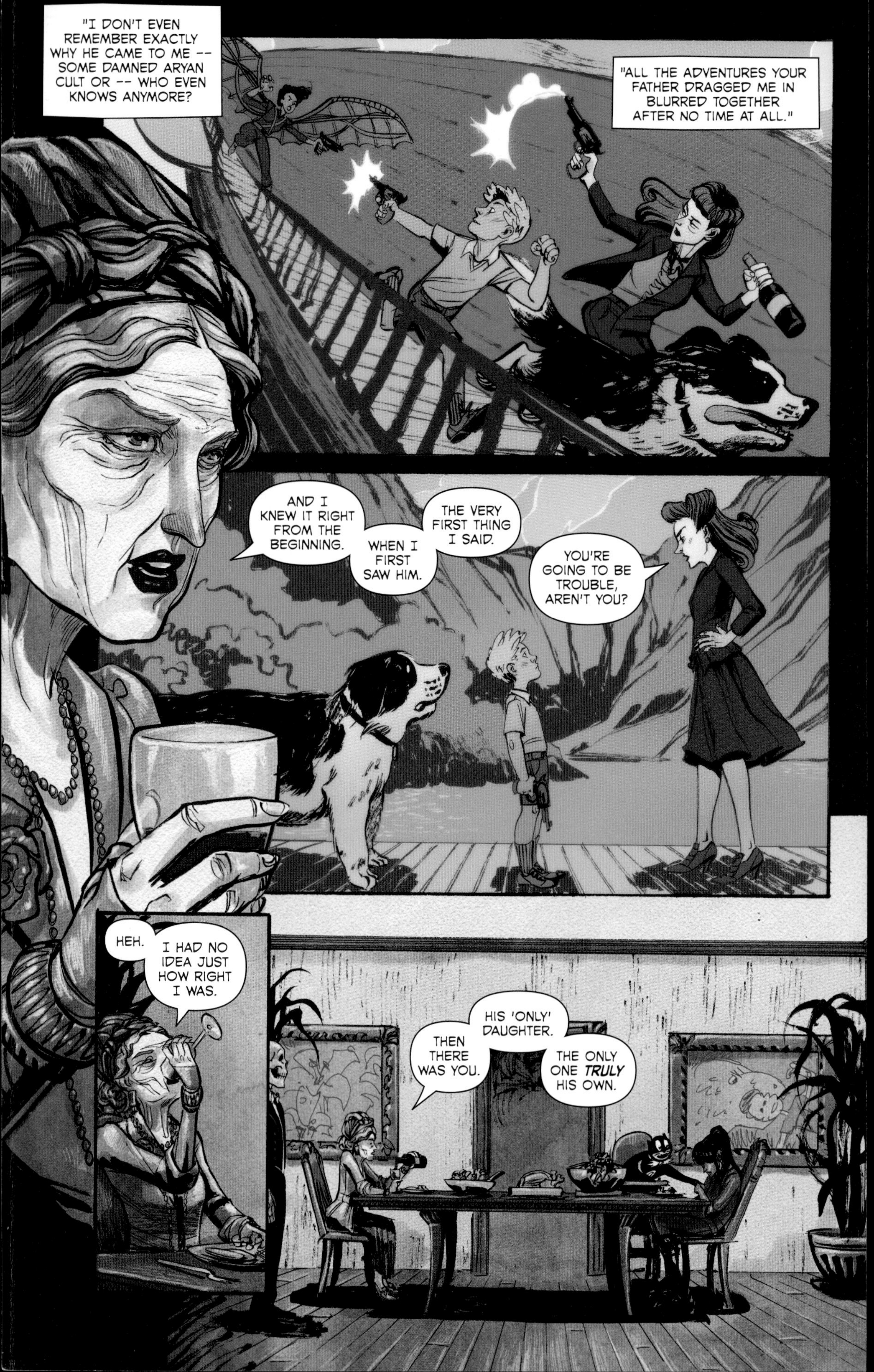
"I DON'T EVEN REMEMBER EXACTLY WHY HE CAME TO ME -- SOME DAMNED ARYAN CULT OR -- WHO EVEN KNOWS ANYMORE?
"ALL THE ADVENTURES YOUR FATHER DRAGGED ME IN BLURRED TOGETHER AFTER NO TIME AT ALL."
AND I KNEW IT RIGHT FROM THE BEGINNING.
WHEN I FIRST SAW HIM.
THE VERY FIRST THING I SAID.
YOU'RE GOING TO BE TROUBLE, AREN'T YOU?
HEH.
I HAD NO IDEA JUST HOW RIGHT I WAS.
THEN THERE WAS YOU.
HIS 'ONLY' DAUGHTER.
THE ONLY ONE TRULY HIS OWN.

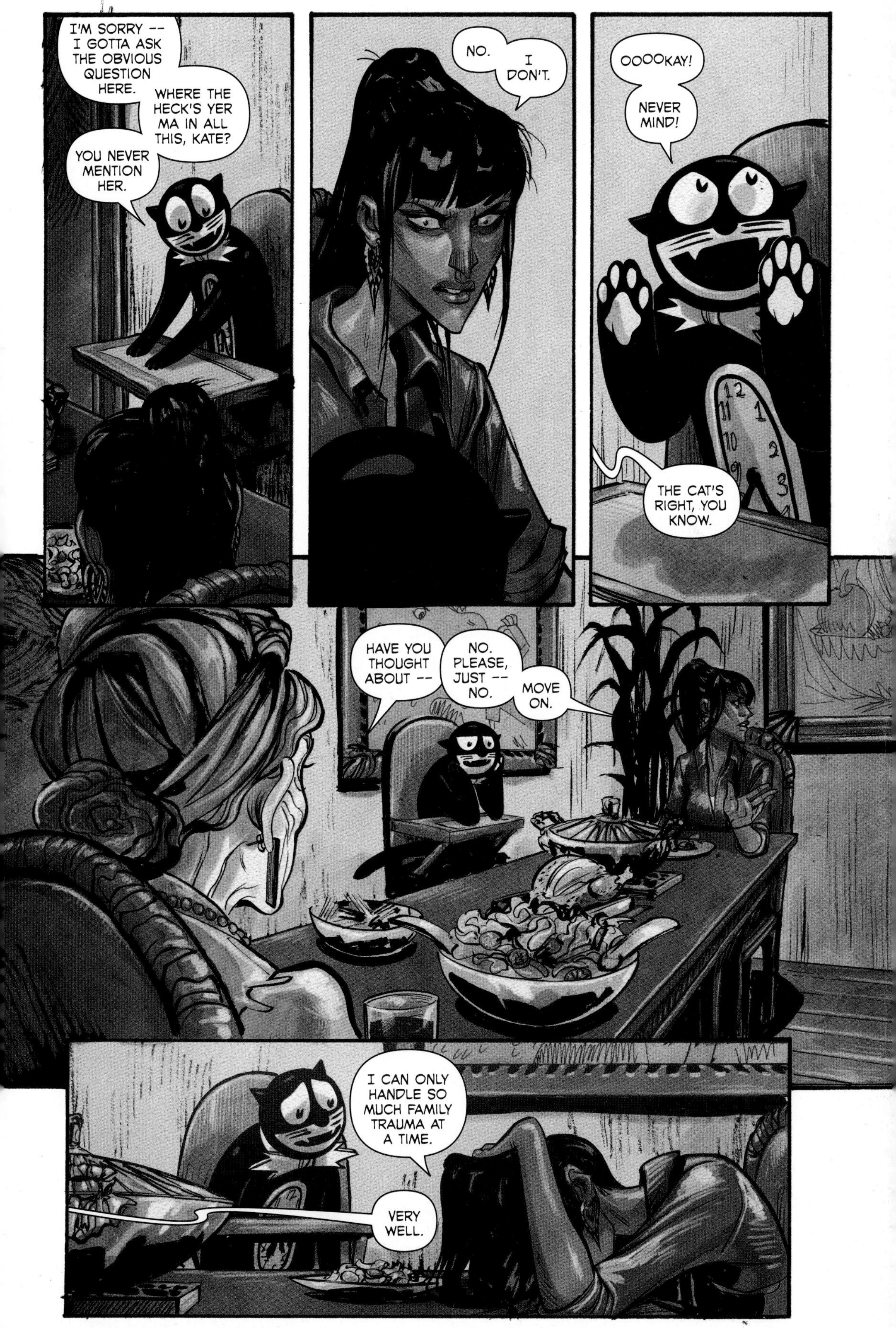
I'M SORRY -- I GOTTA ASK THE OBVIOUS QUESTION HERE.
WHERE THE HECK'S YER MA IN ALL THIS, KATE?
YOU NEVER MENTION HER.
NO.
I DON'T.
OOOOKAY!
NEVER MIND!
THE CAT'S RIGHT, YOU KNOW.
HAVE YOU THOUGHT ABOUT --
NO. PLEASE, JUST -- NO.
MOVE ON.
I CAN ONLY HANDLE SO MUCH FAMILY TRAUMA AT A TIME.
VERY WELL.

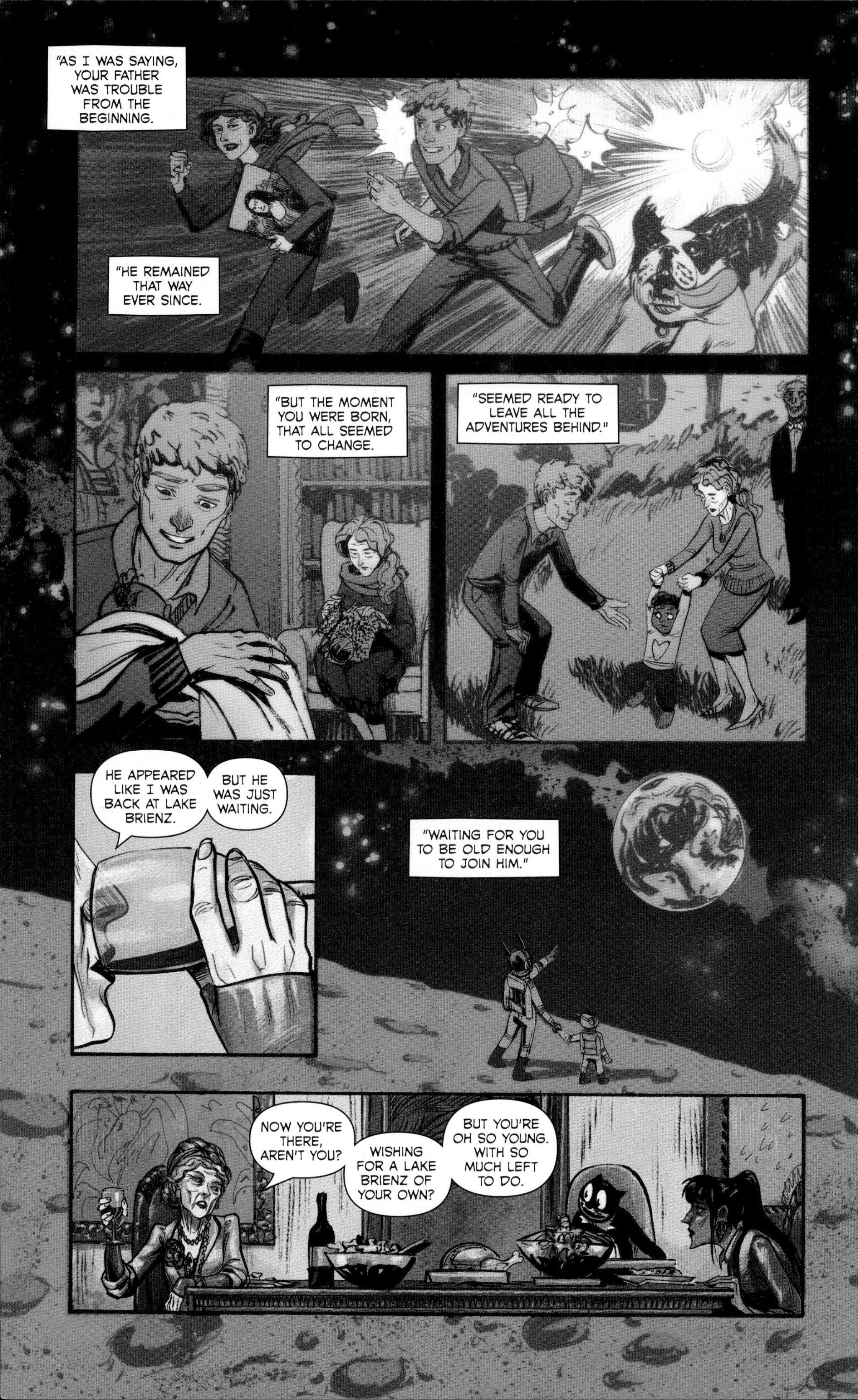
"AS I WAS SAYING, YOUR FATHER WAS TROUBLE FROM THE BEGINNING.
"HE REMAINED THAT WAY EVER SINCE.
"BUT THE MOMENT YOU WERE BORN, THAT ALL SEEMED TO CHANGE.
"SEEMED READY TO LEAVE ALL THE ADVENTURES BEHIND."
HE APPEARED LIKE I WAS BACK AT LAKE BRIENZ.
BUT HE WAS JUST WAITING.
"WAITING FOR YOU TO BE OLD ENOUGH TO JOIN HIM."
NOW YOU'RE THERE, AREN'T YOU?
WISHING FOR A LAKE BRIENZ OF YOUR OWN?
BUT YOU'RE OH SO YOUNG. WITH SO MUCH LEFT TO DO.

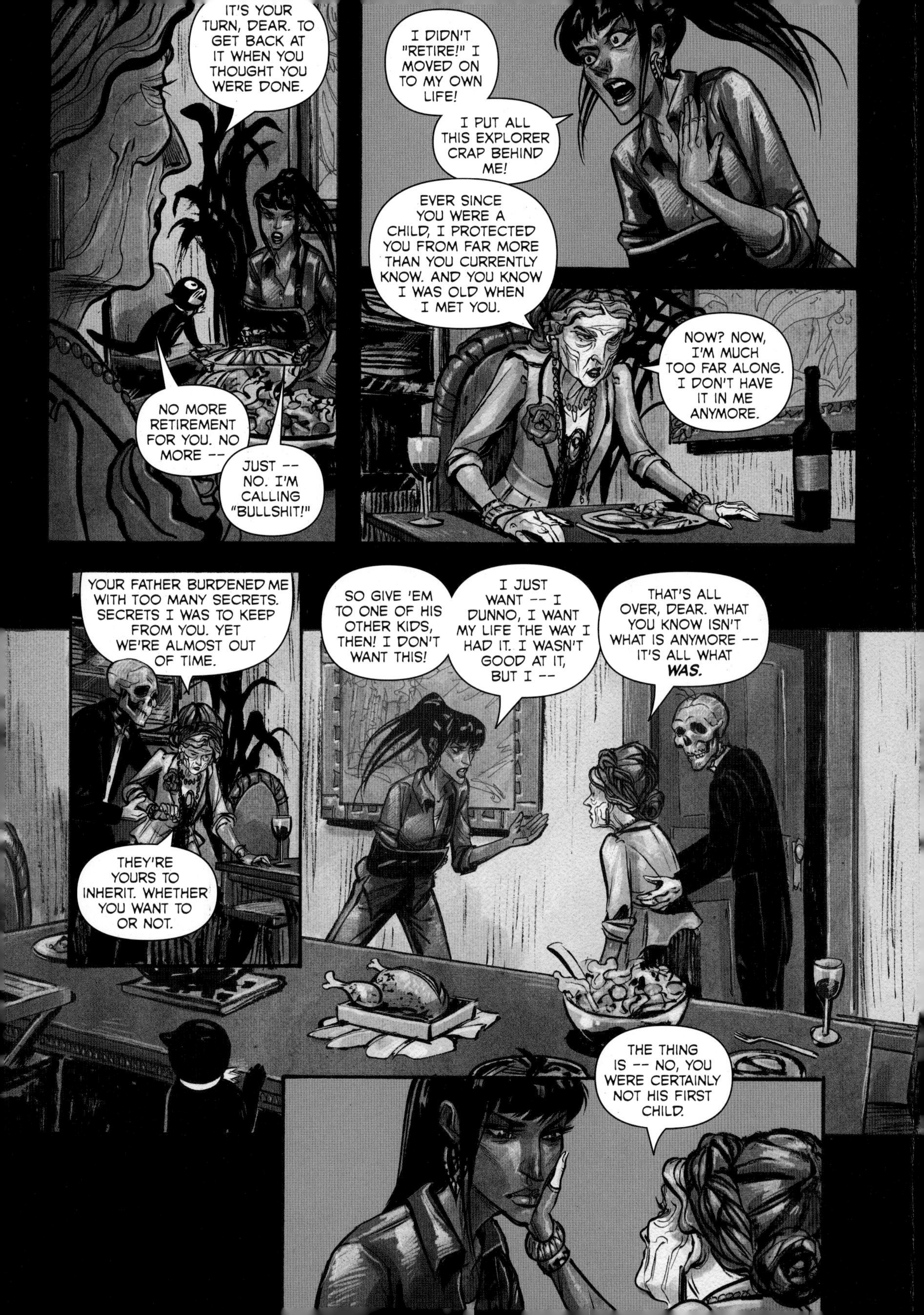
IT'S YOUR TURN, DEAR. TO GET BACK AT IT WHEN YOU THOUGHT YOU WERE DONE.
NO MORE RETIREMENT FOR YOU. NO MORE --
JUST -- NO. I'M CALLING "BULLSHIT!"
I DIDN'T "RETIRE!" I MOVED ON TO MY OWN LIFE!
I PUT ALL THIS EXPLORER CRAP BEHIND ME!
EVER SINCE YOU WERE A CHILD, I PROTECTED YOU FROM FAR MORE THAN YOU CURRENTLY KNOW. AND YOU KNOW I WAS OLD WHEN I MET YOU.
NOW? NOW, I'M MUCH TOO FAR ALONG. I DON'T HAVE IT IN ME ANYMORE.
YOUR FATHER BURDENED ME WITH TOO MANY SECRETS. SECRETS I WAS TO KEEP FROM YOU. YET WE'RE ALMOST OUT OF TIME.
THEY'RE YOURS TO INHERIT. WHETHER YOU WANT TO OR NOT.
SO GIVE 'EM TO ONE OF HIS OTHER KIDS, THEN! I DON'T WANT THIS!
I JUST WANT -- I DUNNO, I WANT MY LIFE THE WAY I HAD IT. I WASN'T GOOD AT IT, BUT I --
THAT'S ALL OVER, DEAR. WHAT YOU KNOW ISN'T WHAT IS ANYMORE -- IT'S ALL WHAT ***WAS.***
THE THING IS -- NO, YOU WERE CERTAINLY NOT HIS FIRST CHILD.

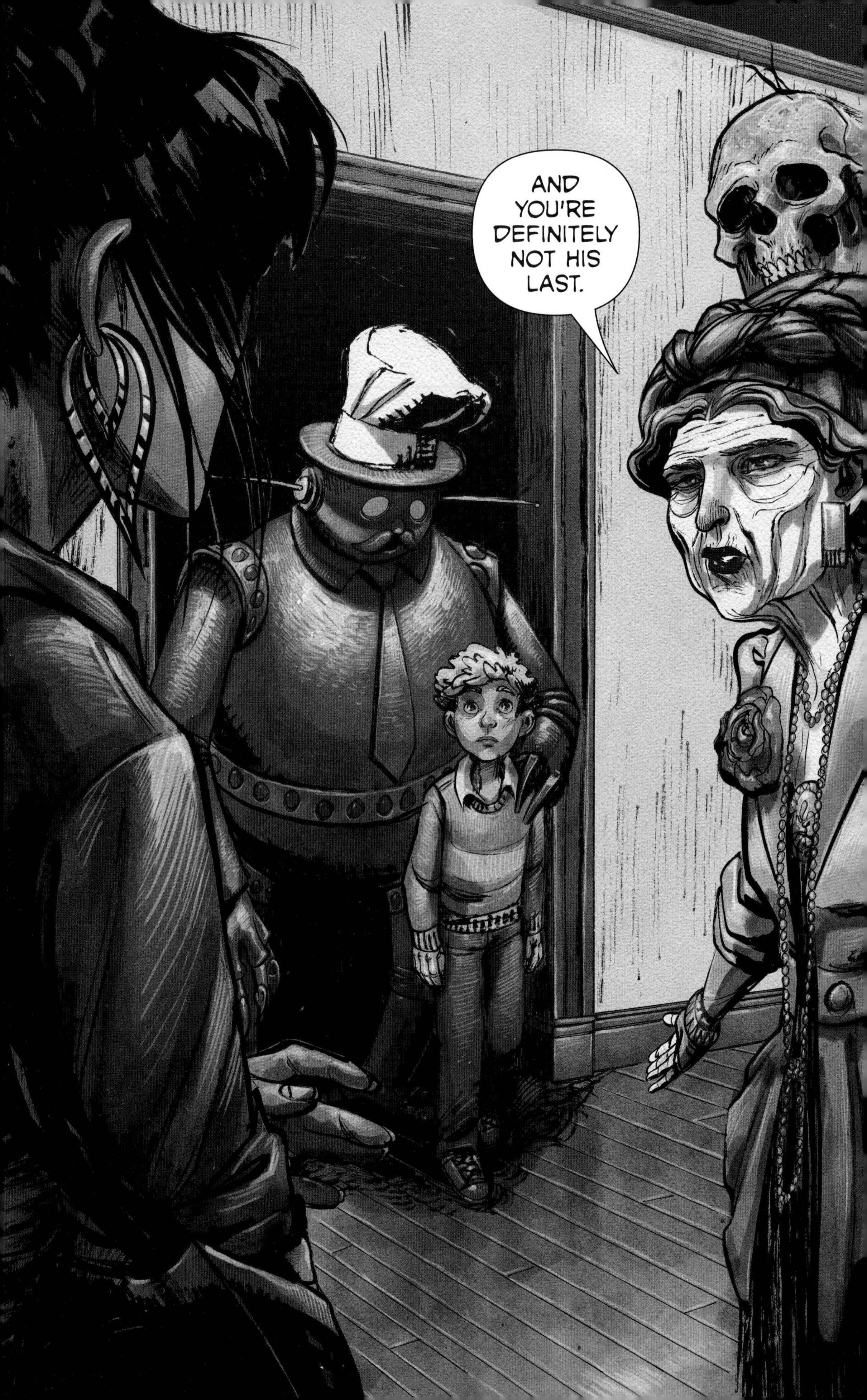
AND YOU'RE DEFINITELY NOT HIS LAST.

CHAPTER 5

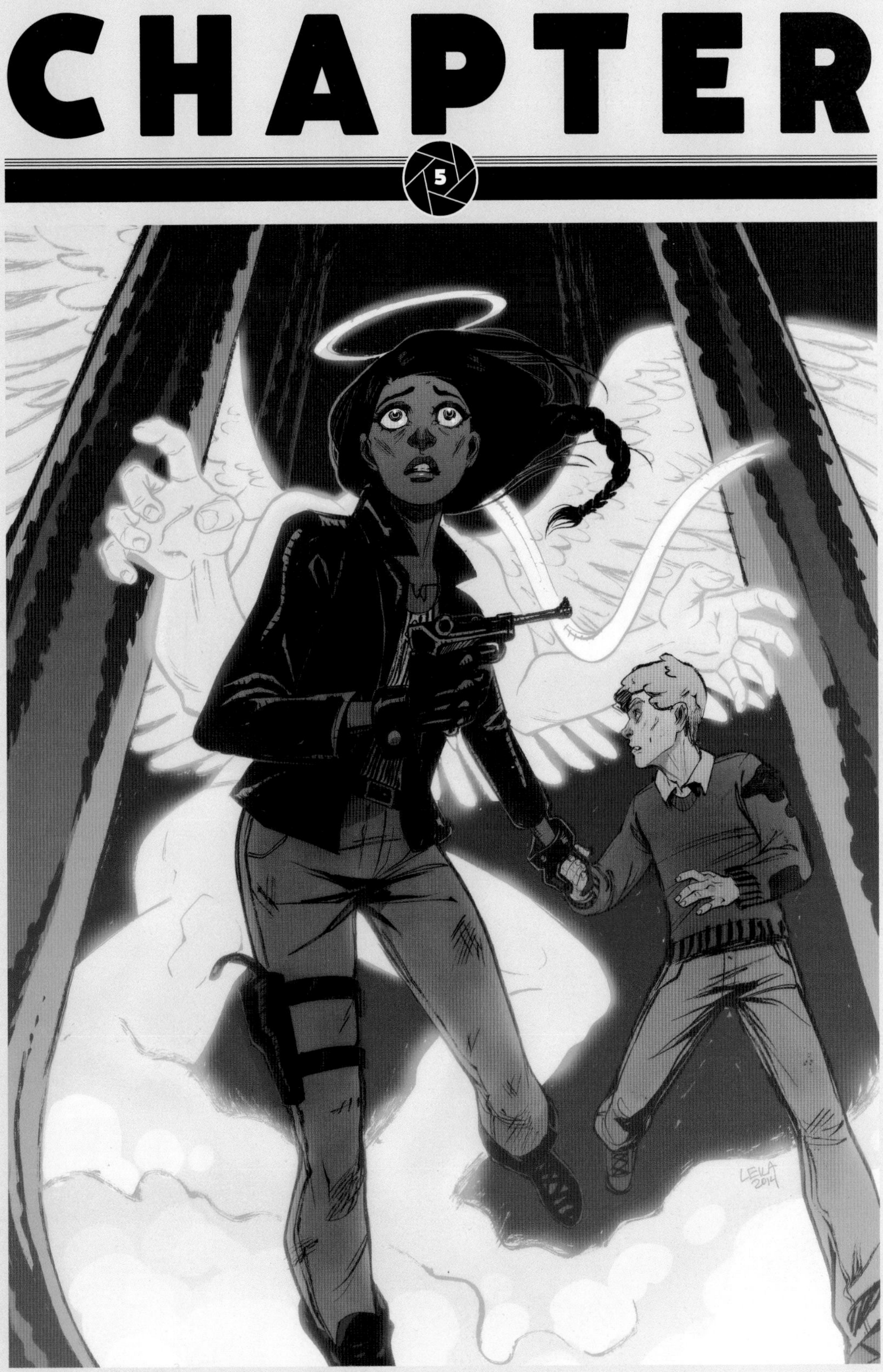

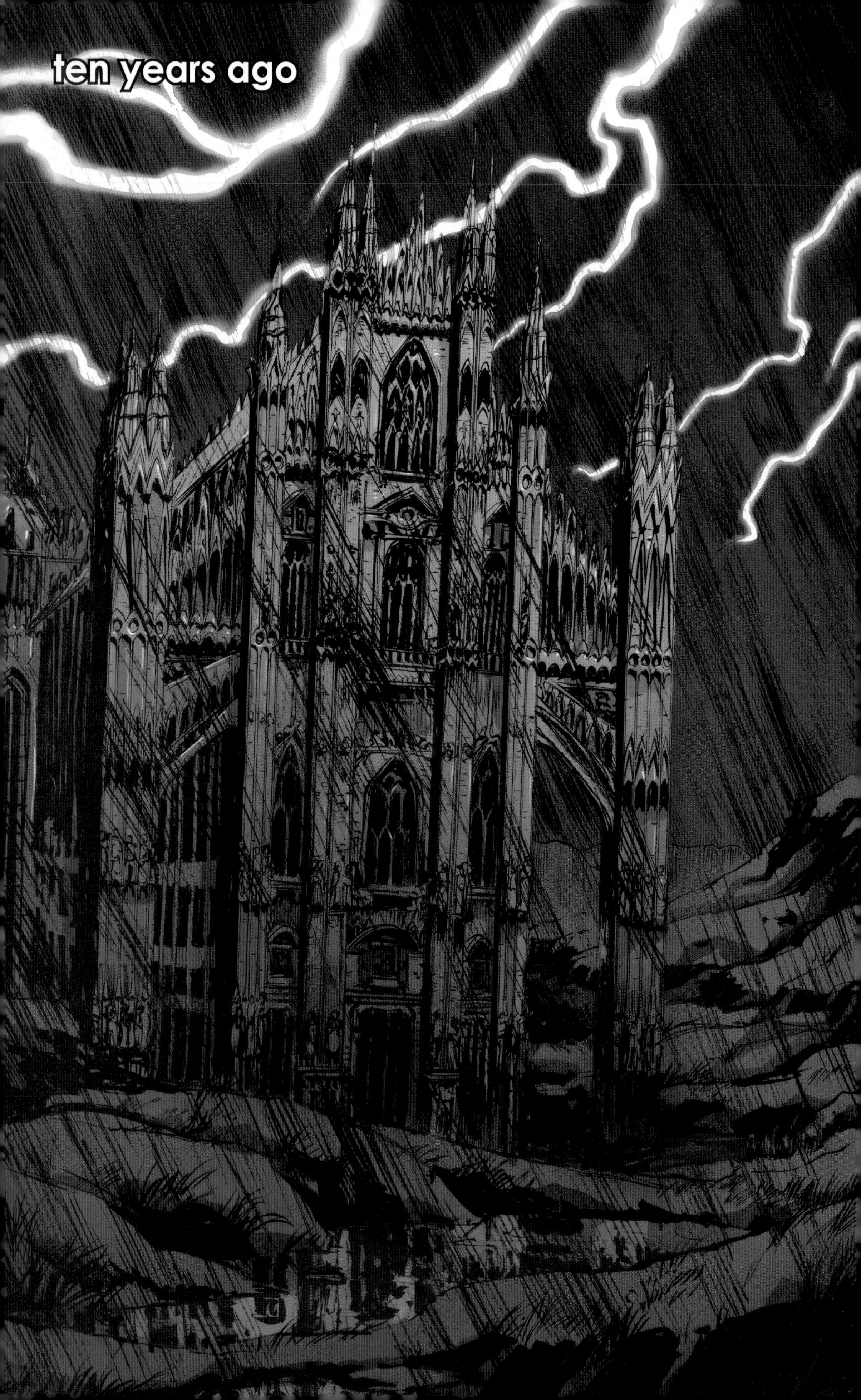
ten years ago

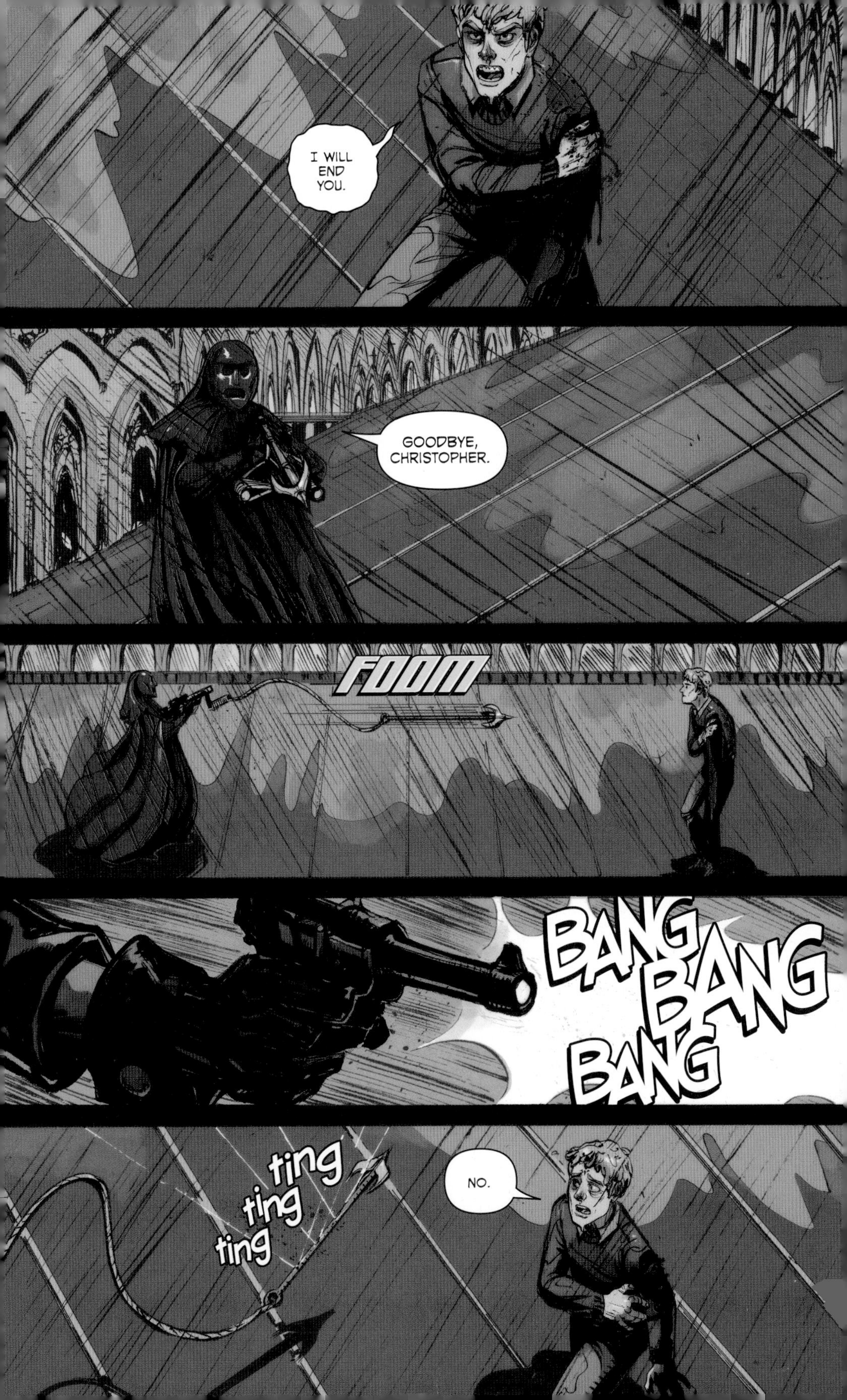
I WILL END YOU.
GOODBYE, CHRISTOPHER.
FOOM
BANG
BANG
BANG
ting
ting
ting
NO.

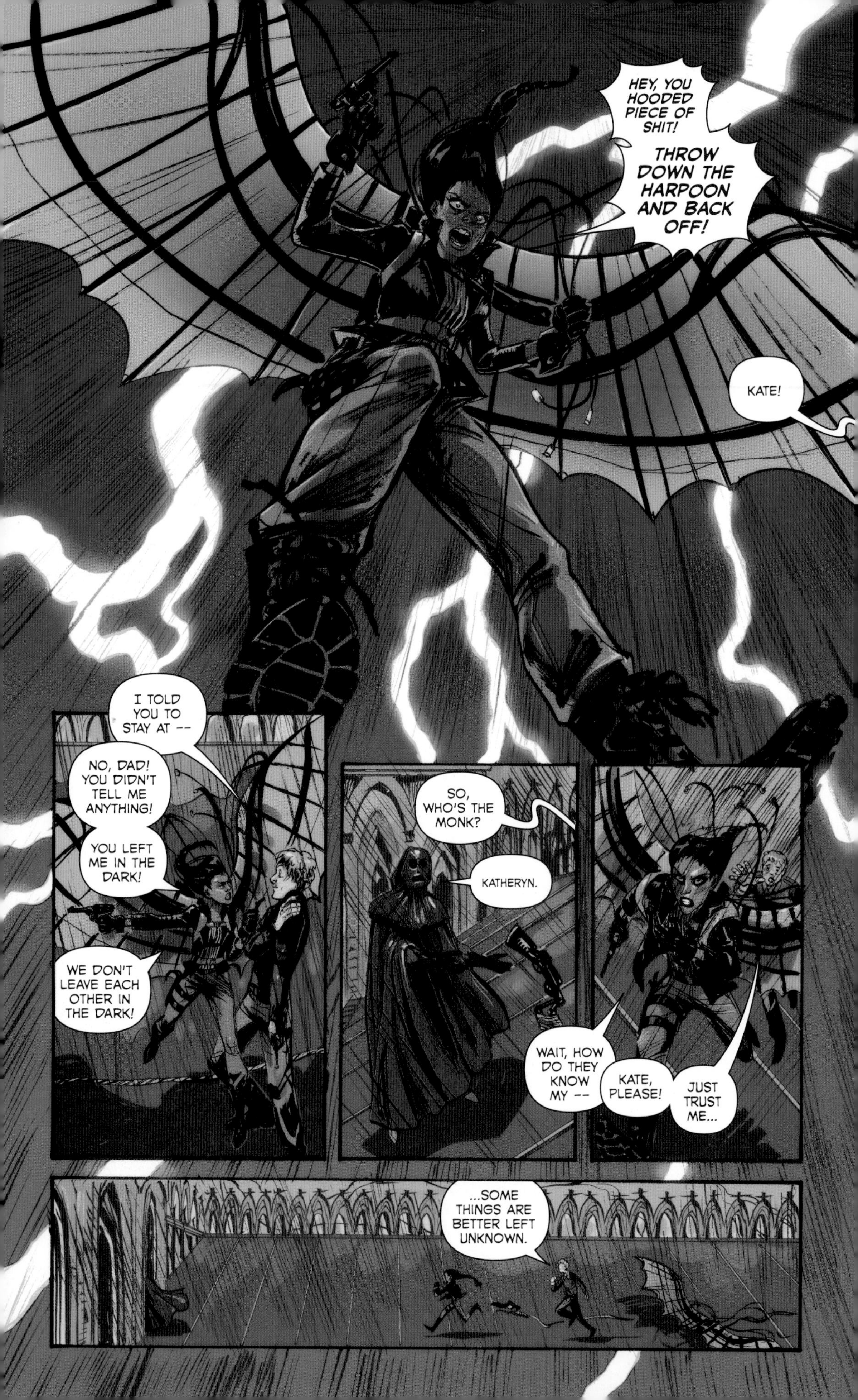
HEY, YOU HOODED PIECE OF SHIT!
THROW DOWN THE HARPOON AND BACK OFF!
KATE!
I TOLD YOU TO STAY AT --
NO, DAD! YOU DIDN'T TELL ME ANYTHING!
YOU LEFT ME IN THE DARK!
WE DON'T LEAVE EACH OTHER IN THE DARK!
SO, WHO'S THE MONK?
KATHERYN.
WAIT, HOW DO THEY KNOW MY --
KATE, PLEASE!
JUST TRUST ME...
...SOME THINGS ARE BETTER LEFT UNKNOWN.

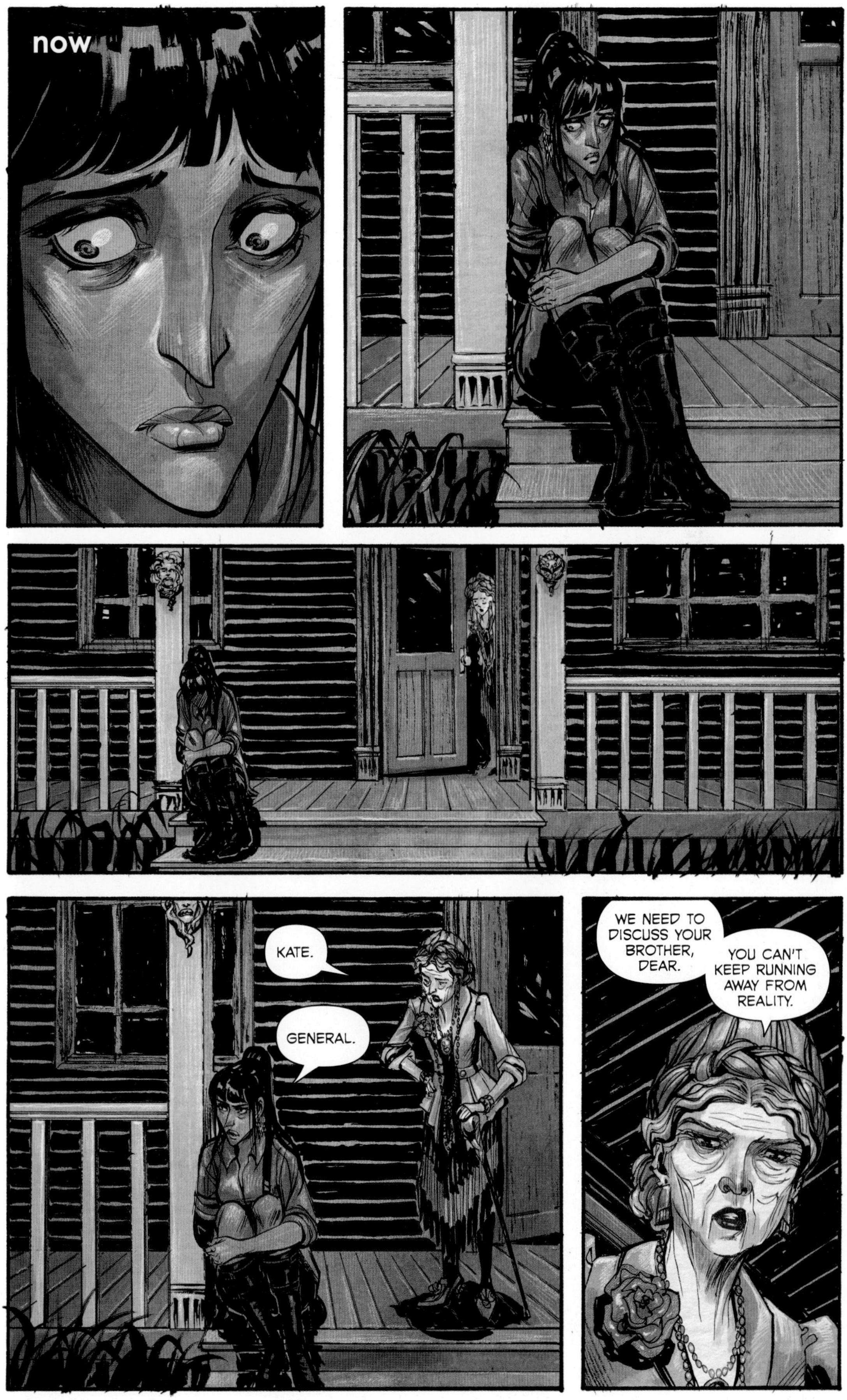
now
KATE.
GENERAL.
WE NEED TO DISCUSS YOUR BROTHER, DEAR.
YOU CAN'T KEEP RUNNING AWAY FROM REALITY.

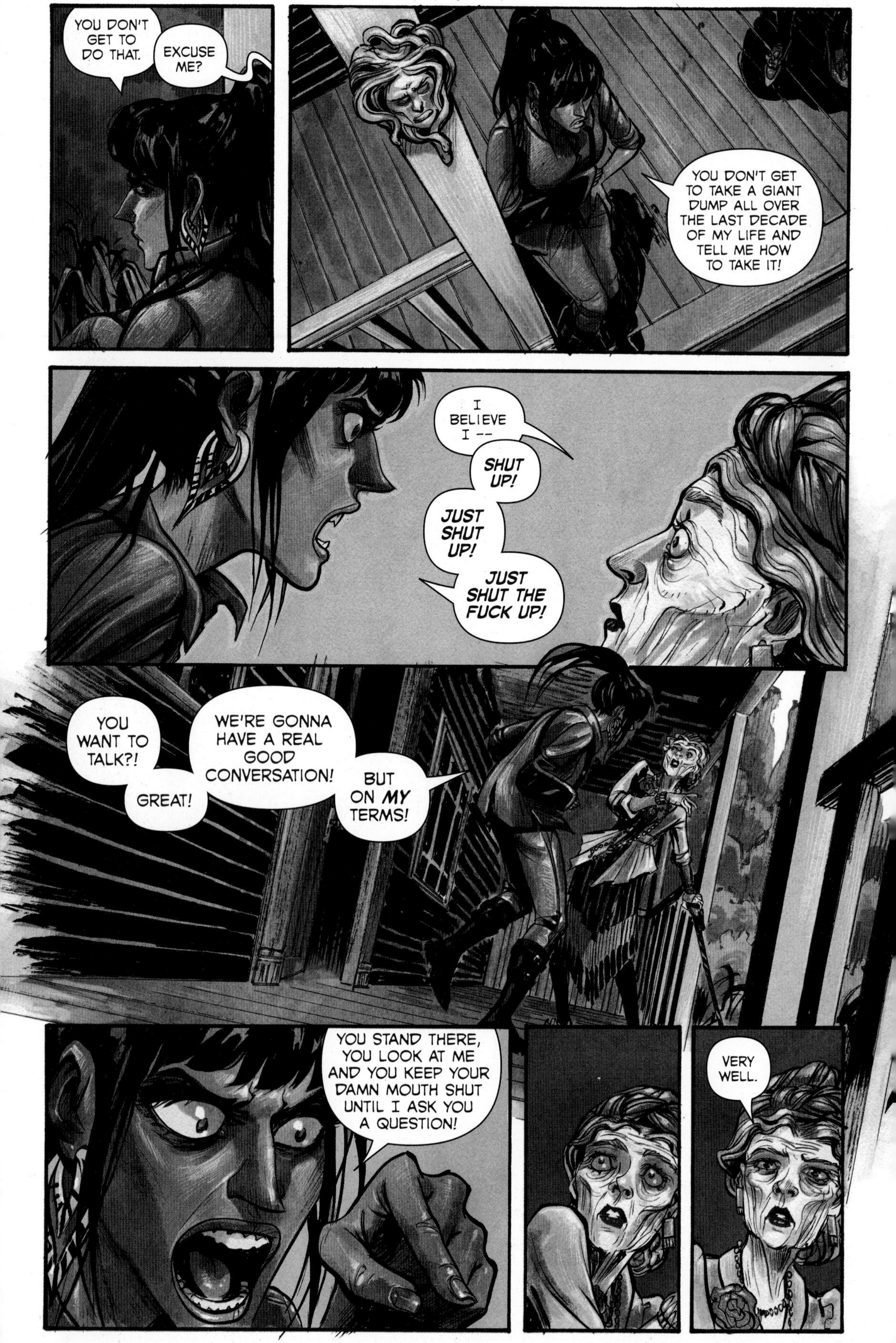
YOU DON'T GET TO DO THAT.
EXCUSE ME?
YOU DON'T GET TO TAKE A GIANT DUMP ALL OVER THE LAST DECADE OF MY LIFE AND TELL ME HOW TO TAKE IT!
I BELIEVE I --
SHUT UP!
JUST SHUT UP!
JUST SHUT THE FUCK UP!
YOU WANT TO TALK?!
GREAT!
WE'RE GONNA HAVE A REAL GOOD CONVERSATION!
BUT ON MY TERMS!
YOU STAND THERE, YOU LOOK AT ME AND YOU KEEP YOUR DAMN MOUTH SHUT UNTIL I ASK YOU A QUESTION!
VERY WELL.

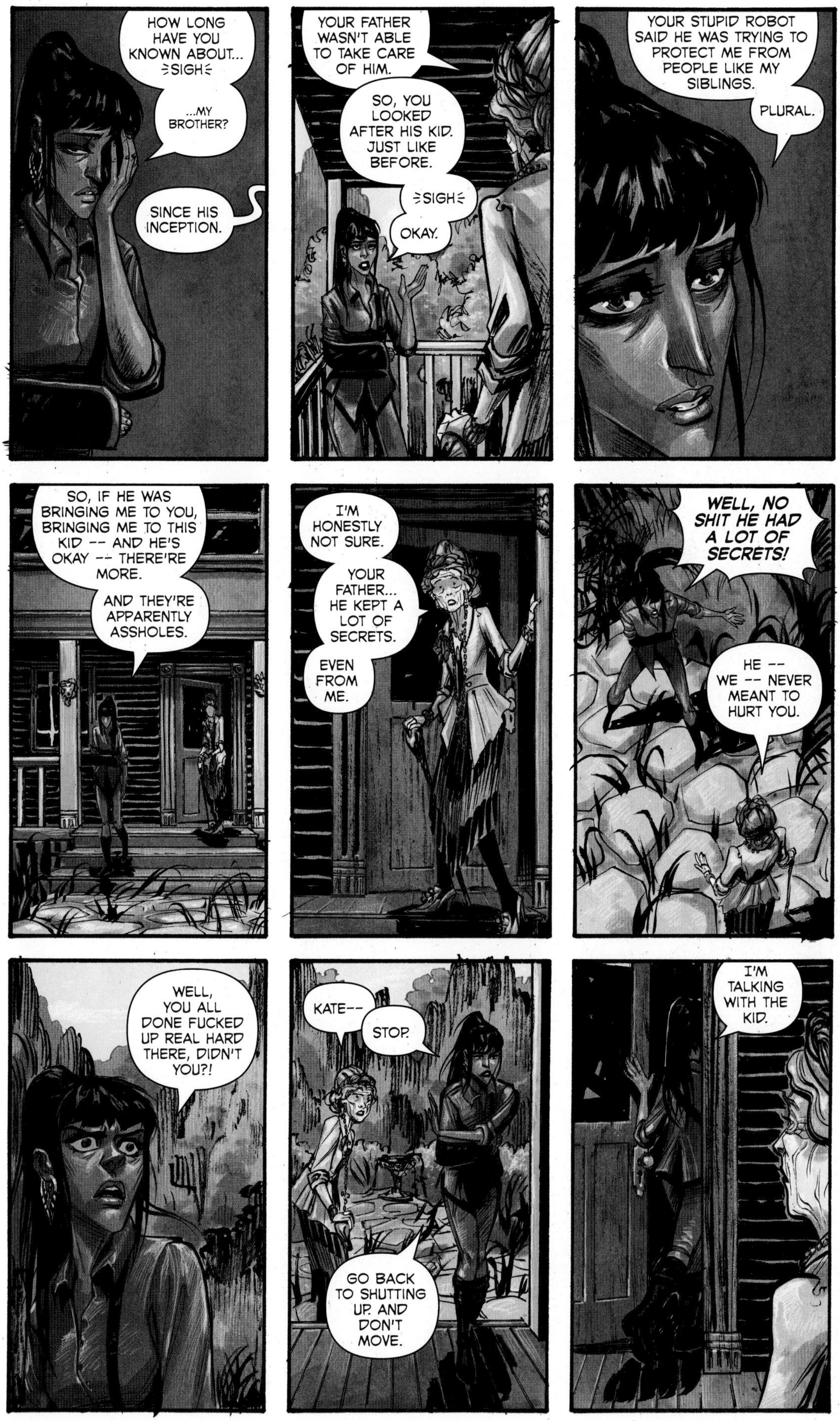
HOW LONG HAVE YOU KNOWN ABOUT... SIGH
...MY BROTHER?
SINCE HIS INCEPTION.
YOUR FATHER WASN'T ABLE TO TAKE CARE OF HIM.
SO, YOU LOOKED AFTER HIS KID. JUST LIKE BEFORE.
SIGH
OKAY.
YOUR STUPID ROBOT SAID HE WAS TRYING TO PROTECT ME FROM PEOPLE LIKE MY SIBLINGS.
PLURAL.
SO, IF HE WAS BRINGING ME TO YOU, BRINGING ME TO THIS KID -- AND HE'S OKAY -- THERE'RE MORE.
AND THEY'RE APPARENTLY ASSHOLES.
I'M HONESTLY NOT SURE.
YOUR FATHER... HE KEPT A LOT OF SECRETS.
EVEN FROM ME.
WELL, NO SHIT HE HAD A LOT OF SECRETS!
HE -- WE -- NEVER MEANT TO HURT YOU.
WELL, YOU ALL DONE FUCKED UP REAL HARD THERE, DIDN'T YOU?!
KATE--
STOP.
GO BACK TO SHUTTING UP. AND DON'T MOVE.
I'M TALKING WITH THE KID.

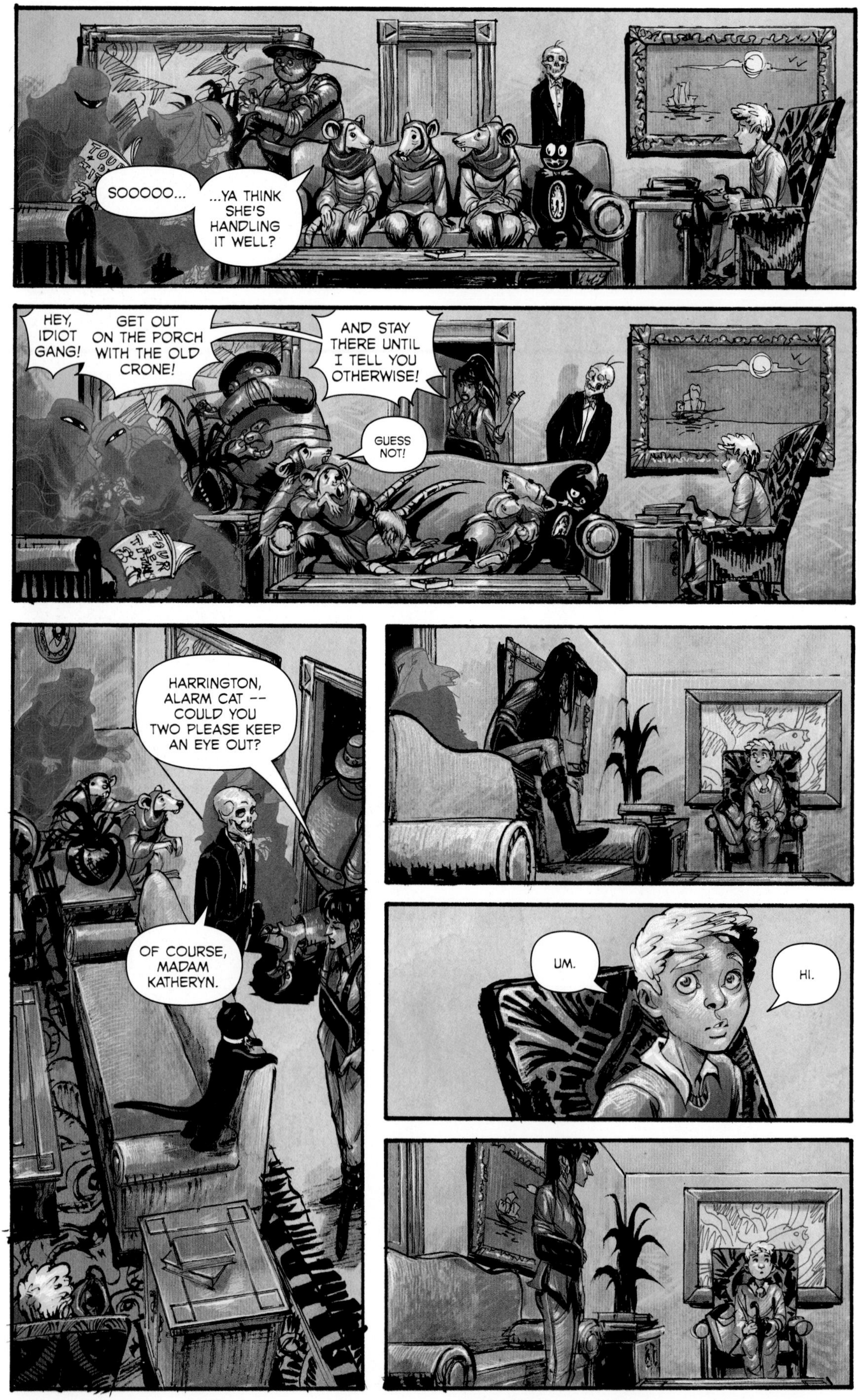
SOOOOO...
...YA THINK SHE'S HANDLING IT WELL?
HEY, IDIOT GANG!
GET OUT ON THE PORCH WITH THE OLD CRONE!
AND STAY THERE UNTIL I TELL YOU OTHERWISE!
GUESS NOT!
HARRINGTON, ALARM CAT -- COULD YOU TWO PLEASE KEEP AN EYE OUT?
OF COURSE, MADAM KATHERYN.
UM.
HI.

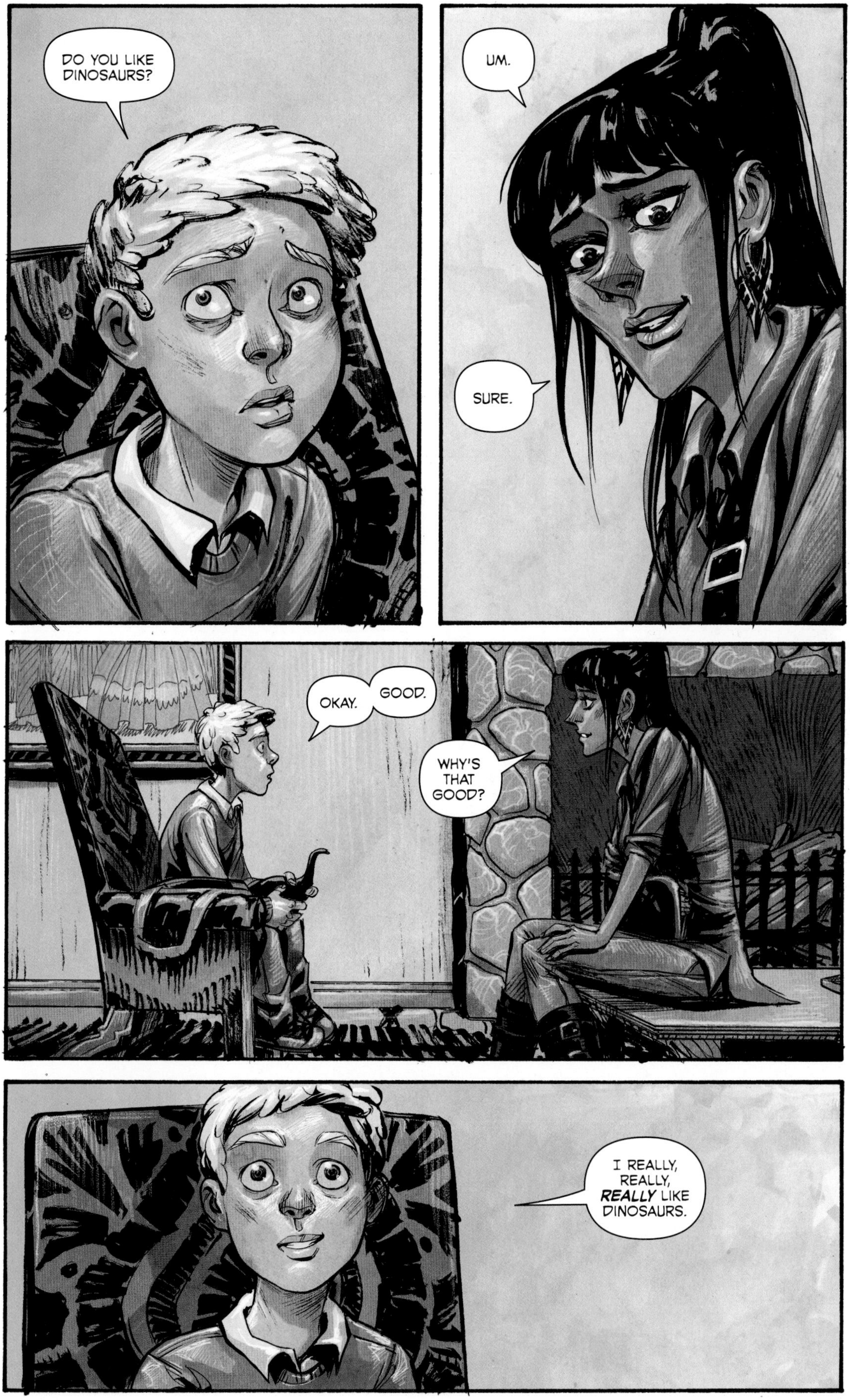
DO YOU LIKE DINOSAURS?
UM.
SURE.
OKAY.
GOOD.
WHY'S THAT GOOD?
I REALLY, REALLY, *REALLY* LIKE DINOSAURS.

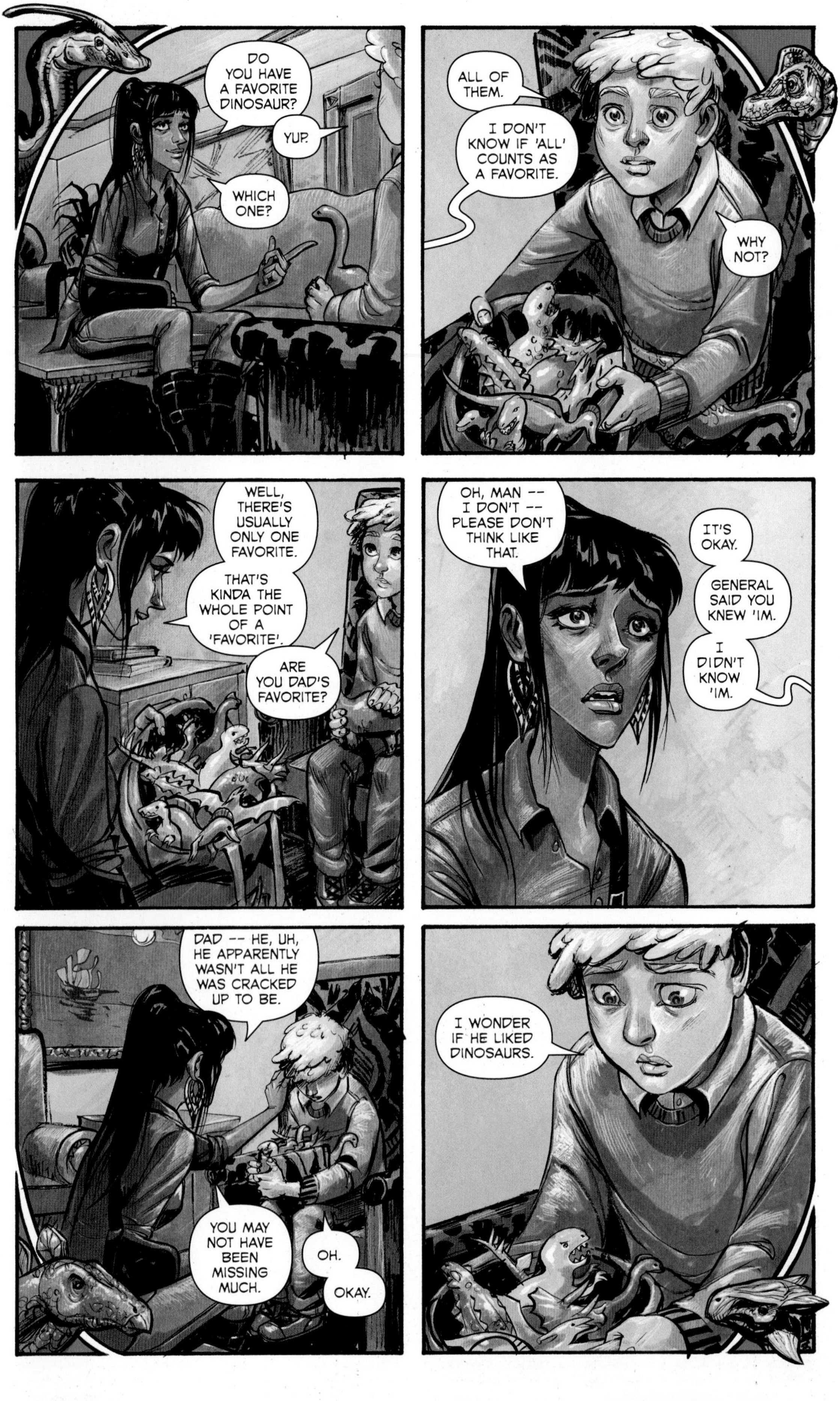
DO YOU HAVE A FAVORITE DINOSAUR?
YUP.
WHICH ONE?
ALL OF THEM.
I DON'T KNOW IF 'ALL' COUNTS AS A FAVORITE.
WHY NOT?
WELL, THERE'S USUALLY ONLY ONE FAVORITE.
THAT'S KINDA THE WHOLE POINT OF A 'FAVORITE'.
ARE YOU DAD'S FAVORITE?
OH, MAN -- I DON'T -- PLEASE DON'T THINK LIKE THAT.
IT'S OKAY.
GENERAL SAID YOU KNEW 'IM.
I DIDN'T KNOW 'IM.
DAD -- HE, UH, HE APPARENTLY WASN'T ALL HE WAS CRACKED UP TO BE.
YOU MAY NOT HAVE BEEN MISSING MUCH.
OH.
OKAY.
I WONDER IF HE LIKED DINOSAURS.

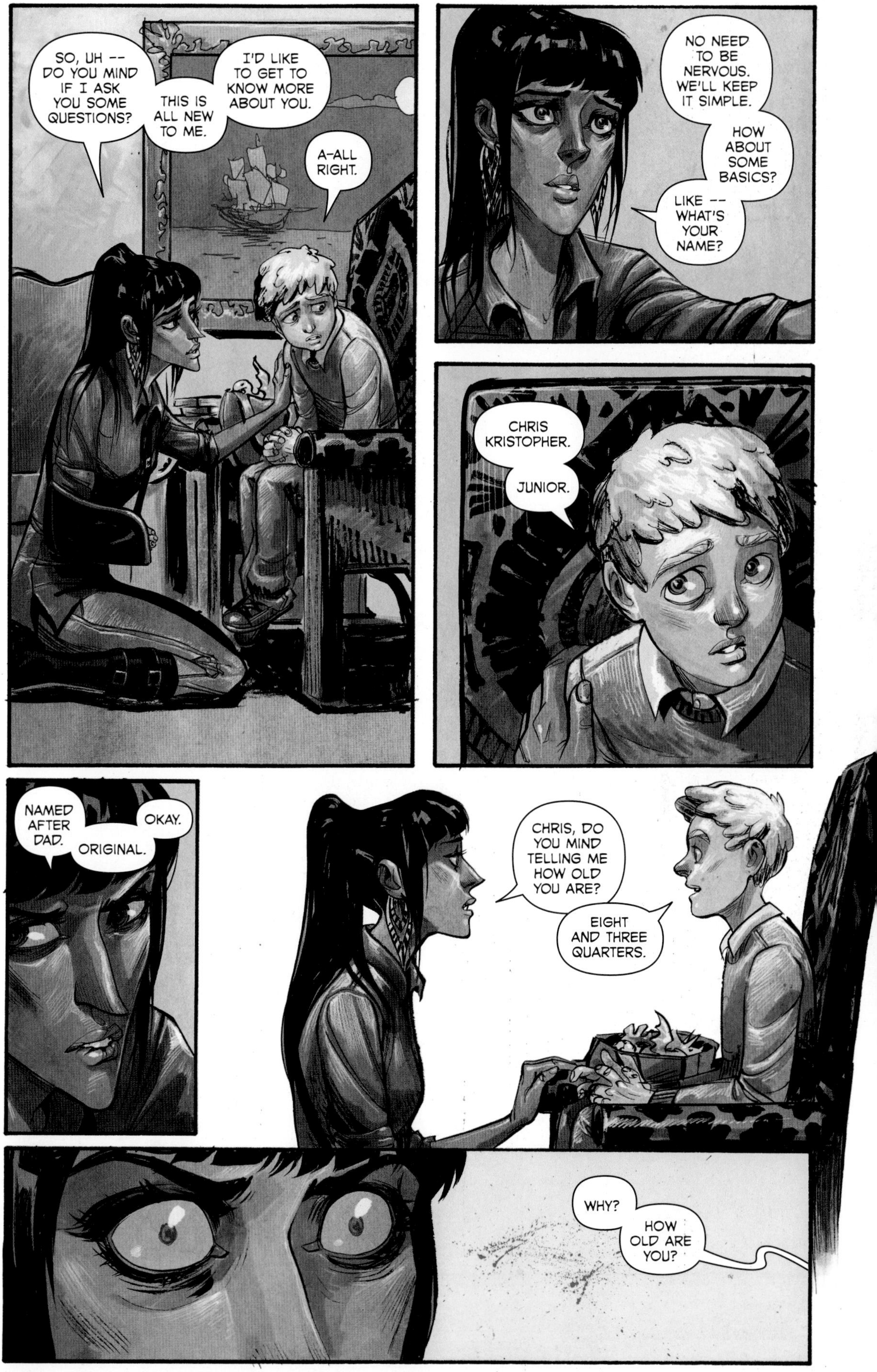
SO, UH -- DO YOU MIND IF I ASK YOU SOME QUESTIONS?
THIS IS ALL NEW TO ME.
I'D LIKE TO GET TO KNOW MORE ABOUT YOU.
A-ALL RIGHT.
NO NEED TO BE NERVOUS. WE'LL KEEP IT SIMPLE.
HOW ABOUT SOME BASICS?
LIKE -- WHAT'S YOUR NAME?
CHRIS KRISTOPHER.
JUNIOR.
NAMED AFTER DAD.
ORIGINAL.
OKAY.
CHRIS, DO YOU MIND TELLING ME HOW OLD YOU ARE?
EIGHT AND THREE QUARTERS.
WHY?
HOW OLD ARE YOU?

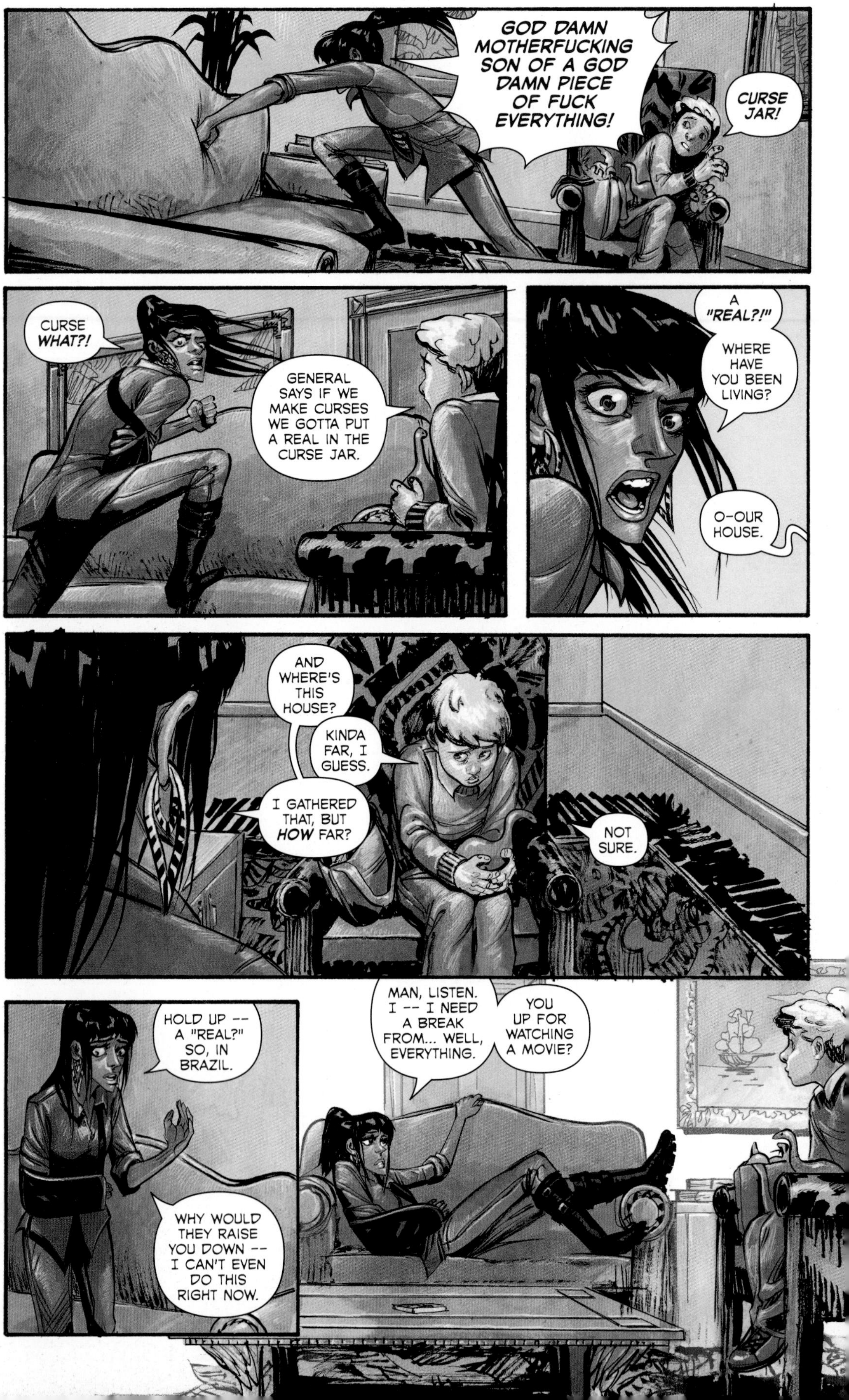
GOD DAMN MOTHERFUCKING SON OF A GOD DAMN PIECE OF FUCK EVERYTHING!
CURSE JAR!
CURSE *WHAT?!*
GENERAL SAYS IF WE MAKE CURSES WE GOTTA PUT A REAL IN THE CURSE JAR.
A *"REAL?!"*
WHERE HAVE YOU BEEN LIVING?
O-OUR HOUSE.
AND WHERE'S THIS HOUSE?
KINDA FAR, I GUESS.
I GATHERED THAT, BUT *HOW* FAR?
NOT SURE.
HOLD UP -- A "REAL?" SO, IN BRAZIL.
WHY WOULD THEY RAISE YOU DOWN -- I CAN'T EVEN DO THIS RIGHT NOW.
MAN, LISTEN. I -- I NEED A BREAK FROM... WELL, EVERYTHING.
YOU UP FOR WATCHING A MOVIE?

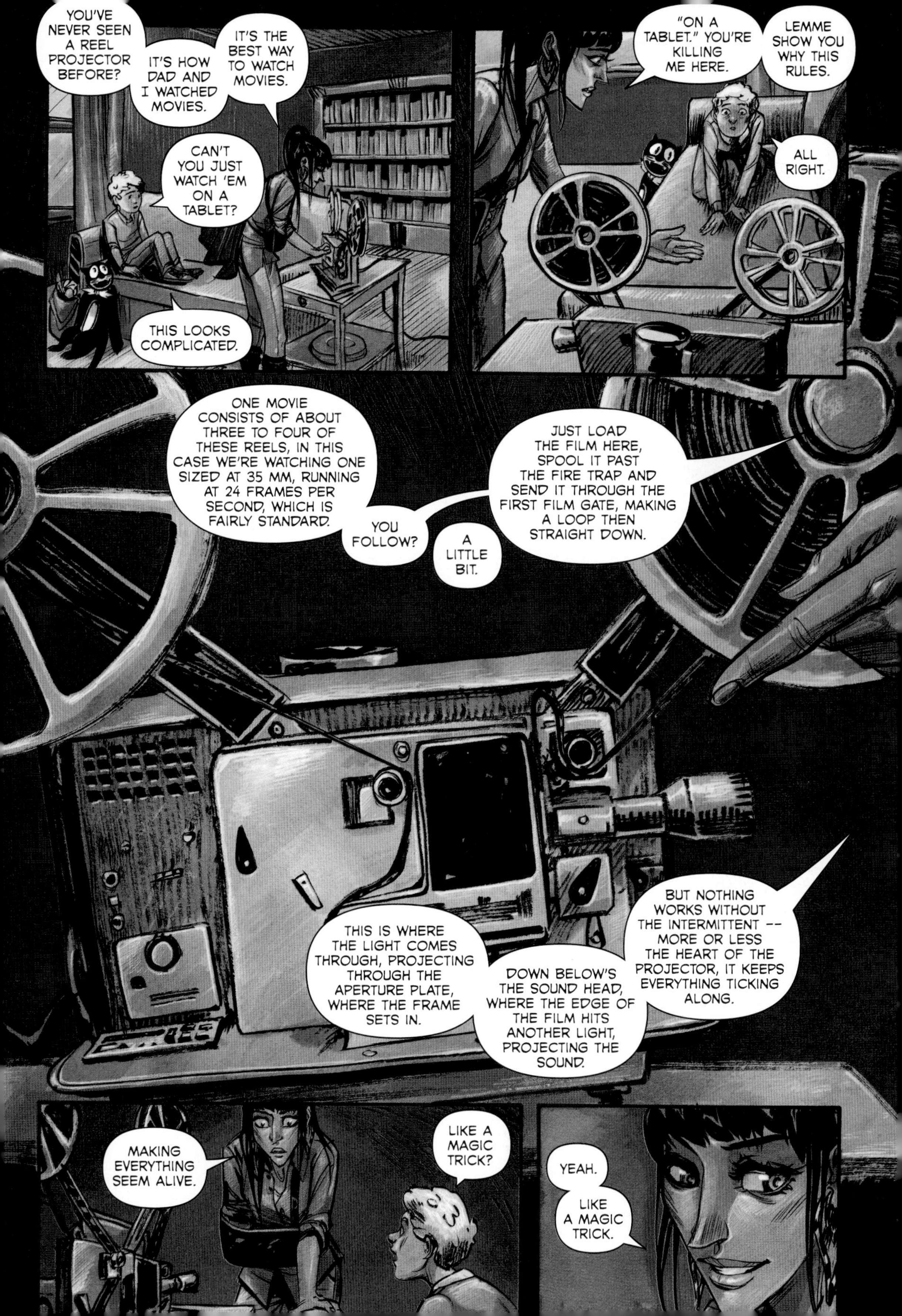
YOU'VE NEVER SEEN A REEL PROJECTOR BEFORE?
IT'S HOW DAD AND I WATCHED MOVIES.
IT'S THE BEST WAY TO WATCH MOVIES.
CAN'T YOU JUST WATCH 'EM ON A TABLET?
THIS LOOKS COMPLICATED.
"ON A TABLET." YOU'RE KILLING ME HERE.
LEMME SHOW YOU WHY THIS RULES.
ALL RIGHT.
ONE MOVIE CONSISTS OF ABOUT THREE TO FOUR OF THESE REELS, IN THIS CASE WE'RE WATCHING ONE SIZED AT 35 MM, RUNNING AT 24 FRAMES PER SECOND, WHICH IS FAIRLY STANDARD.
YOU FOLLOW?
A LITTLE BIT.
JUST LOAD THE FILM HERE, SPOOL IT PAST THE FIRE TRAP AND SEND IT THROUGH THE FIRST FILM GATE, MAKING A LOOP THEN STRAIGHT DOWN.
THIS IS WHERE THE LIGHT COMES THROUGH, PROJECTING THROUGH THE APERTURE PLATE, WHERE THE FRAME SETS IN.
DOWN BELOW'S THE SOUND HEAD, WHERE THE EDGE OF THE FILM HITS ANOTHER LIGHT, PROJECTING THE SOUND.
BUT NOTHING WORKS WITHOUT THE INTERMITTENT -- MORE OR LESS THE HEART OF THE PROJECTOR, IT KEEPS EVERYTHING TICKING ALONG.
MAKING EVERYTHING SEEM ALIVE.
LIKE A MAGIC TRICK?
YEAH.
LIKE A MAGIC TRICK.

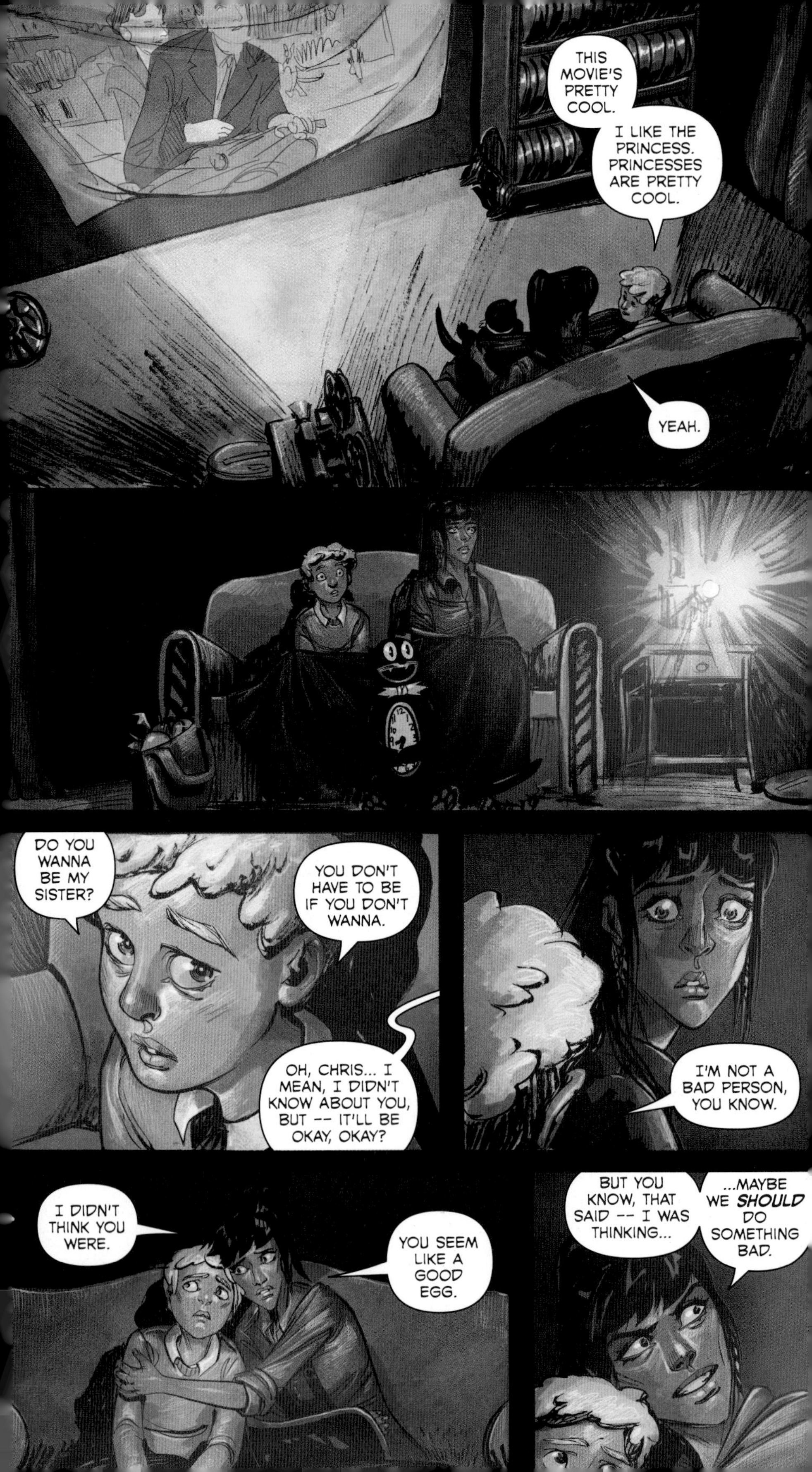
THIS MOVIE'S PRETTY COOL.
I LIKE THE PRINCESS. PRINCESSES ARE PRETTY COOL.
YEAH.
DO YOU WANNA BE MY SISTER?
YOU DON'T HAVE TO BE IF YOU DON'T WANNA.
OH, CHRIS... I MEAN, I DIDN'T KNOW ABOUT YOU, BUT -- IT'LL BE OKAY, OKAY?
I'M NOT A BAD PERSON, YOU KNOW.
I DIDN'T THINK YOU WERE.
YOU SEEM LIKE A GOOD EGG.
BUT YOU KNOW, THAT SAID -- I WAS THINKING...
...MAYBE WE *SHOULD* DO SOMETHING BAD.

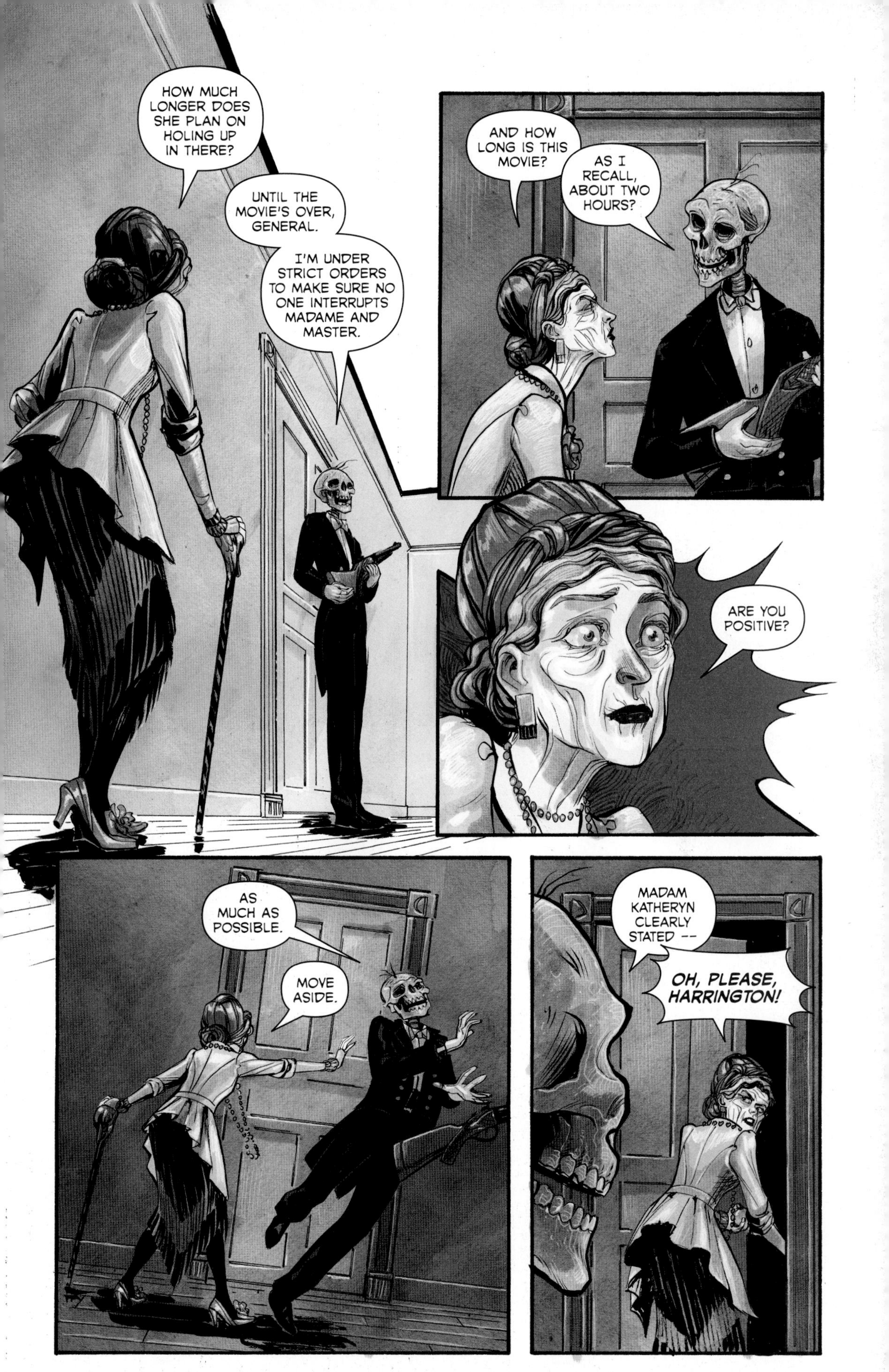
HOW MUCH LONGER DOES SHE PLAN ON HOLING UP IN THERE?
UNTIL THE MOVIE'S OVER, GENERAL.
I'M UNDER STRICT ORDERS TO MAKE SURE NO ONE INTERRUPTS MADAME AND MASTER.
AND HOW LONG IS THIS MOVIE?
AS I RECALL, ABOUT TWO HOURS?
ARE YOU POSITIVE?
AS MUCH AS POSSIBLE.
MOVE ASIDE.
MADAM KATHERYN CLEARLY STATED --
OH, PLEASE, HARRINGTON!

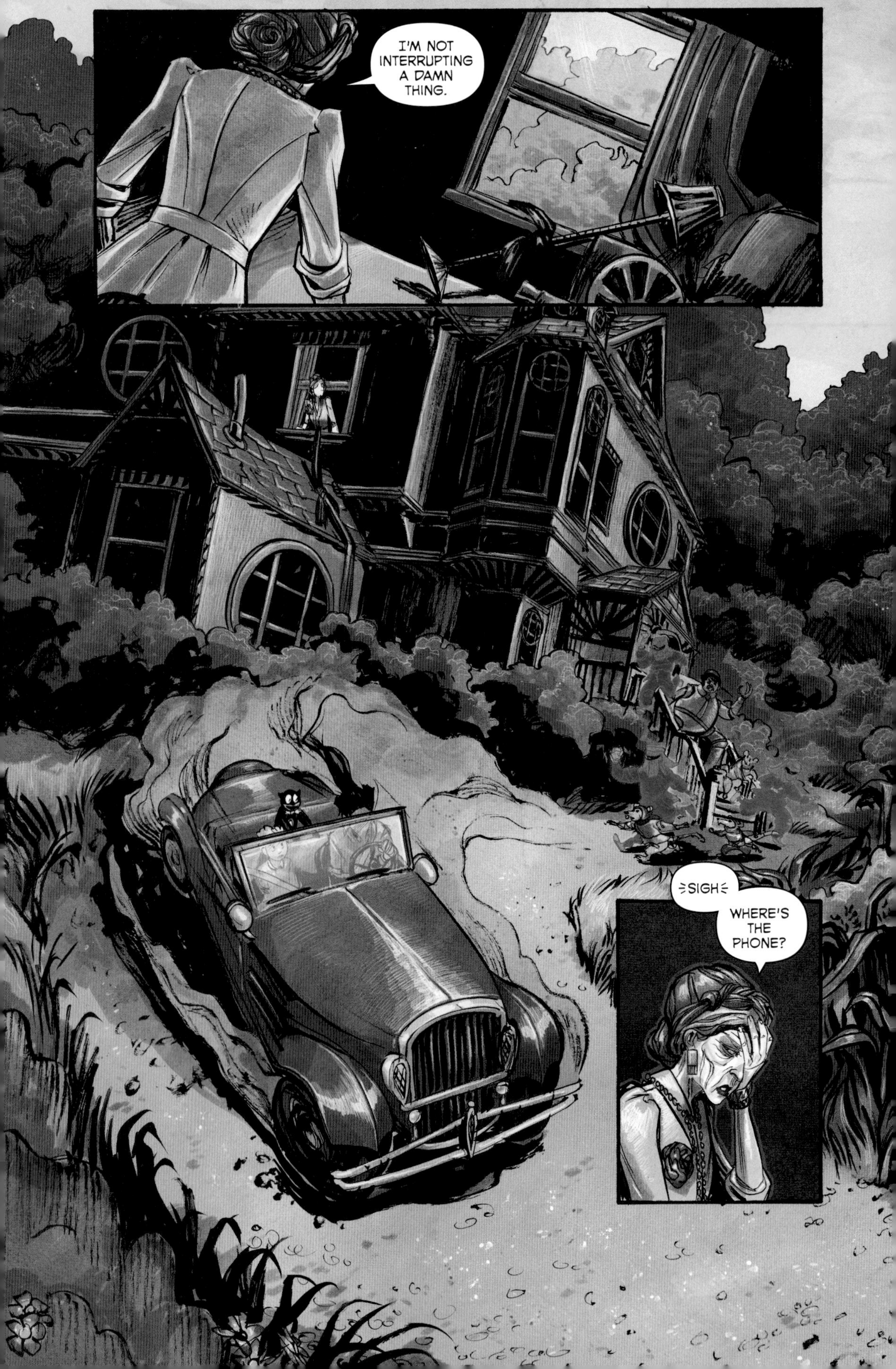
I'M NOT INTERRUPTING A DAMN THING.
≡SIGH≡
WHERE'S THE PHONE?

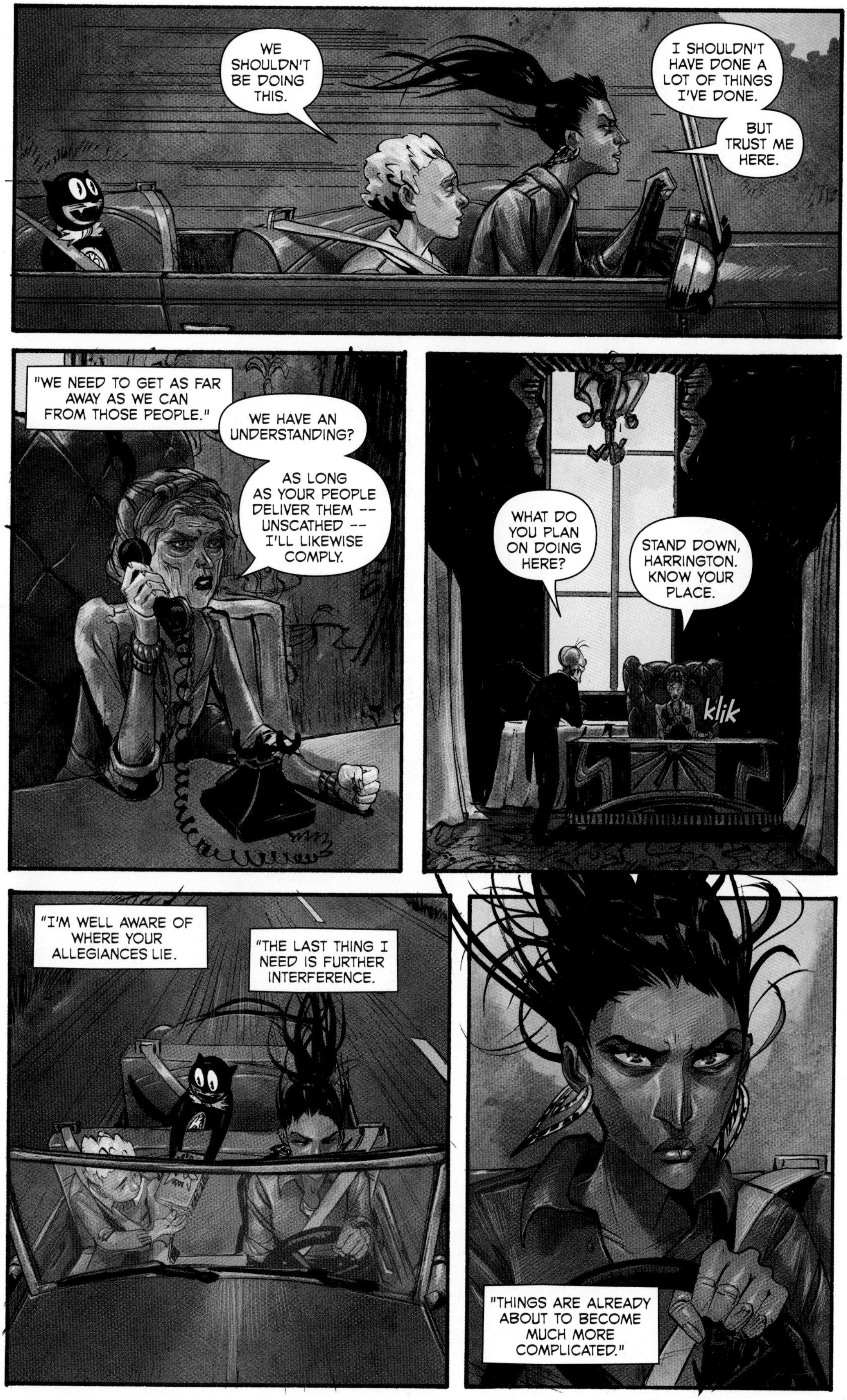
WE SHOULDN'T BE DOING THIS.
I SHOULDN'T HAVE DONE A LOT OF THINGS I'VE DONE.
BUT TRUST ME HERE.
"WE NEED TO GET AS FAR AWAY AS WE CAN FROM THOSE PEOPLE."
WE HAVE AN UNDERSTANDING?
AS LONG AS YOUR PEOPLE DELIVER THEM -- UNSCATHED -- I'LL LIKEWISE COMPLY.
WHAT DO YOU PLAN ON DOING HERE?
STAND DOWN, HARRINGTON. KNOW YOUR PLACE.
klik
"I'M WELL AWARE OF WHERE YOUR ALLEGIANCES LIE.
"THE LAST THING I NEED IS FURTHER INTERFERENCE.
"THINGS ARE ALREADY ABOUT TO BECOME MUCH MORE COMPLICATED."

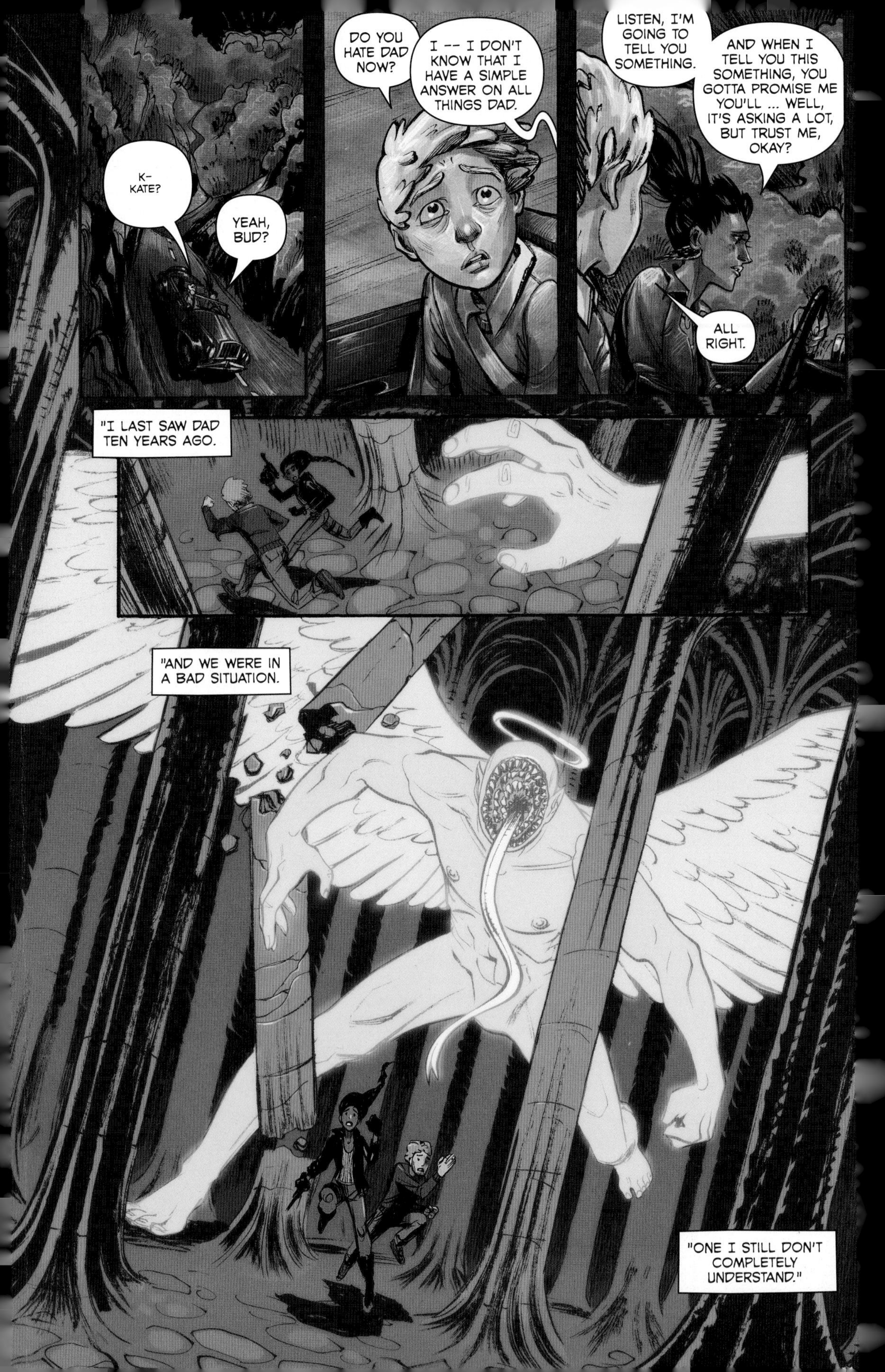
K-KATE?
YEAH, BUD?
DO YOU HATE DAD NOW?
I -- I DON'T KNOW THAT I HAVE A SIMPLE ANSWER ON ALL THINGS DAD.
LISTEN, I'M GOING TO TELL YOU SOMETHING.
AND WHEN I TELL YOU THIS SOMETHING, YOU GOTTA PROMISE ME YOU'LL ... WELL, IT'S ASKING A LOT, BUT TRUST ME, OKAY?
ALL RIGHT.
"I LAST SAW DAD TEN YEARS AGO.
"AND WE WERE IN A BAD SITUATION.
"ONE I STILL DON'T COMPLETELY UNDERSTAND."

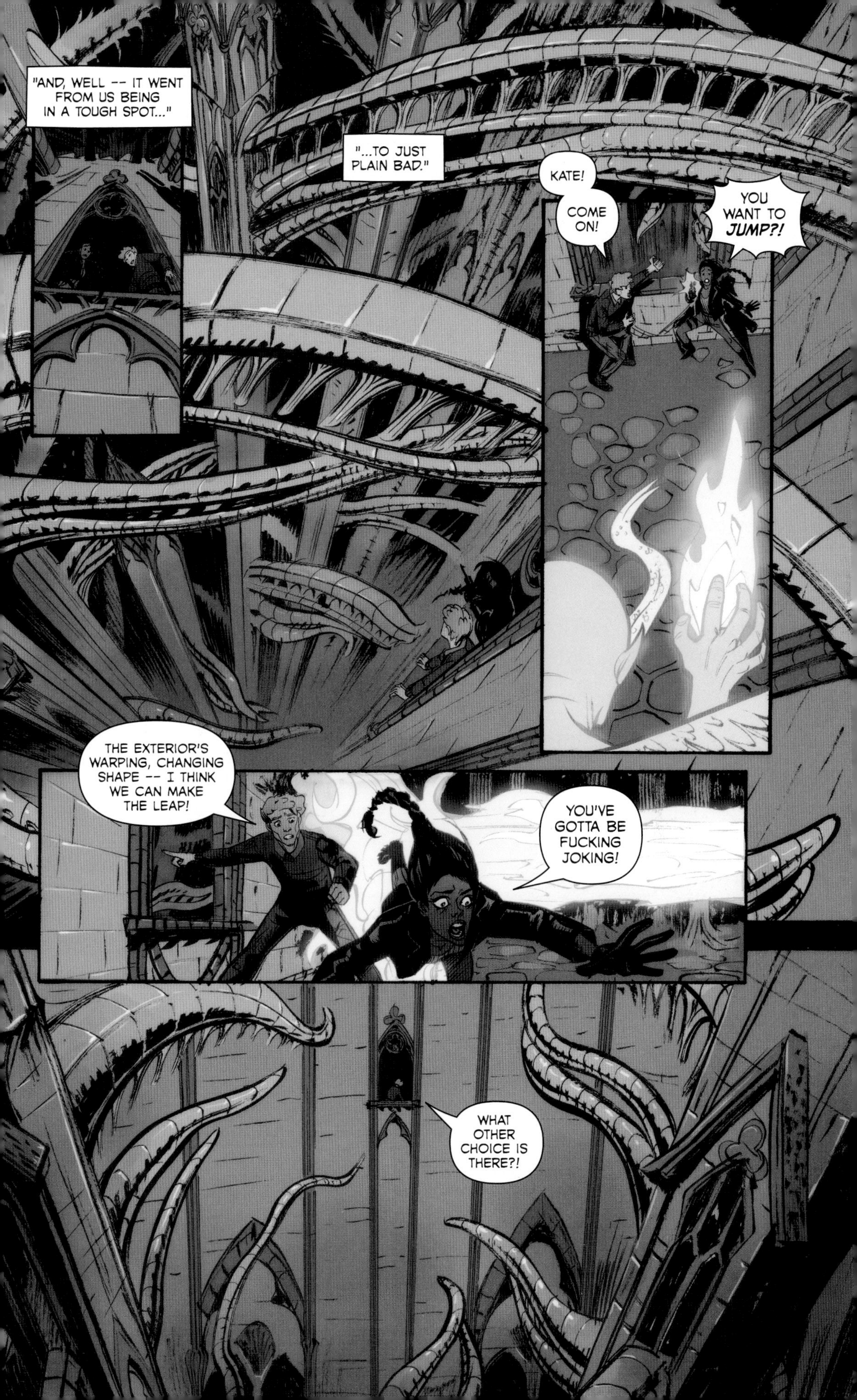
"AND, WELL -- IT WENT FROM US BEING IN A TOUGH SPOT..."
"...TO JUST PLAIN BAD."
KATE!
COME ON!
YOU WANT TO JUMP?!
THE EXTERIOR'S WARPING, CHANGING SHAPE -- I THINK WE CAN MAKE THE LEAP!
YOU'VE GOTTA BE FUCKING JOKING!
WHAT OTHER CHOICE IS THERE?!

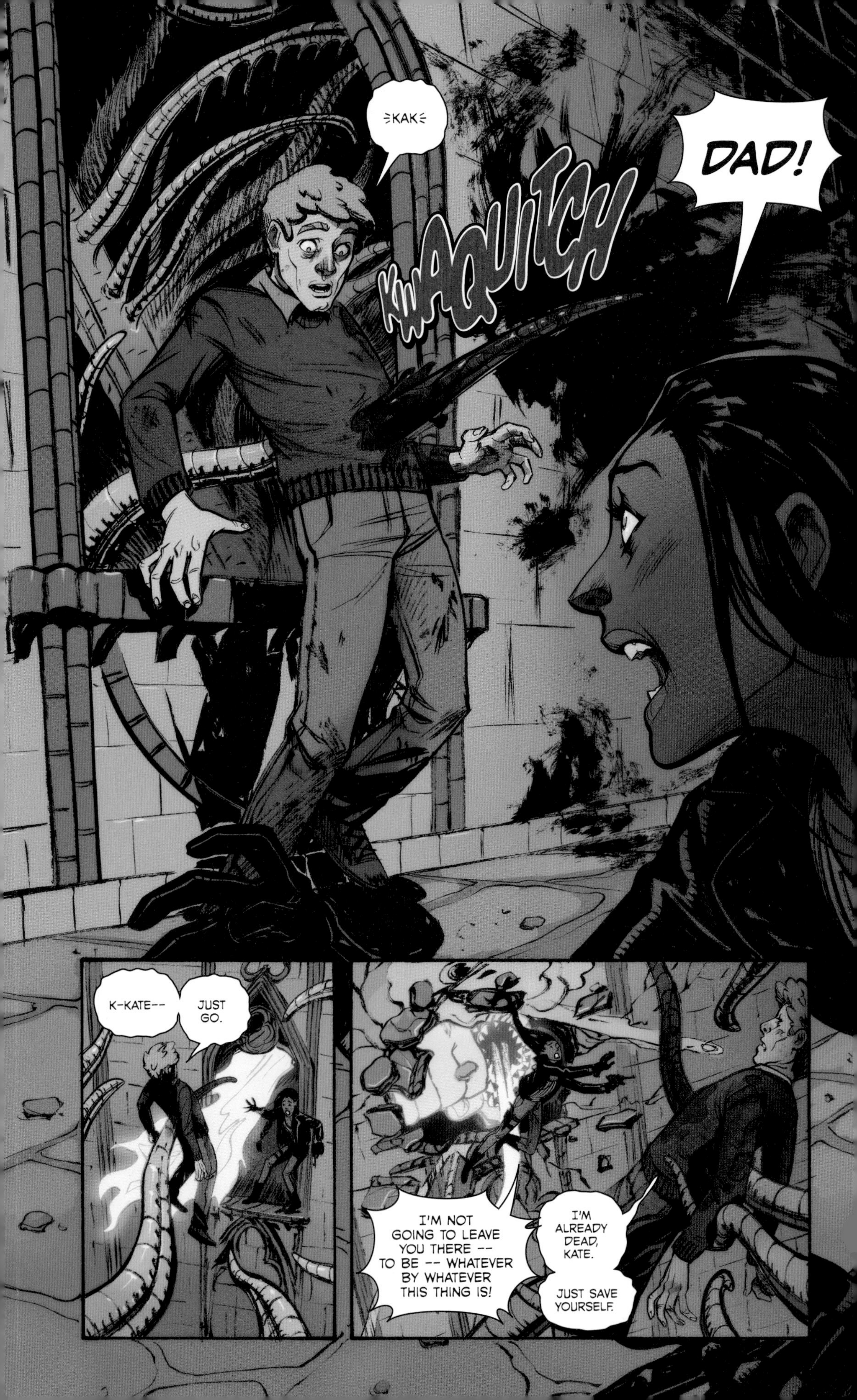
KAK
KWAQUITCH
DAD!
K-KATE--
JUST GO.
I'M NOT GOING TO LEAVE YOU THERE -- TO BE -- WHATEVER BY WHATEVER THIS THING IS!
I'M ALREADY DEAD, KATE.
JUST SAVE YOURSELF.

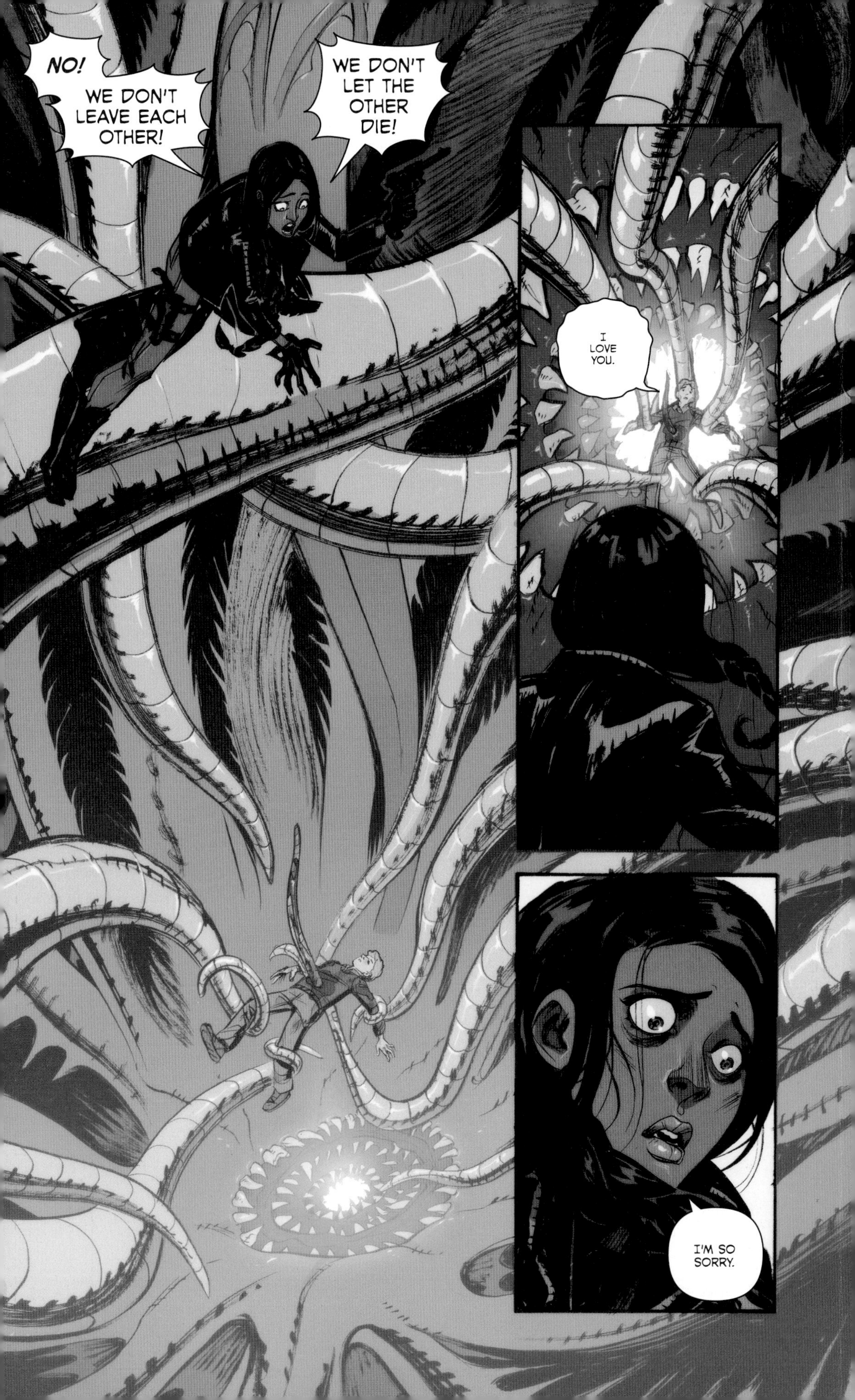
NO!
WE DON'T LEAVE EACH OTHER!
WE DON'T LET THE OTHER DIE!
I LOVE YOU.
I'M SO SORRY.

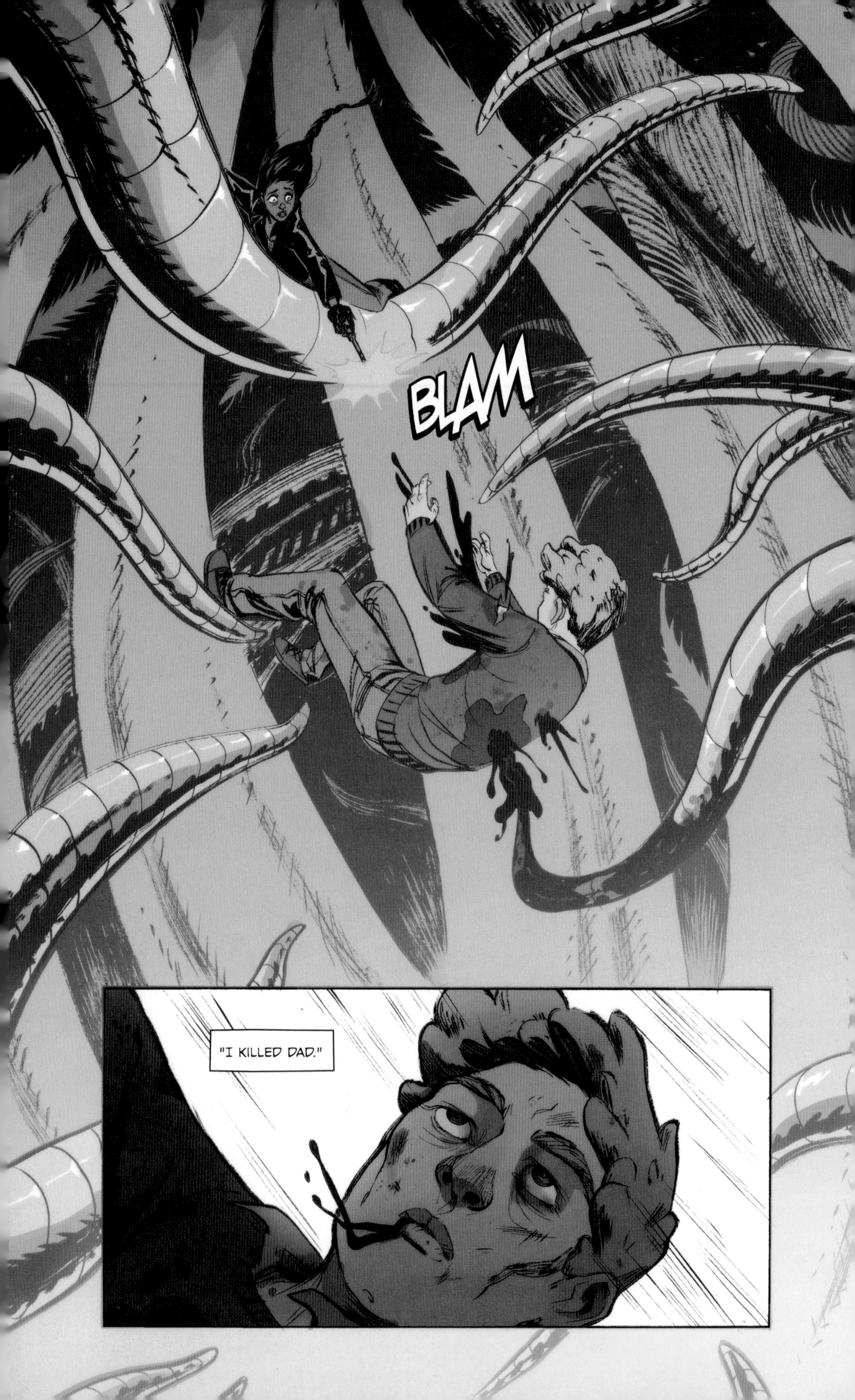
BLAM
"I KILLED DAD."

CHAPTER

6

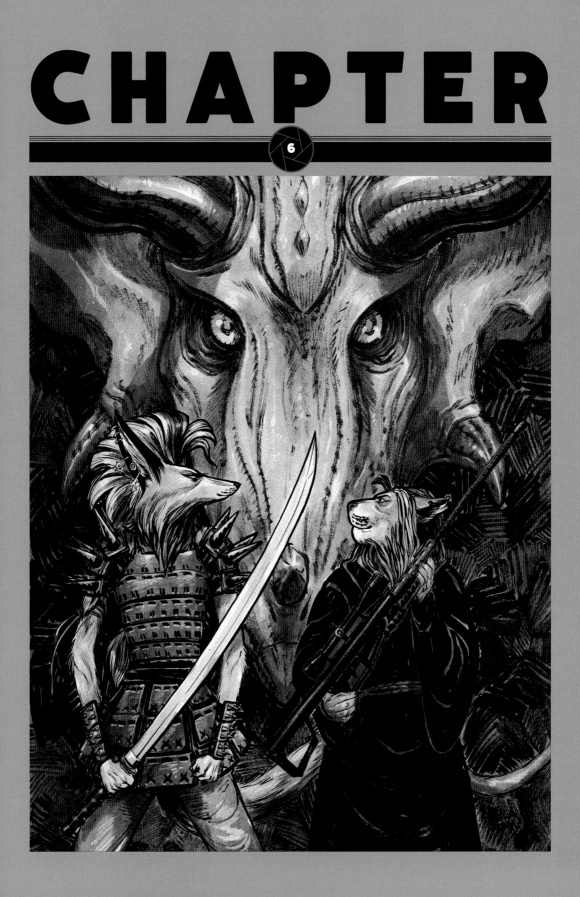

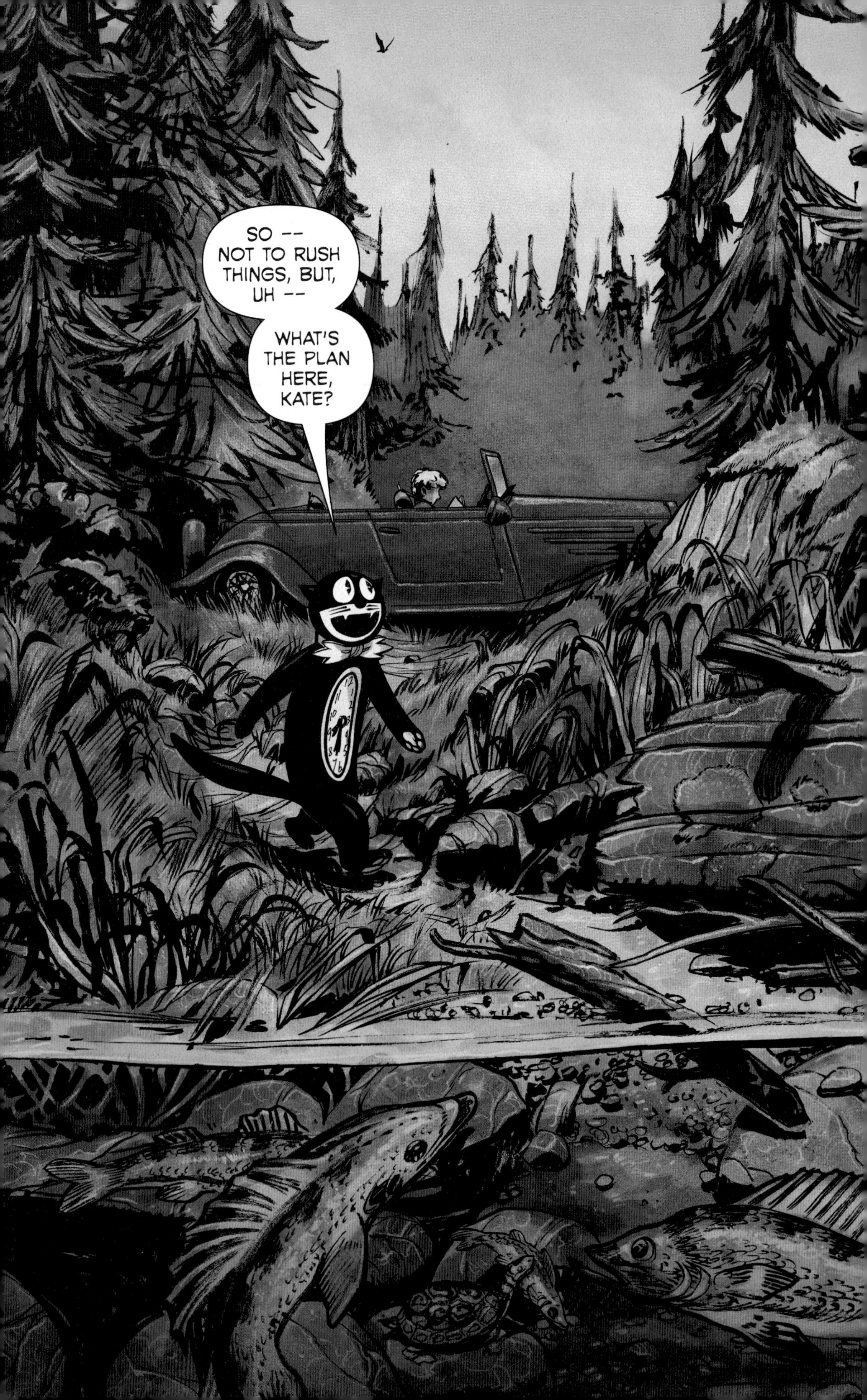
SO -- NOT TO RUSH THINGS, BUT, UH --
WHAT'S THE PLAN HERE, KATE?

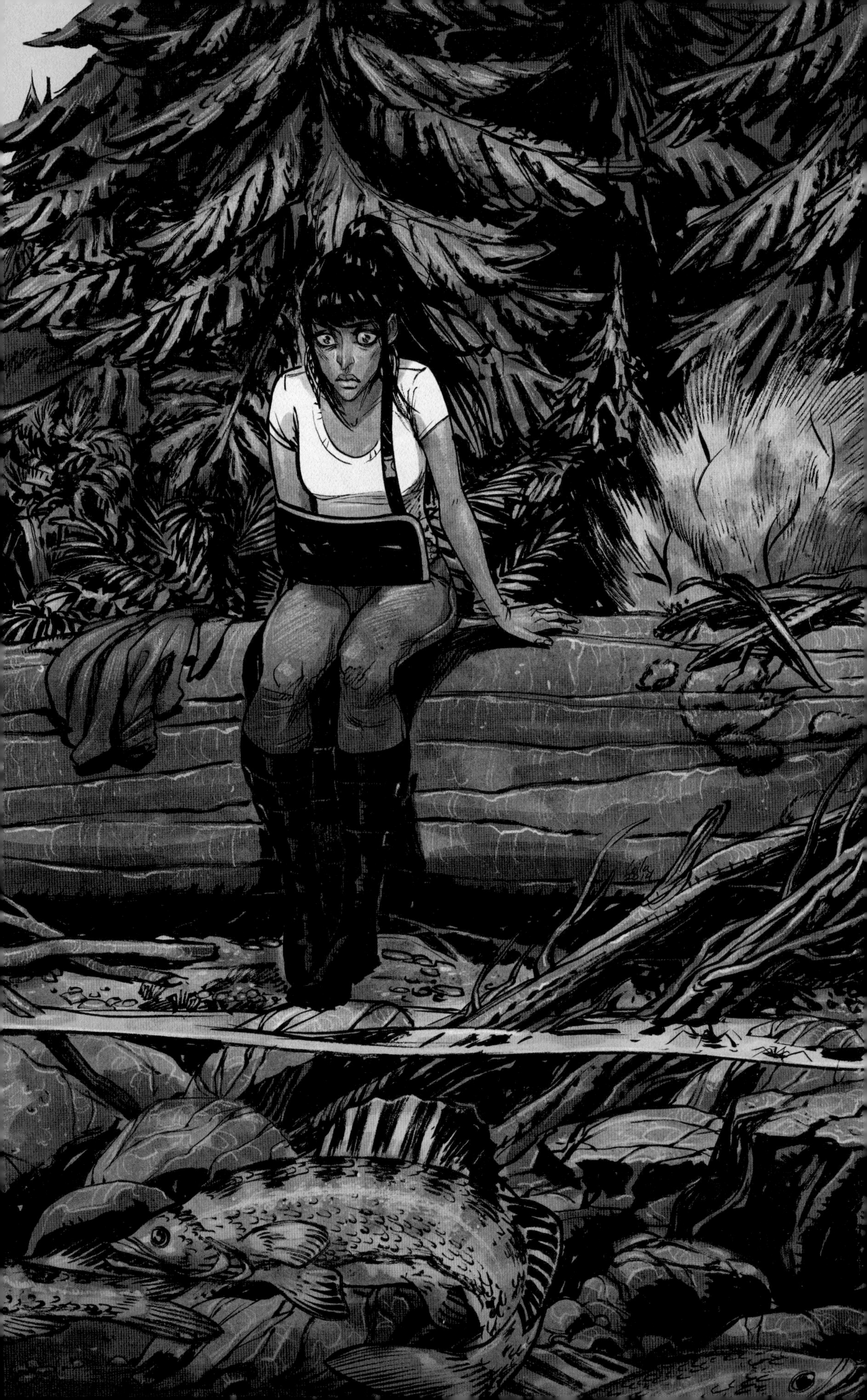

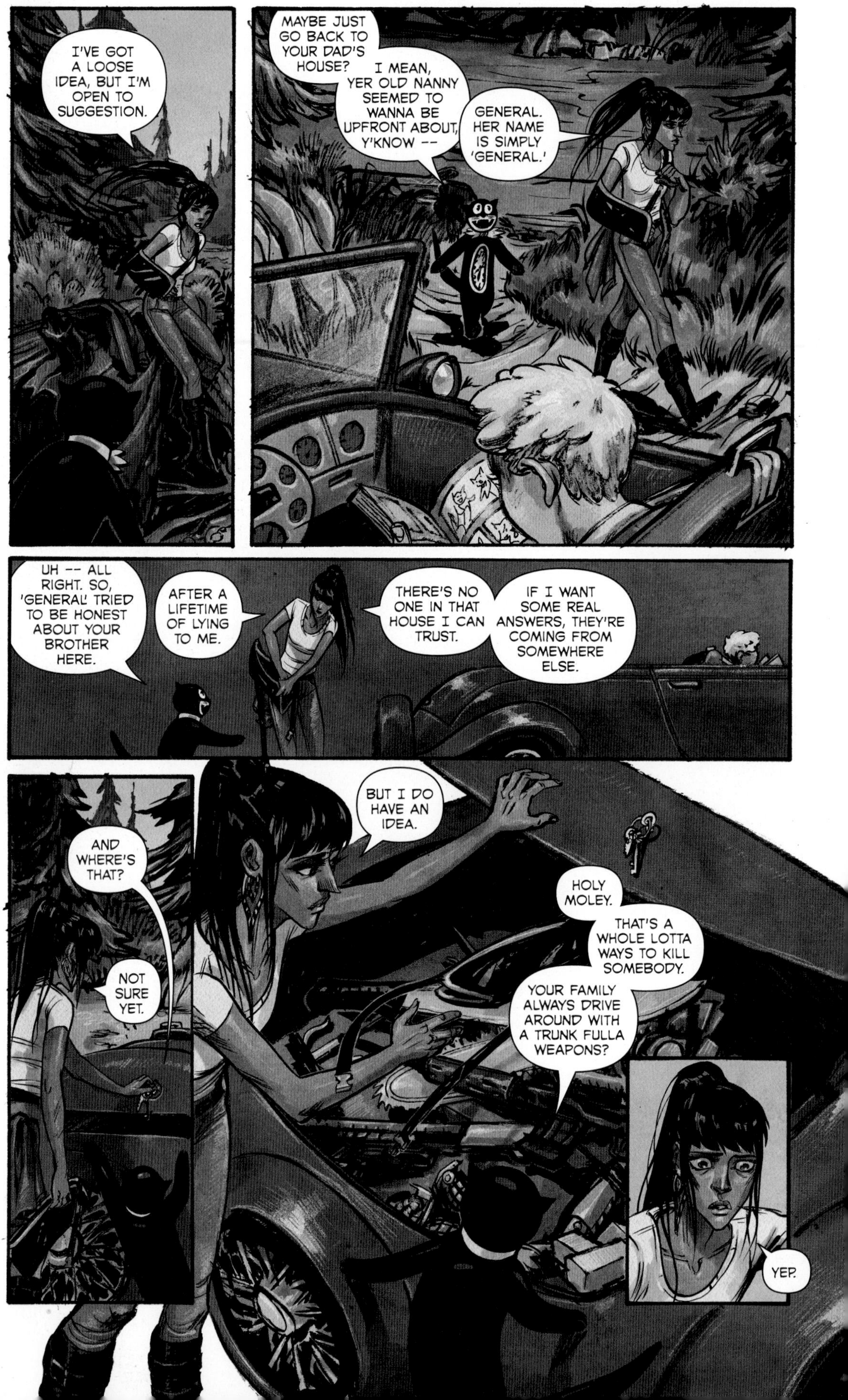
I'VE GOT A LOOSE IDEA, BUT I'M OPEN TO SUGGESTION.
MAYBE JUST GO BACK TO YOUR DAD'S HOUSE?
I MEAN, YER OLD NANNY SEEMED TO WANNA BE UPFRONT ABOUT, Y'KNOW --
GENERAL. HER NAME IS SIMPLY 'GENERAL.'
UH -- ALL RIGHT. SO, 'GENERAL' TRIED TO BE HONEST ABOUT YOUR BROTHER HERE.
AFTER A LIFETIME OF LYING TO ME.
THERE'S NO ONE IN THAT HOUSE I CAN TRUST.
IF I WANT SOME REAL ANSWERS, THEY'RE COMING FROM SOMEWHERE ELSE.
AND WHERE'S THAT?
NOT SURE YET.
BUT I DO HAVE AN IDEA.
HOLY MOLEY.
THAT'S A WHOLE LOTTA WAYS TO KILL SOMEBODY.
YOUR FAMILY ALWAYS DRIVE AROUND WITH A TRUNK FULLA WEAPONS?
YEP.

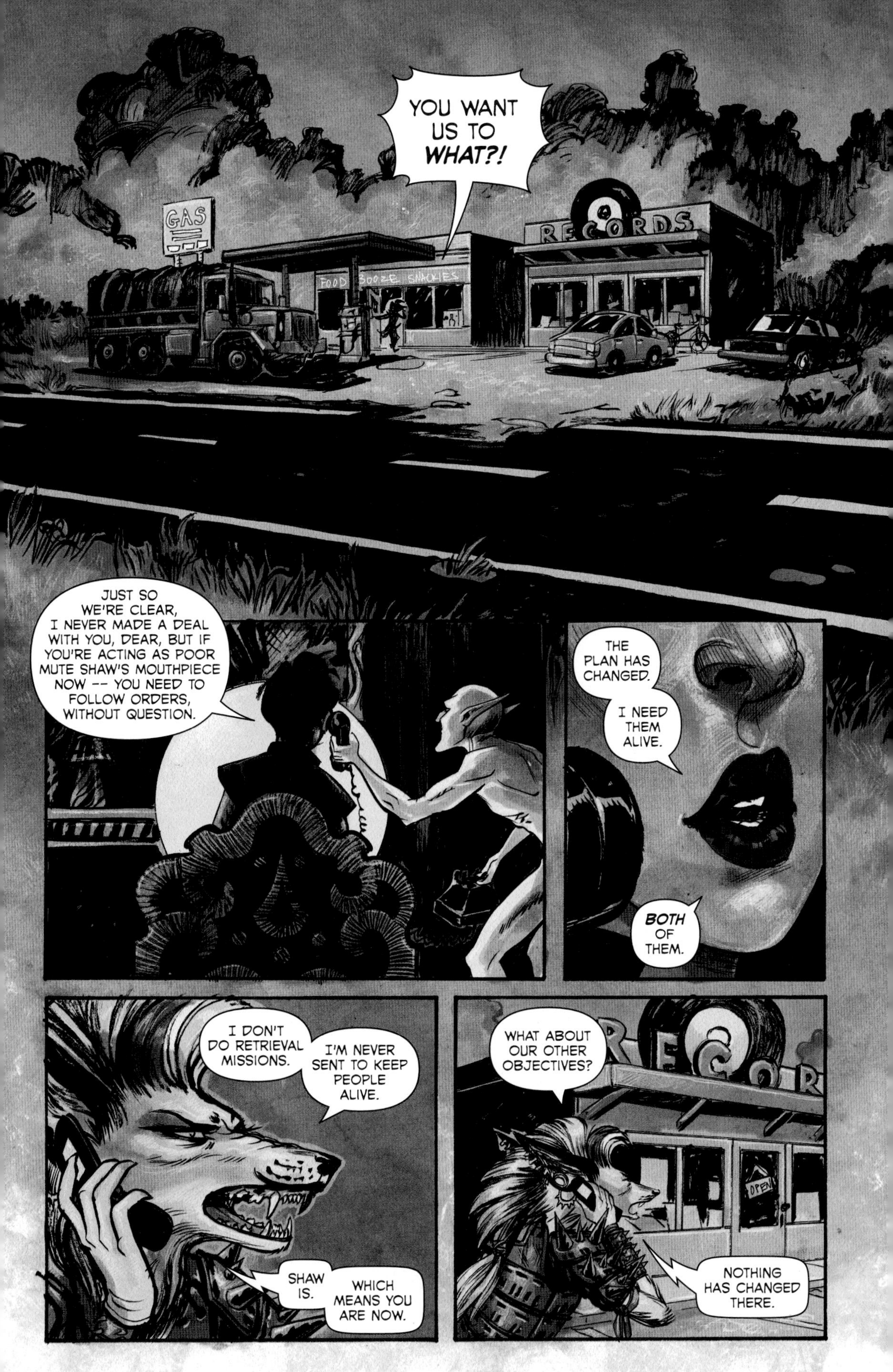
YOU WANT US TO *WHAT?!*
GAS
RECORDS
FOOD BOOZE SNACKIES
JUST SO WE'RE CLEAR, I NEVER MADE A DEAL WITH YOU, DEAR, BUT IF YOU'RE ACTING AS POOR MUTE SHAW'S MOUTHPIECE NOW -- YOU NEED TO FOLLOW ORDERS, WITHOUT QUESTION.
THE PLAN HAS CHANGED.
I NEED THEM ALIVE.
BOTH OF THEM.
I DON'T DO RETRIEVAL MISSIONS.
I'M NEVER SENT TO KEEP PEOPLE ALIVE.
SHAW IS.
WHICH MEANS YOU ARE NOW.
WHAT ABOUT OUR OTHER OBJECTIVES?
OPEN
NOTHING HAS CHANGED THERE.

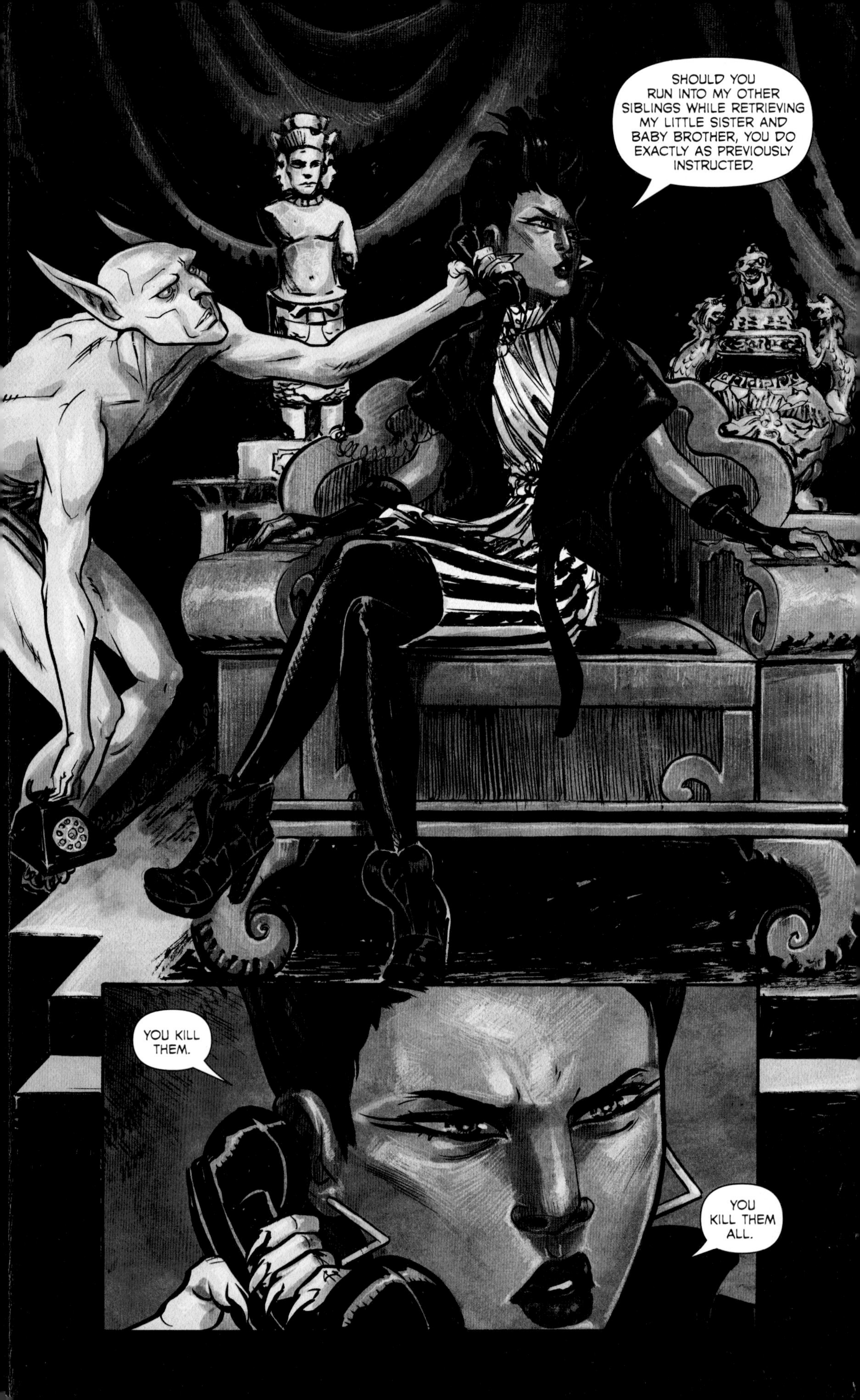
SHOULD YOU RUN INTO MY OTHER SIBLINGS WHILE RETRIEVING MY LITTLE SISTER AND BABY BROTHER, YOU DO EXACTLY AS PREVIOUSLY INSTRUCTED.
YOU KILL THEM.
YOU KILL THEM ALL.

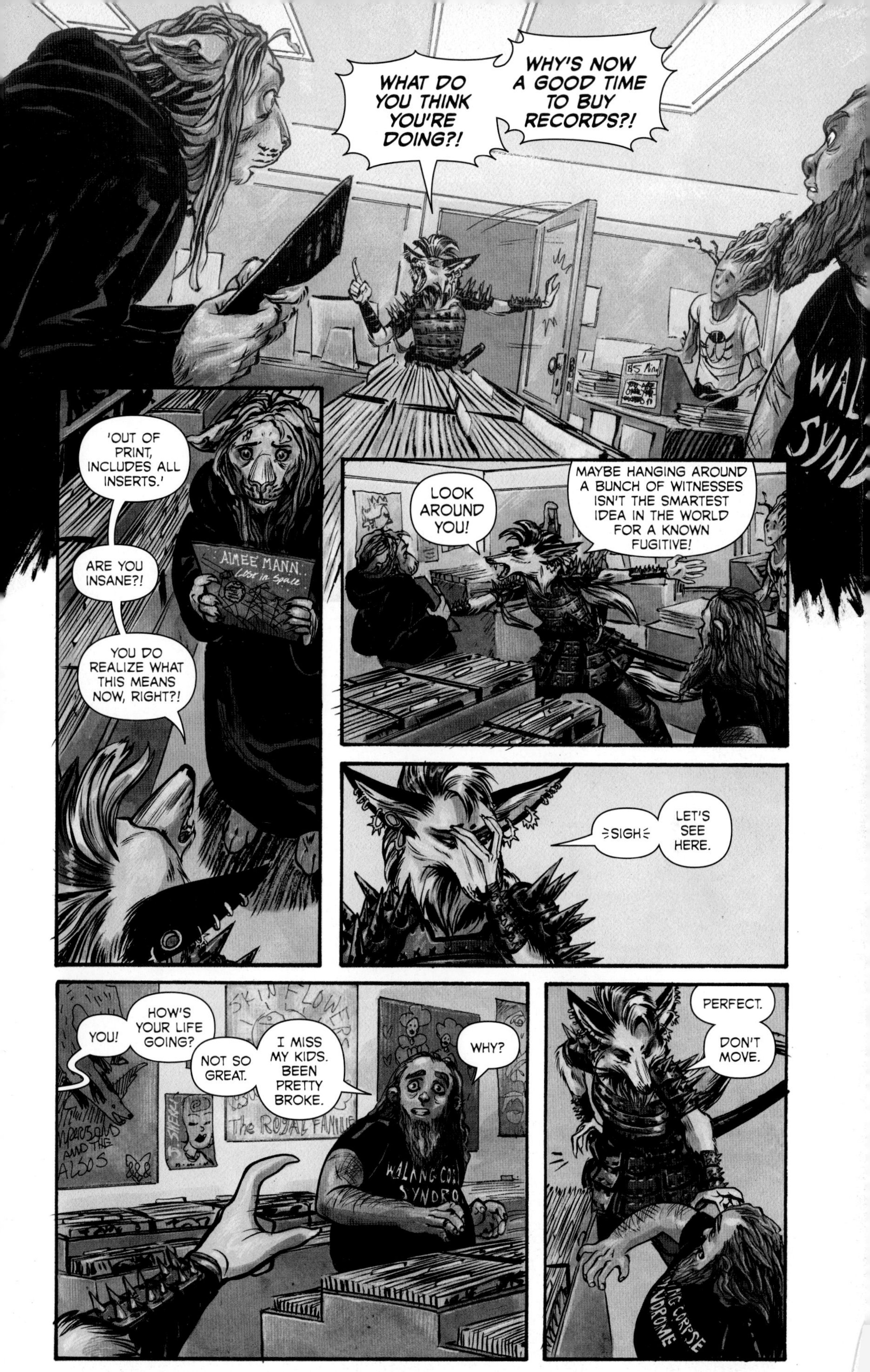
WHAT DO YOU THINK YOU'RE DOING?!
WHY'S NOW A GOOD TIME TO BUY RECORDS?!
'OUT OF PRINT, INCLUDES ALL INSERTS.'
AIMEE MANN
Lost in Space
ARE YOU INSANE?!
YOU DO REALIZE WHAT THIS MEANS NOW, RIGHT?!
LOOK AROUND YOU!
MAYBE HANGING AROUND A BUNCH OF WITNESSES ISN'T THE SMARTEST IDEA IN THE WORLD FOR A KNOWN FUGITIVE!
SIGH
LET'S SEE HERE.
YOU!
HOW'S YOUR LIFE GOING?
NOT SO GREAT.
I MISS MY KIDS. BEEN PRETTY BROKE.
WHY?
The ROYAL FAMILIE
PERFECT.
DON'T MOVE.

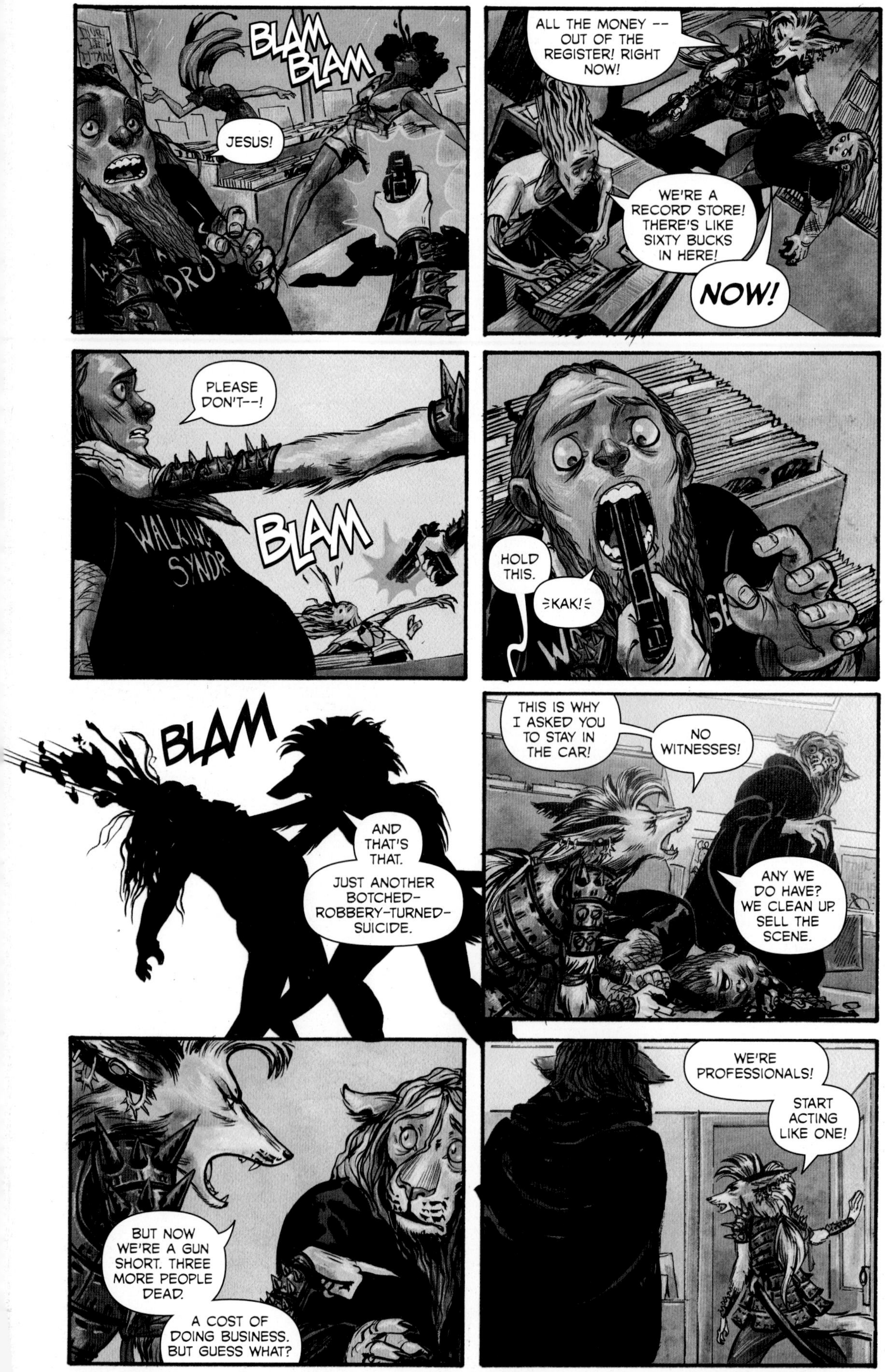
BLAM BLAM
JESUS!
ALL THE MONEY -- OUT OF THE REGISTER! RIGHT NOW!
WE'RE A RECORD STORE! THERE'S LIKE SIXTY BUCKS IN HERE!
NOW!
PLEASE DON'T--!
BLAM
HOLD THIS.
KAK!
BLAM
AND THAT'S THAT.
JUST ANOTHER BOTCHED-ROBBERY-TURNED-SUICIDE.
THIS IS WHY I ASKED YOU TO STAY IN THE CAR!
NO WITNESSES!
ANY WE DO HAVE? WE CLEAN UP. SELL THE SCENE.
BUT NOW WE'RE A GUN SHORT. THREE MORE PEOPLE DEAD.
A COST OF DOING BUSINESS. BUT GUESS WHAT?
WE'RE PROFESSIONALS!
START ACTING LIKE ONE!

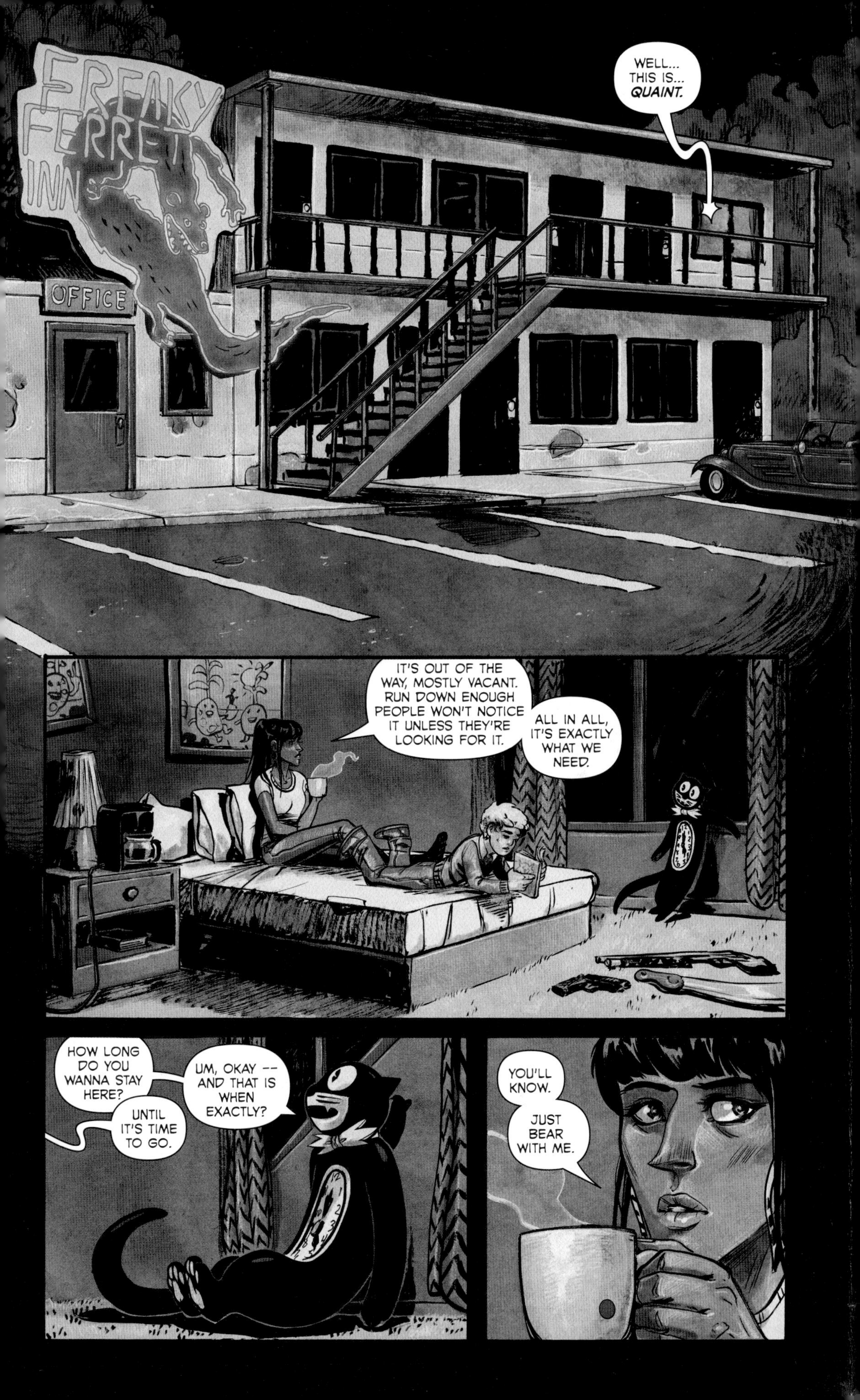
FREAKY FERRET INN
OFFICE
WELL... THIS IS... QUAINT.
IT'S OUT OF THE WAY, MOSTLY VACANT. RUN DOWN ENOUGH PEOPLE WON'T NOTICE IT UNLESS THEY'RE LOOKING FOR IT.
ALL IN ALL, IT'S EXACTLY WHAT WE NEED.
HOW LONG DO YOU WANNA STAY HERE?
UNTIL IT'S TIME TO GO.
UM, OKAY -- AND THAT IS WHEN EXACTLY?
YOU'LL KNOW.
JUST BEAR WITH ME.

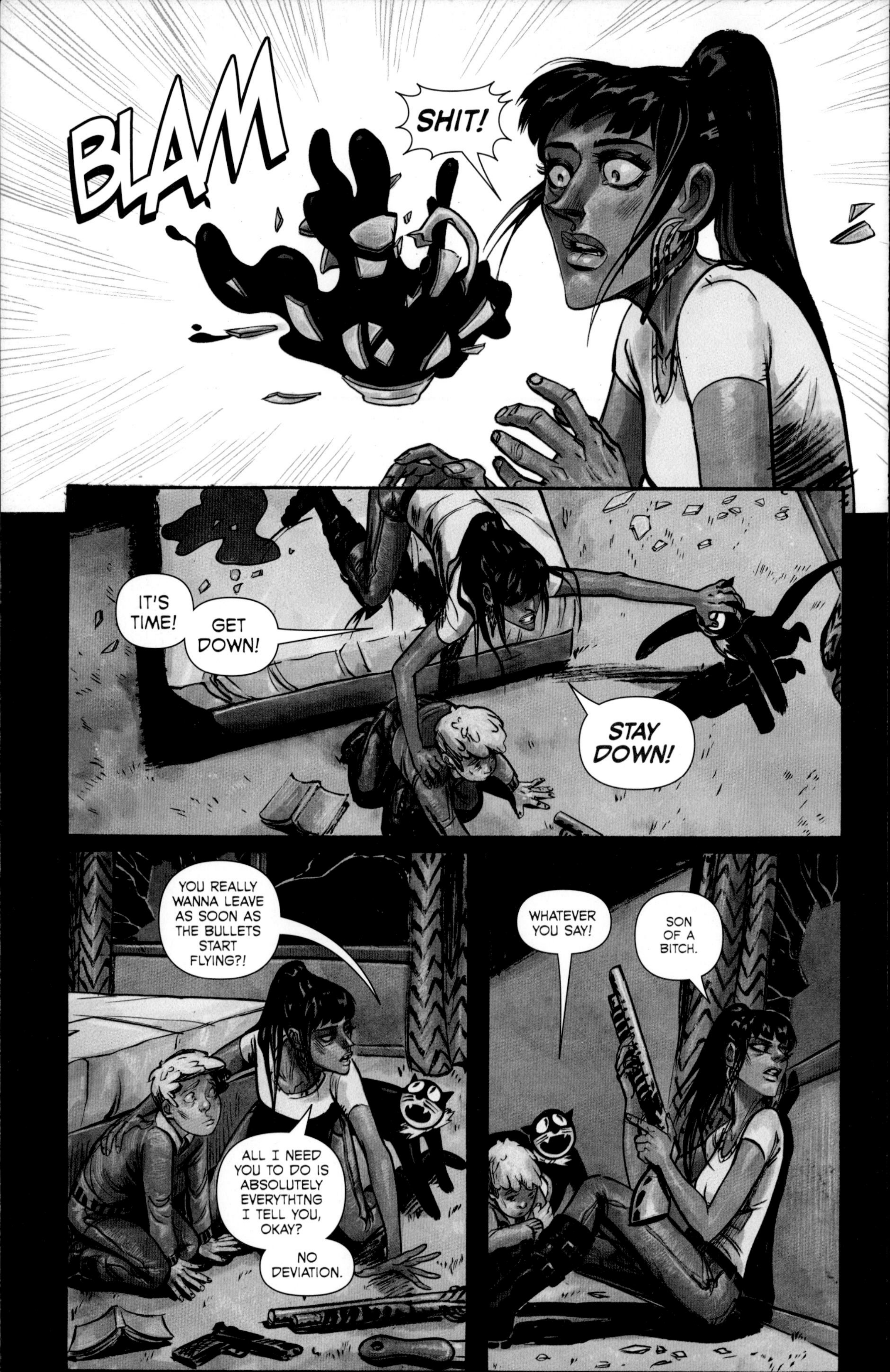
BLAM
SHIT!
IT'S TIME!
GET DOWN!
STAY DOWN!
YOU REALLY WANNA LEAVE AS SOON AS THE BULLETS START FLYING?!
ALL I NEED YOU TO DO IS ABSOLUTELY EVERYTHTNG I TELL YOU, OKAY?
NO DEVIATION.
WHATEVER YOU SAY!
SON OF A BITCH.

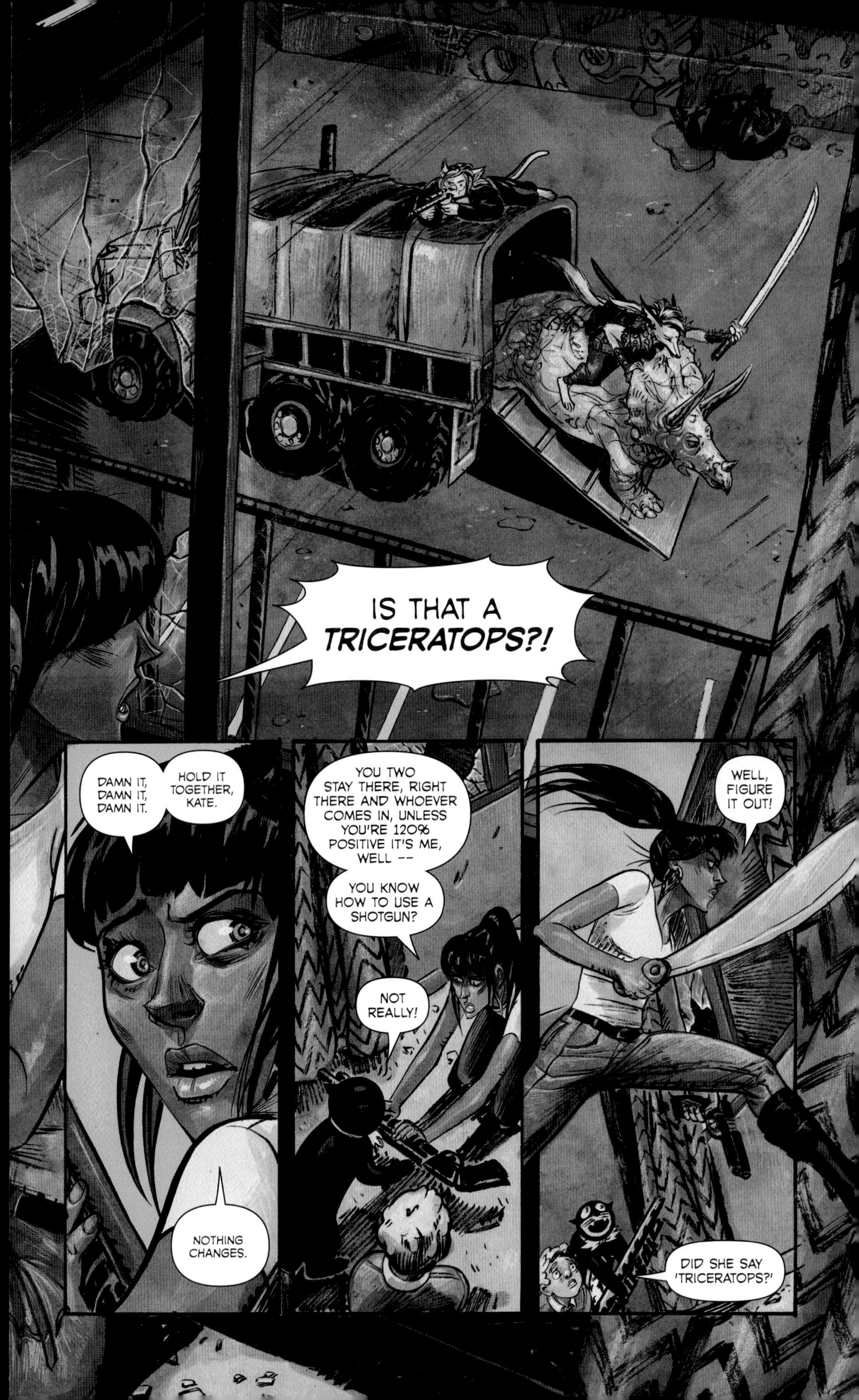
IS THAT A TRICERATOPS?!
DAMN IT, DAMN IT, DAMN IT.
HOLD IT TOGETHER, KATE.
NOTHING CHANGES.
YOU TWO STAY THERE, RIGHT THERE AND WHOEVER COMES IN, UNLESS YOU'RE 120% POSITIVE IT'S ME, WELL --
YOU KNOW HOW TO USE A SHOTGUN?
NOT REALLY!
WELL, FIGURE IT OUT!
DID SHE SAY 'TRICERATOPS?'

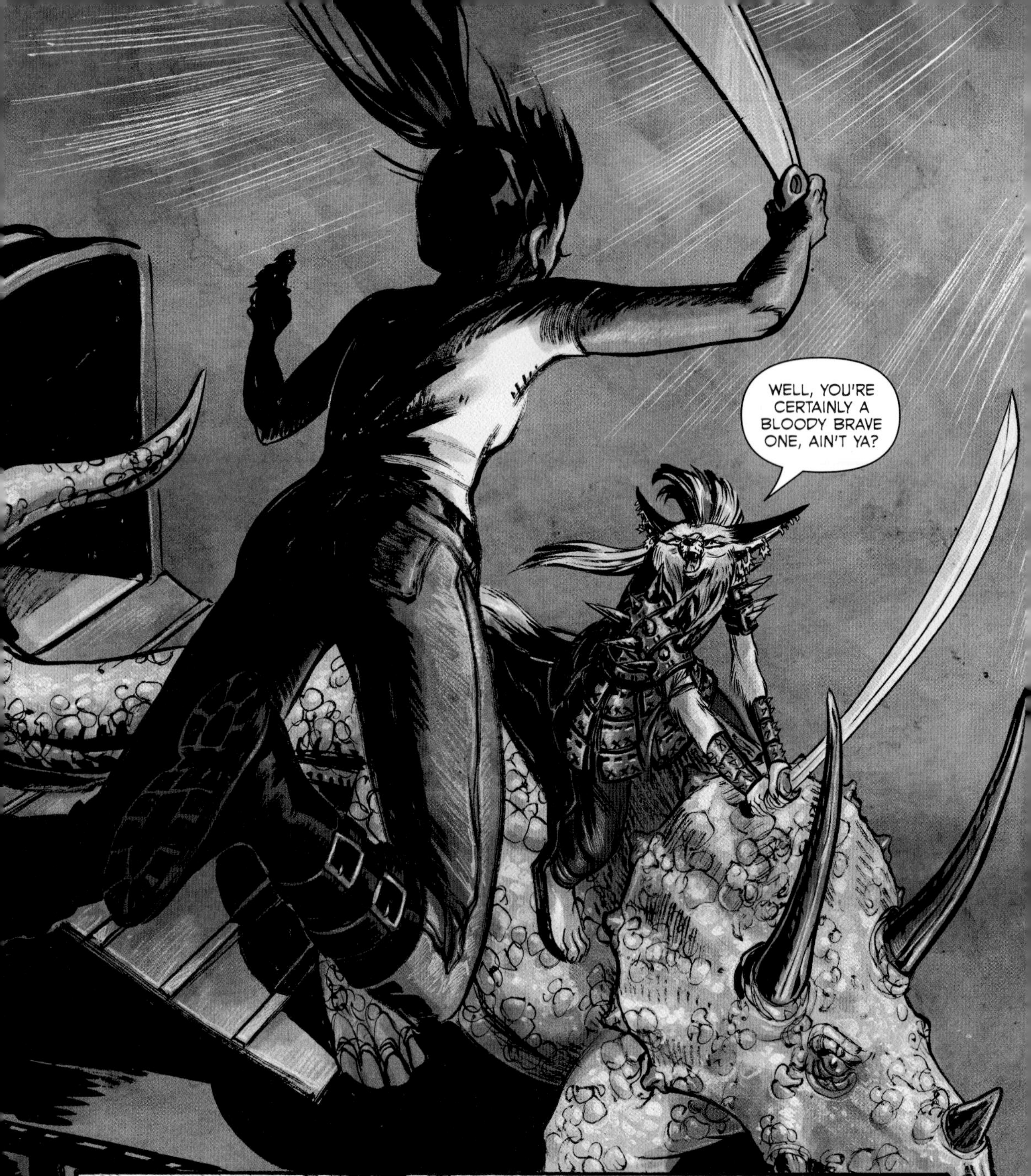
WELL, YOU'RE CERTAINLY A BLOODY BRAVE ONE, AIN'T YA?

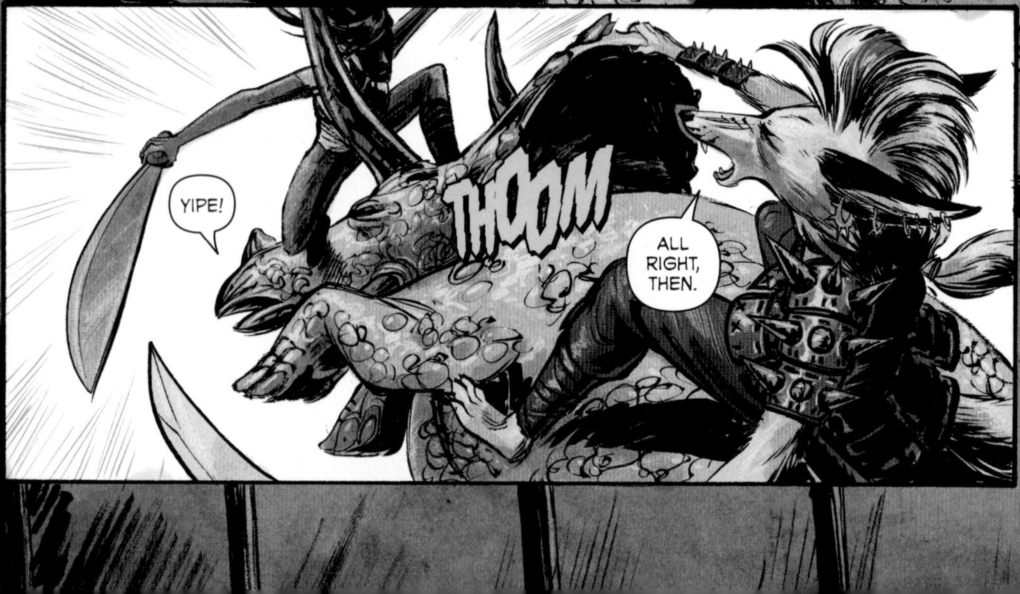
YIPE!
THOOM
ALL RIGHT, THEN.

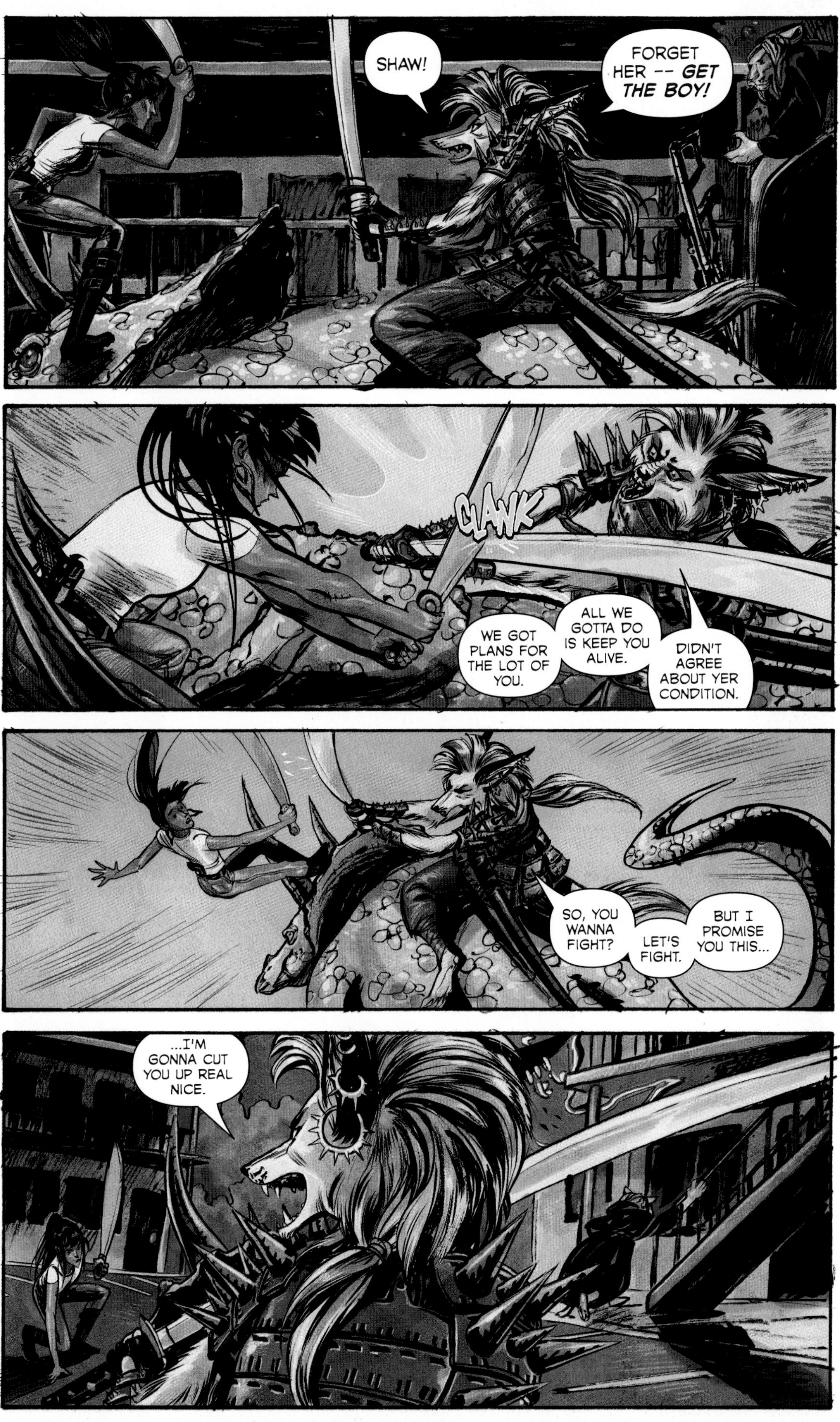
SHAW!
FORGET HER -- GET THE BOY!
CLANK
WE GOT PLANS FOR THE LOT OF YOU.
ALL WE GOTTA DO IS KEEP YOU ALIVE.
DIDN'T AGREE ABOUT YER CONDITION.
SO, YOU WANNA FIGHT?
LET'S FIGHT.
BUT I PROMISE YOU THIS...
...I'M GONNA CUT YOU UP REAL NICE.

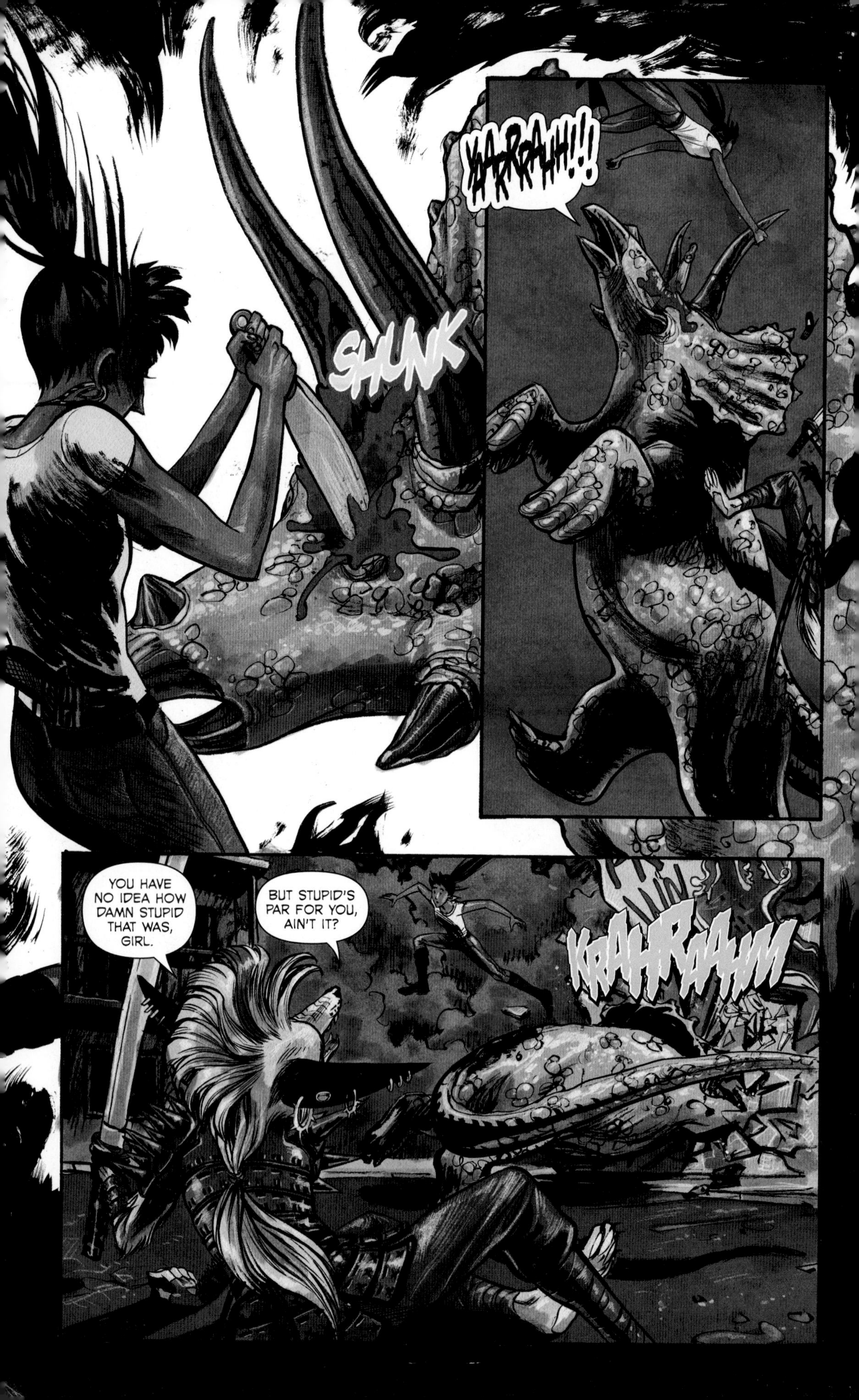
YAARRAAH!!!
SHUNK
YOU HAVE NO IDEA HOW DAMN STUPID THAT WAS, GIRL.
BUT STUPID'S PAR FOR YOU, AIN'T IT?
KRAHRAAAM

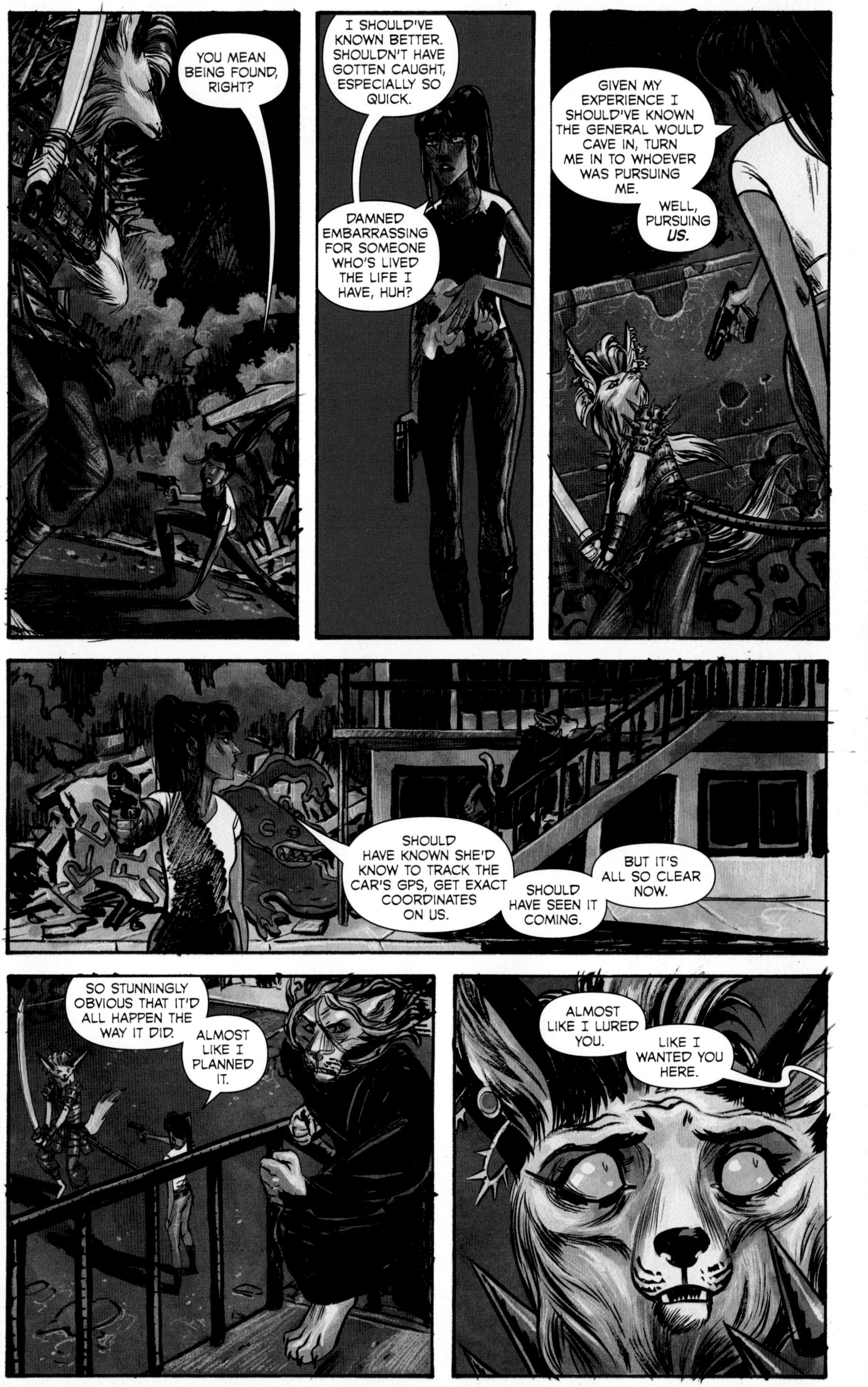
YOU MEAN BEING FOUND, RIGHT?
I SHOULD'VE KNOWN BETTER. SHOULDN'T HAVE GOTTEN CAUGHT, ESPECIALLY SO QUICK.
DAMNED EMBARRASSING FOR SOMEONE WHO'S LIVED THE LIFE I HAVE, HUH?
GIVEN MY EXPERIENCE I SHOULD'VE KNOWN THE GENERAL WOULD CAVE IN, TURN ME IN TO WHOEVER WAS PURSUING ME.
WELL, PURSUING *US.*
SHOULD HAVE KNOWN SHE'D KNOW TO TRACK THE CAR'S GPS, GET EXACT COORDINATES ON US.
SHOULD HAVE SEEN IT COMING.
BUT IT'S ALL SO CLEAR NOW.
SO STUNNINGLY OBVIOUS THAT IT'D ALL HAPPEN THE WAY IT DID.
ALMOST LIKE I PLANNED IT.
ALMOST LIKE I LURED YOU.
LIKE I WANTED YOU HERE.

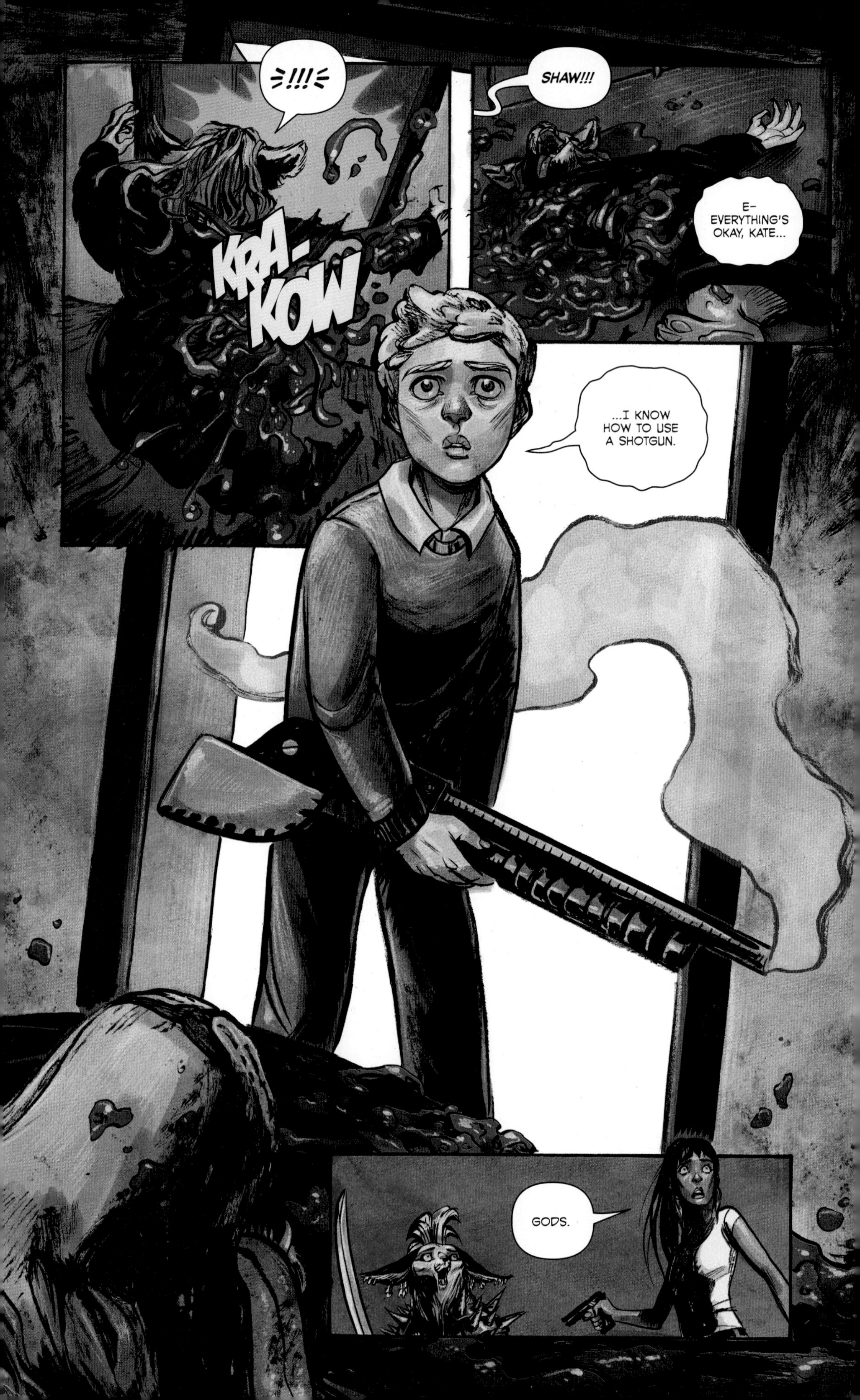
!!!
KRA-KOW
SHAW!!!
E-EVERYTHING'S OKAY, KATE...
...I KNOW HOW TO USE A SHOTGUN.
GODS.

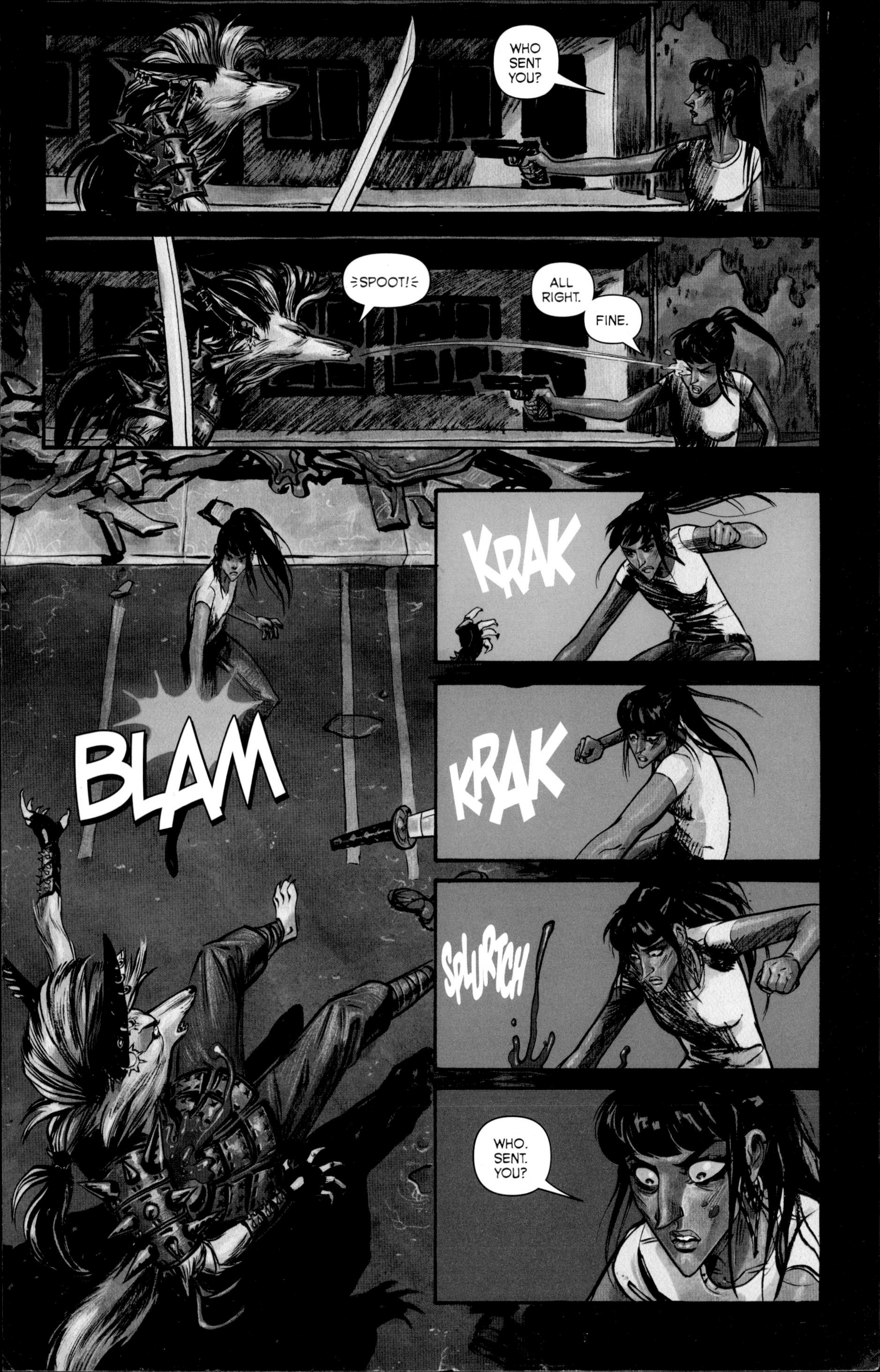
WHO SENT YOU?
SPOOT!
ALL RIGHT.
FINE.
BLAM
KRAK
KRAK
SPLURTCH
WHO. SENT. YOU?

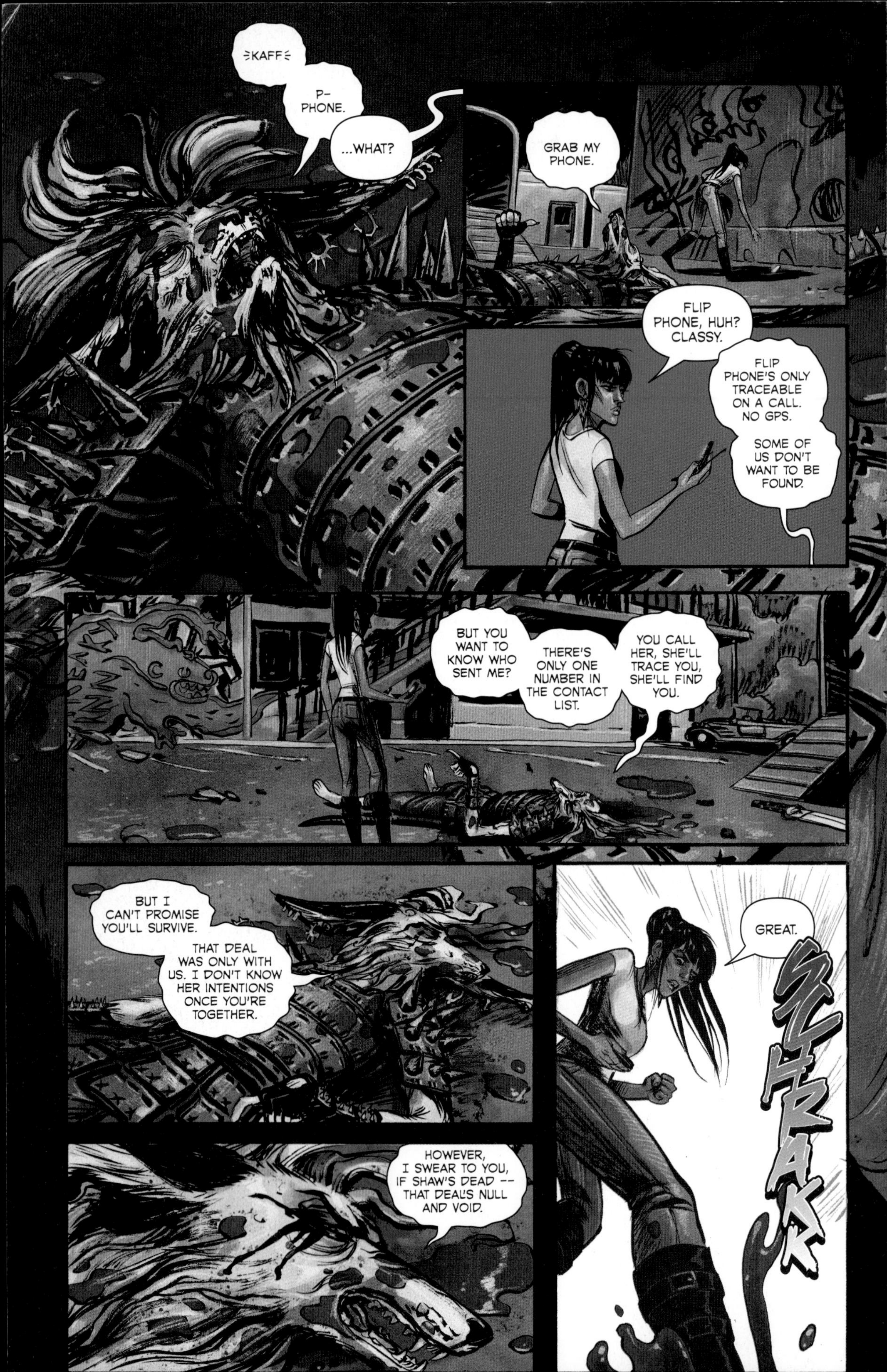
KAFF
P-
PHONE.
...WHAT?
GRAB MY PHONE.
FLIP PHONE, HUH? CLASSY.
FLIP PHONE'S ONLY TRACEABLE ON A CALL. NO GPS.
SOME OF US DON'T WANT TO BE FOUND.
BUT YOU WANT TO KNOW WHO SENT ME?
THERE'S ONLY ONE NUMBER IN THE CONTACT LIST.
YOU CALL HER, SHE'LL TRACE YOU, SHE'LL FIND YOU.
BUT I CAN'T PROMISE YOU'LL SURVIVE.
THAT DEAL WAS ONLY WITH US. I DON'T KNOW HER INTENTIONS ONCE YOU'RE TOGETHER.
HOWEVER, I SWEAR TO YOU, IF SHAW'S DEAD -- THAT DEAL'S NULL AND VOID.
GREAT.
SCHRAKK

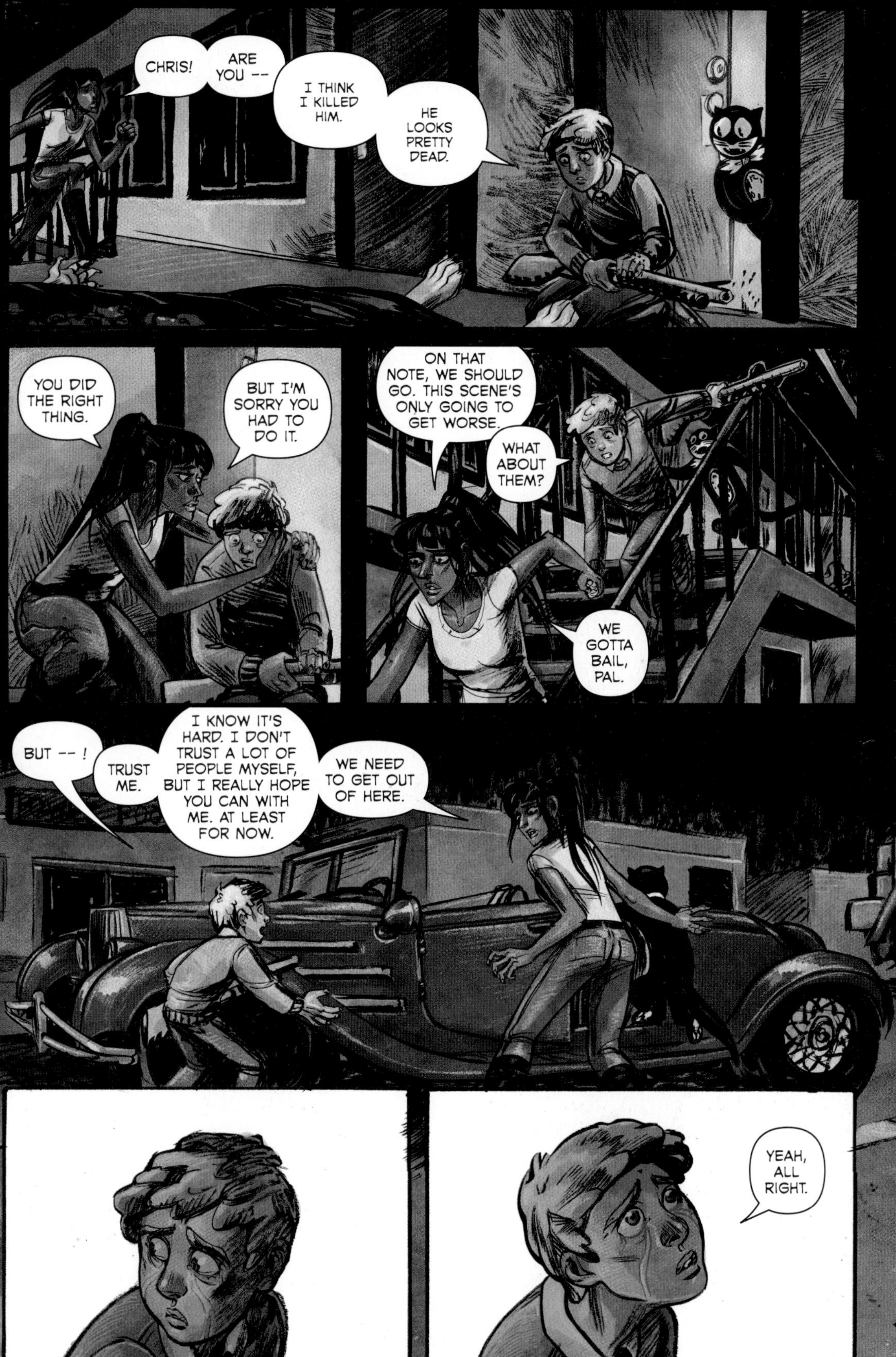
CHRIS!
ARE YOU --
I THINK I KILLED HIM.
HE LOOKS PRETTY DEAD.
YOU DID THE RIGHT THING.
BUT I'M SORRY YOU HAD TO DO IT.
ON THAT NOTE, WE SHOULD GO. THIS SCENE'S ONLY GOING TO GET WORSE.
WHAT ABOUT THEM?
WE GOTTA BAIL, PAL.
BUT -- !
TRUST ME.
I KNOW IT'S HARD. I DON'T TRUST A LOT OF PEOPLE MYSELF, BUT I REALLY HOPE YOU CAN WITH ME. AT LEAST FOR NOW.
WE NEED TO GET OUT OF HERE.
YEAH, ALL RIGHT.

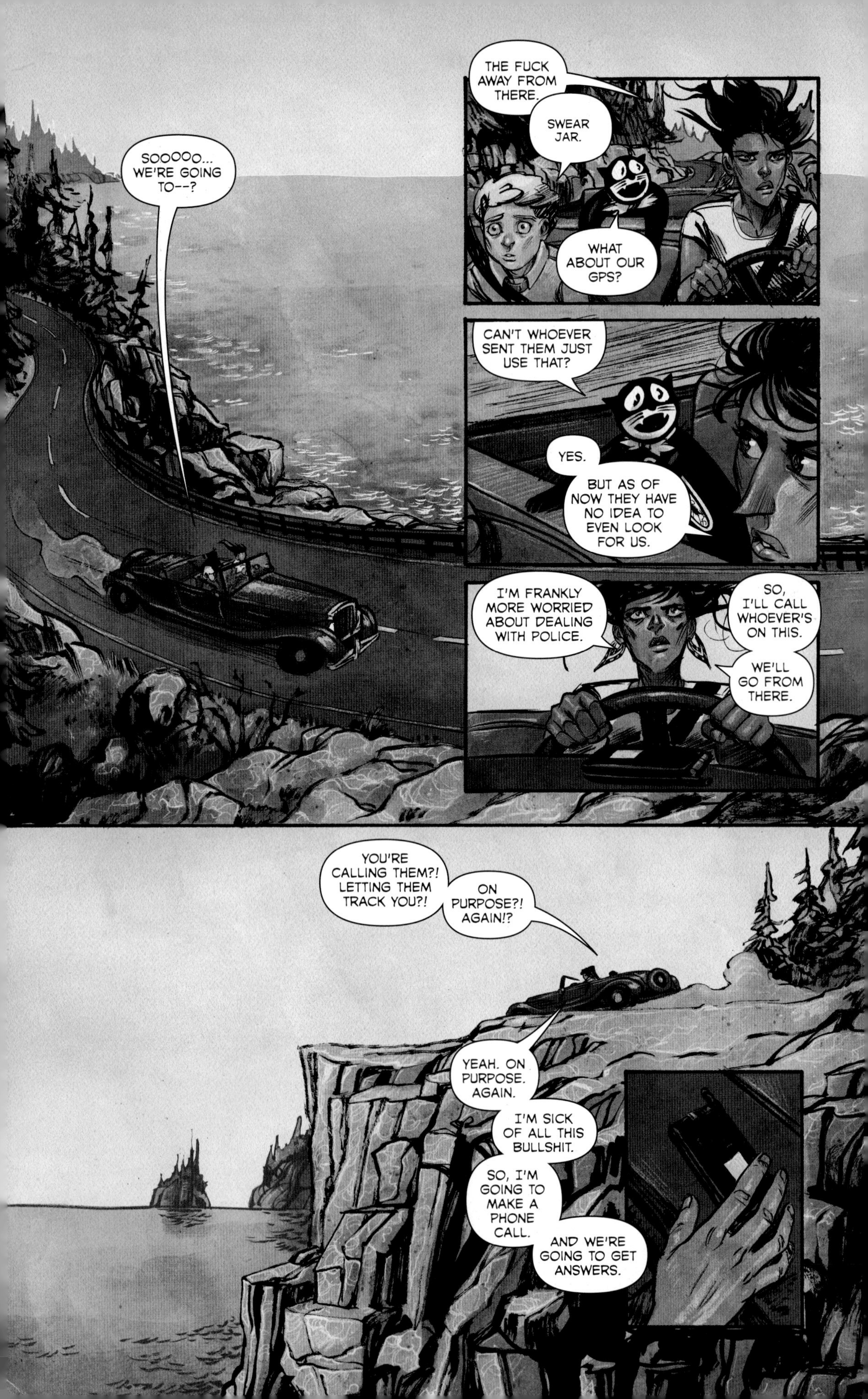
SOOOOO... WE'RE GOING TO--?
THE FUCK AWAY FROM THERE.
SWEAR JAR.
WHAT ABOUT OUR GPS?
CAN'T WHOEVER SENT THEM JUST USE THAT?
YES.
BUT AS OF NOW THEY HAVE NO IDEA TO EVEN LOOK FOR US.
I'M FRANKLY MORE WORRIED ABOUT DEALING WITH POLICE.
SO, I'LL CALL WHOEVER'S ON THIS.
WE'LL GO FROM THERE.
YOU'RE CALLING THEM?! LETTING THEM TRACK YOU?!
ON PURPOSE?! AGAIN!?
YEAH. ON PURPOSE. AGAIN.
I'M SICK OF ALL THIS BULLSHIT.
SO, I'M GOING TO MAKE A PHONE CALL.
AND WE'RE GOING TO GET ANSWERS.

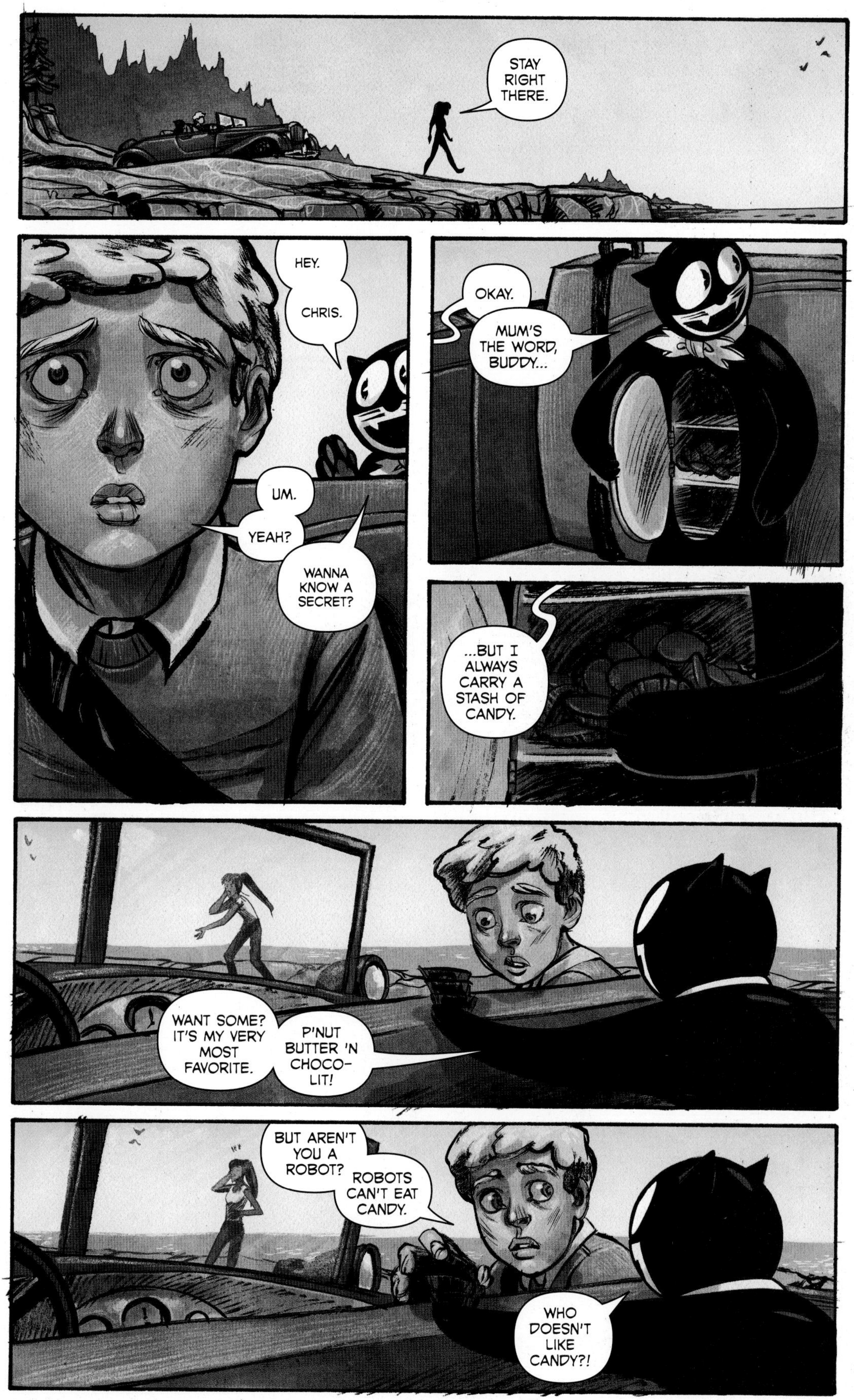
STAY RIGHT THERE.
HEY.
CHRIS.
UM.
YEAH?
WANNA KNOW A SECRET?
OKAY.
MUM'S THE WORD, BUDDY...
...BUT I ALWAYS CARRY A STASH OF CANDY.
WANT SOME? IT'S MY VERY MOST FAVORITE.
P'NUT BUTTER 'N CHOCO-LIT!
BUT AREN'T YOU A ROBOT?
ROBOTS CAN'T EAT CANDY.
WHO DOESN'T LIKE CANDY?!

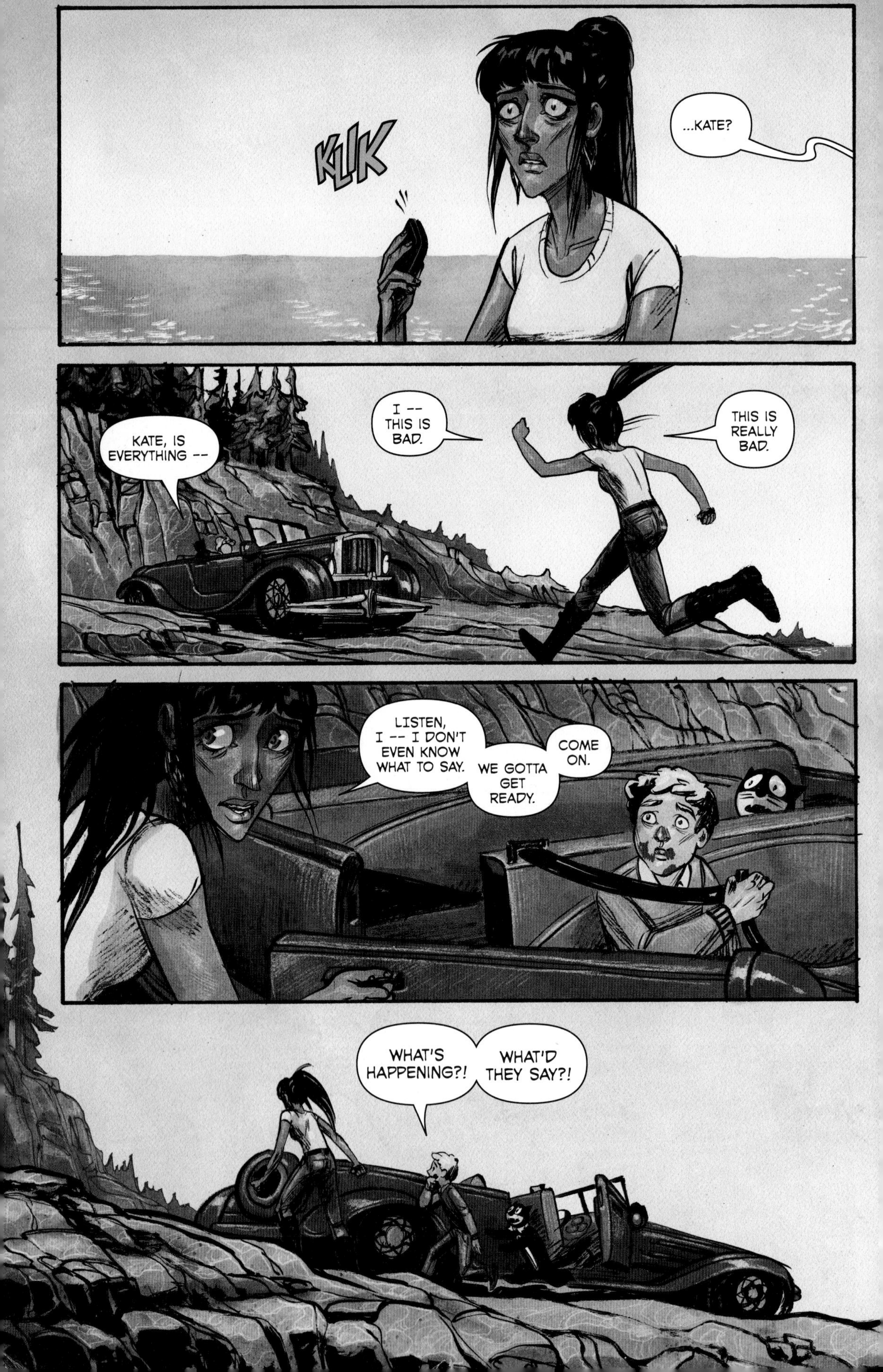
KLIK
...KATE?
KATE, IS EVERYTHING --
I -- THIS IS BAD.
THIS IS REALLY BAD.
LISTEN, I -- I DON'T EVEN KNOW WHAT TO SAY.
WE GOTTA GET READY.
COME ON.
WHAT'S HAPPENING?!
WHAT'D THEY SAY?!

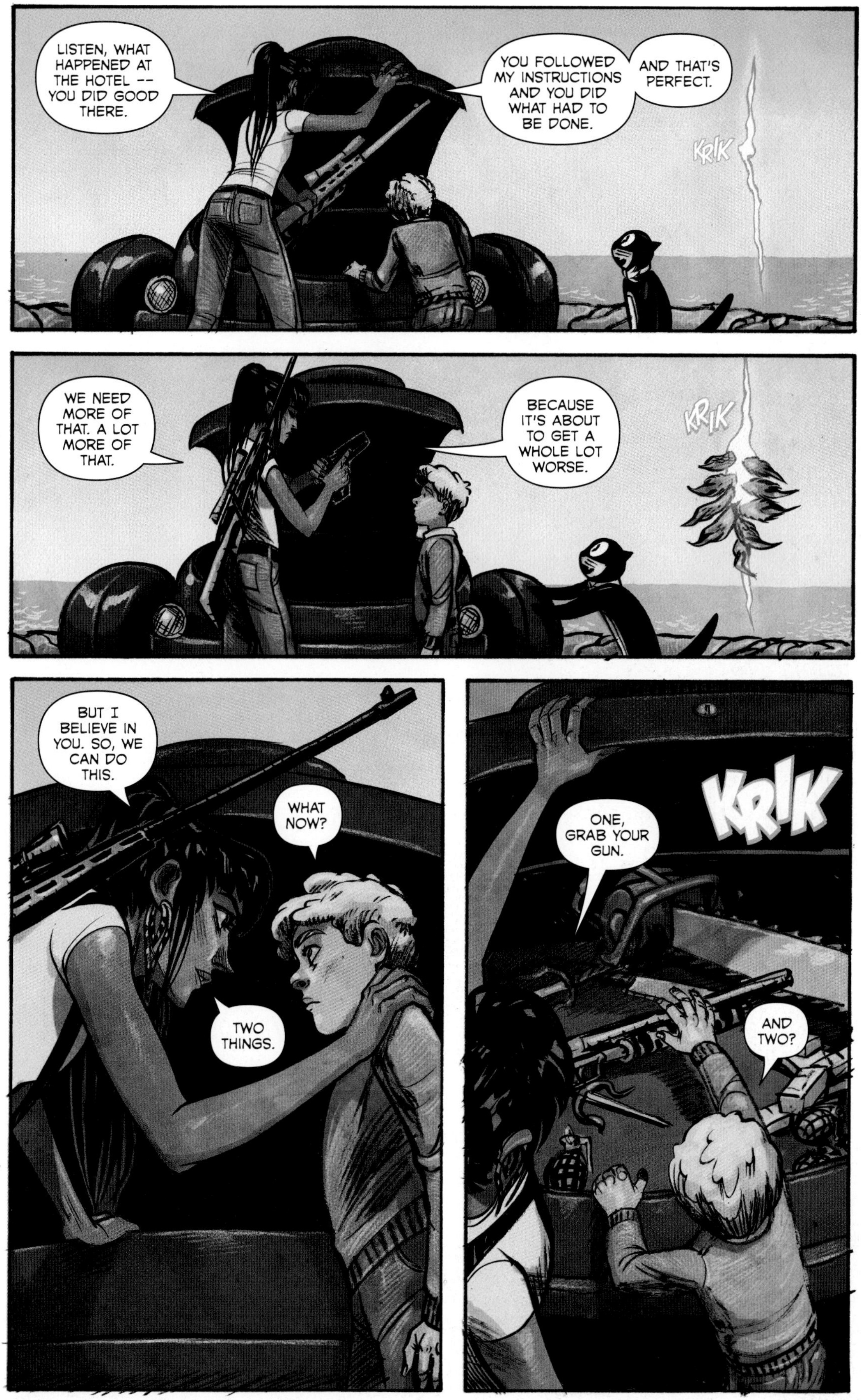
LISTEN, WHAT HAPPENED AT THE HOTEL -- YOU DID GOOD THERE.
YOU FOLLOWED MY INSTRUCTIONS AND YOU DID WHAT HAD TO BE DONE.
AND THAT'S PERFECT.
KRIK
WE NEED MORE OF THAT. A LOT MORE OF THAT.
BECAUSE IT'S ABOUT TO GET A WHOLE LOT WORSE.
KRIK
BUT I BELIEVE IN YOU. SO, WE CAN DO THIS.
WHAT NOW?
TWO THINGS.
KRIK
ONE, GRAB YOUR GUN.
AND TWO?

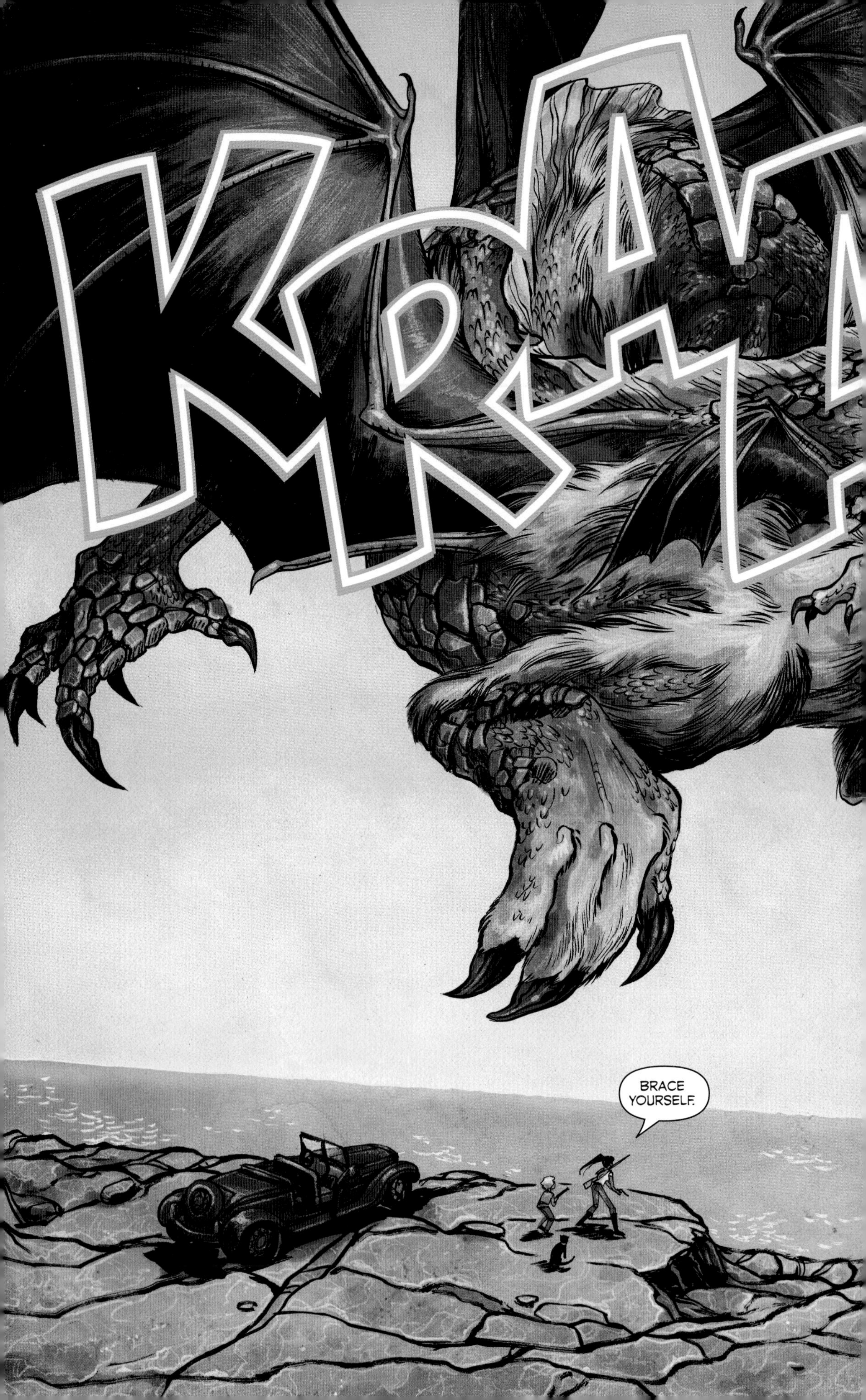
BRACE YOURSELF.

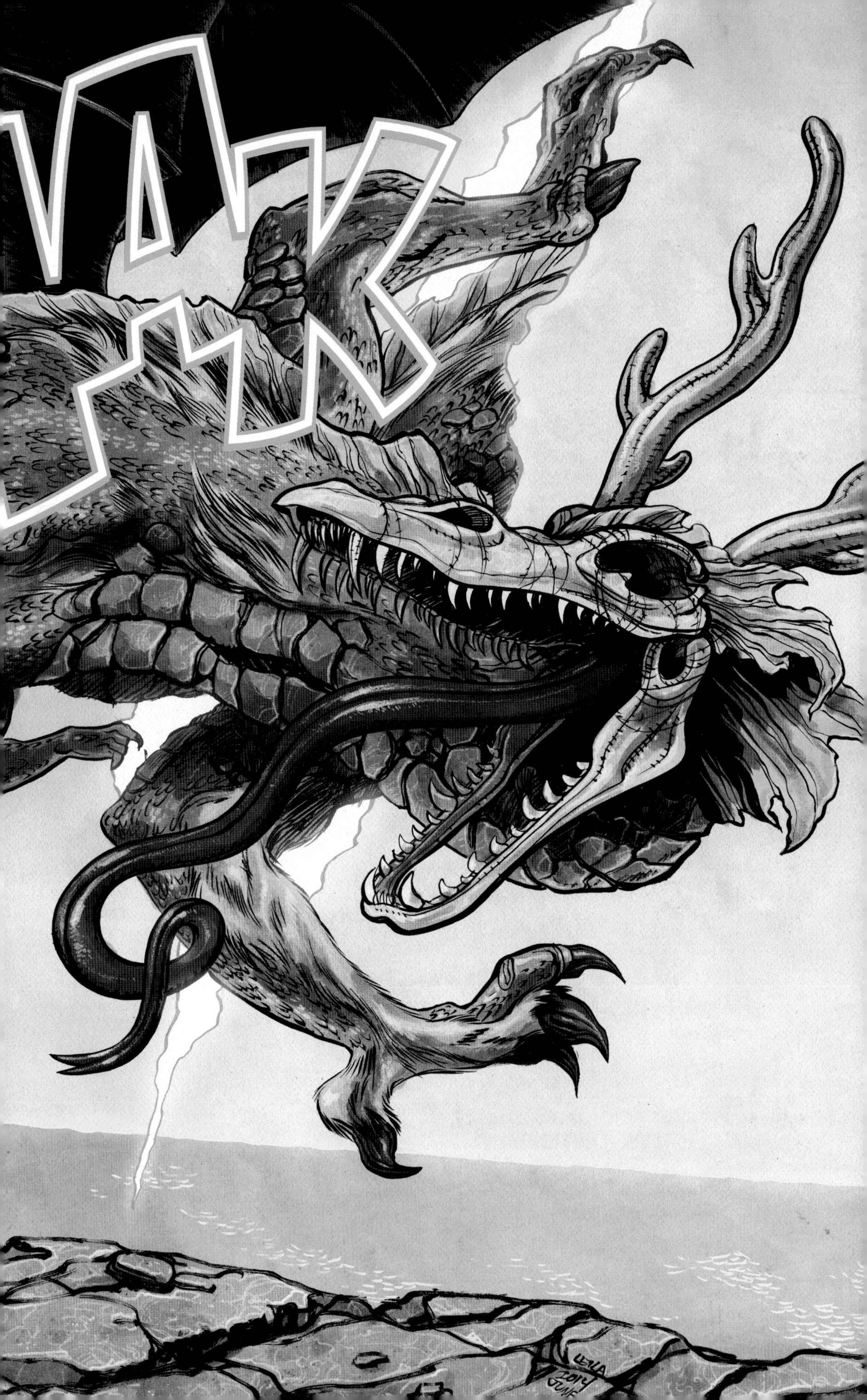

JOE KEATINGE - WRITER

LEILA DEL DUCA - ARTIST

OWEN GIENI - COLORIST

ED BRISSON - LETTERER

COVER DESIGN BY LEILA DEL DUCA
AND DREW GILL

CHAPTER BREAKS DESIGNED BY
TIM LEONG AND MONICA GARCIA

IMAGE COMICS, INC.
Robert Kirkman - chief operating officer
Erik Larsen - chief financial officer
Todd McFarlane - president
Marc Silvestri - chief executive officer
Jim Valentino - vice-president
www.imagecomics.com

Eric Stephenson - publisher
Ron Richards - director of business development
Jennifer de Guzman - director of trade book sales
Kat Salazar - director of pr & marketing
Corey Murphy - director of Retail Sales
Jeremy Sullivan - director of digital sales
Emilio Bautista - sales assistant

Branwyn Bigglestone - senior accounts manager
Emily Miller - accounts manager
Jessica Ambriz - administrative assistant
Tyler Shainline - events coordinator
David Brothers - content manager
Jonathan Chan - production manager

Drew Gill - art director
Meredith Wallace - print manager
Addison Duke - production artist
Vincent Kukua - production artist
Tricia Ramos - production assistant